AF543056

Dalit and Backward Women

Dalit *and* Backward Women

Rakesh K. Sinha

MOHIT PUBLICATIONS
New Delhi - 110002 (India)

First Published : 2010

© *Reserved*

ISBN : 978-81-7445-525-3

Published by :
MOHIT PUBLICATIONS
4675/21, Ansari Road, Daryaganj-110002
Phone : 23255141; Fax. : 23284126

PRINTED IN INDIA

Published by Sangita Goel for Mohit Publications, New Delhi-02, Typeset by Abhijeet Typesetters and Printed at Nav Prabhat Printing Press Delhi.

Preface

The difficult lives of Dalit women are perhaps best revealed by studying the social, economic, educational, health and political conditions of Dalit women. India has celebrated its 62th year of Independence. The country is now recording 2-digit economic growth every year and successfully takes quite an important and dominant position in international politics and in the economic arena. The success of India is built up with the international reputation of well-educated human resources, "democratic and stabled" political circumstances, and promises of land, benefits and other resources to the foreign and national investors-which are all based on exploitation of Dalit women.

Brahmanism and Hindu religion are primarily responsible for the past and present of the Dalits. Dalit liberation has been a myth due to the poison of Varna hierarchy and the concept of purity and pollution of castes and foods by sared scriptures of Hindu religion and culture. Both Dalit women and men wonder why they have been discriminated so inhumanely by those who belong to the same religion, that is Hindu. Due to extreme and cruel caste-based discrimination in Hindu religion, many Dalit women and men have changed their religion to Christianity and Buddhism for their liberation. Those who have changed their religion generally do not face such problems. Many of them have received opportunities to get good education and jobs. For example some Dalit women work as nurses in hospitals and clinics run by Christian missionary.

Political under-representation of women has emerged as one of the key concerns for women's movements in the nineties. Arguments relating to it revolve around two broad issues: the representative character of democratic institutions and their public accountability on women's issues. Recent developments in feminist politics in India not only indicate growing concern with under-representation of women in elected and decision-making bodies, but also with arguments for some form of reservation or affirmative action to redress existing gender imbalances. These arguments are advanced precisely because gender balanced representation is expected to alter development priorities, perspectives, and concerns and thereby increase accountability. The notion of affirmative action has always been contested both in terms of its meaning and the goals and practices it encompasses.

The preamble of Indian constitution adequately empowers the central and state government to eliminate human rights violation in the country. Inspite of these international and national declarations and resolutions, human rights are violated in different countries all over the world. In Indian society, due to the social barriers such as castetism, untouchability, patriarchy, disparity, superstition, religious exploitation and class variations, specific groups are becoming weaker and marginalised. The Indian state is caught up in formidable pressure from the global forces at one level and that of the excluded sections at another level. The unavoidable inference is that it will lead to greater legitimacy crisis and larger suffering of the poorer sections of the society.

—Author

Contents

CHAPTER

1 Social and Economic Conditions of Dalit Women

Brahmanism and Hindu religion are primarily responsible for the past and present of the Dalits. Dalit liberation has been a myth due to the poison of Varna hierarchy and the concept of purity and pollution of castes and foods by sared scriptures of Hindu religion and culture. Both Dalit women and men wonder why they have been discriminated so inhumanely by those who belong to the same religion, that is Hindu. Due to extreme and cruel caste-based discrimination in Hindu religion, many Dalit women and men have changed their religion to Christianity and Buddhism for their liberation. Those who have changed their religion generally do not face such problems. Many of them have received opportunities to get good education and jobs. For example some Dalit women work as nurses in hospitals and clinics run by Christian missionary.

Recently, Hindu caste hierarchy has poisoned Christian community in Nepal as well. The dominant caste groups, namely bahun-Chhetris, occupy most of the high positions such as pastors. Some of these "high caste" christians practice caste-based discrimination against Dalit Christians. Such practices may be seen in denial of entry inside the house to the Dalits and marriage relationship between "high caste" Christians and Dalit Christians. Similarlyk those Dalits who have turned into Buddhism are also becoming victims of such discrimination.

Use of Mother Tongues

A problem related to mother tongue is a concern of two types of dalits, Newar Dalit and Madhesi Dalits. It is not a problem of other Hill Dalits, such as Damai, Kami and Sarki because their mother tongue, like Bahun-Chhetris, is Khas Nepali language, the only official language of Nepal. The Newar dalits such as Kasai, Chyame and Pode speak Nepal Bhasa Newar Language) and Madhesi Dalits such as Chamar, Musahar, Dusadh and Dom speak Maithili, Bhojpuri and Awadhi languages. Due to discriminatory language policy of the government many Dalit women and girl child are deprived of education, including basic and primary, and non-formal education. They are deprived of using their mother tongues in the government offices and schools. Lack of education has further deprived them from jobs and other opportunities.

Lack of Awareness

There is a lack of awareness among the Dalit women and men. They continue to become victims from brahmanistic thoughts, polices and practives but they are not aware about it. According to Hisila Yami, "Dalit women are suffering from three types discrimination. On the one hand, they, being women, are exploited by partiarchy and being Dalit, on the other hand, they are exploited by the "high castes". Again, within the households, they suffer from their male family members. Thus Dalit women are living a life of more Dalit within their own community." If Dalit women would have been aware about such exploitations, they would have initiated strong movements and insurgencies.

Dalit Women in Women's and Dalit Movement

The history of both women's and Dalit movements are five decades old. So far women belonging to the dominant caste-Bahun-Chhetris and the newars dominate women's movement. Most of the leaders of women's right movement do not like an idea of social, cultural and religious pluralism among women. Unfortunately, they wrongly believe that it is divisive and communal. Dalit women and women belonging to other minority groups hardly get any opportunity to hold key positions in such movements. Therefore, we see negligible presence of Dalit women in the activities and programs organized by the organizations leading women's movement. Dalit movement is also gaining momentum. Although most of the leaders of the Dalit movement are Dalit men, nevertheless Dalit women leaders are also coming up. Dalit women are organized under the feminist Dalit

Organization and Dalit NGO Federation with more than fifty affiliated Dalit NGOs is led by many Dalit women. There is no doubt whatsoever that Dalit women can contribute significantly to both women's and Dalit movement in eliminating gender-based and caste-based discrimination respectively. Similarly, Dalit movement also needs strong support of the women's movement. Unfortunately, both movements are heading in two opposite directions concerning mutual help and cooperation.

Victimization by Development Industry and NGOs

In Nepal donors open their wallets for women's empowerment (or gender issues) and poverty alleviation or reduction. Both development industry and NGOs claim to work for women and poor but in reality they sustain status quo. They indeed never reach out to the poorest of the poor, that is Dalit women. Whether it is the government or non-government, in both sectors high caste men and women reap the harvest. The development industry run by both the government and non-government is more project-oriented than movement-oriented. Democracy is the system that is of the people, to the people and by the people but in Nepal there are organizations which work to the or for the Dalit but they never give opportunity to the Dalit to work by themselves. Some smart Dalit women and men are co-opted by these " main-stream" governmental and non-governmental organizations killing the movement.

Feminization of Poverty and Dalitization

It is indeed true that there has been a feminization of poverty in Nepal. It is also true that there has been dalitization of poverty in Nepal. Combined together Dalit women are at the bottom of poverty and socio-economic discrimination. Clearly they are the double victims of poverty, one as the women and the other as the Dalit. CARE-Nepal (1996:4) has indetified the disadvantaged groups as those groups who are at the lowest social and economic positions, including illiteracy or low literacy. According to this definition, Dalits and indigenous people belong to the disadvantaged groups. If we add another criterion, that is women, in CARE-Nepal's definition of disadvantaged group, Dalit women remain at the bottom.

If we look at the economic and social indicators of Dalits provided by Dr. Shiva Sharma, it becomes clear that there is

Dalitization of poverty within the Dalit community the gender proportion of economically active population is 85:101.

Economic Condition

The overall economic condition of most of the Dalits is miserable. It is unfortunate that the Dalits who have traditional skills in sustaining agrarian economy live in poverty.

Lack of Access to and Control Over Resources

Due to dominance of patriarchy originating from Hindu religious norms and values, most of the Nepalese women are deprived from access to and control over economic and other resources. Dalit women have access neither in private sphere nor in public sphere due to continuing practices of patriarchy and untouchability. Few Dalit women, as exceptions, may have some access to resources but they may not have any control over them. Displacement from traditional occupation and lack of employment in both agriculture and non-agriculture sectors are common problems of Dalit women and men. Dr. Haribansha Jha (1999), an economist, has estimated that about 68 percent total Nepalese population who live below the absolute poverty line most of them are Dalits. In a country where Dalit men are suffering from the problem of unemployment it is difficult to imagine about employment of Dalit women.

There is no doubt whatsoever those Dalit women and men are rich in skills related to their traditional occupations. The processes of modernization or Westernization, urbanization, globalization and liberalization that have been unfolding in the last five decades have further marginalized knowledge, skills and products based on the Dalits' traditional occupations. Dr. Haribansha Jha (1999:4) has noted that the Hill Dalits, such as Tatma, Khatbe, Mushar and Dom have lost market of their traditional skills and products. Such processes of marginalization have pushed them to rely on agriculture or non-agriculture sector but there too they have no place for employment. In such a situation women become the hardest hit victims of poverty. In Nepal, ownership of land means a lot in terms of wealth, power and prestige.

For the middle and low class people, ownership of land means self-employment and non-ownership means unemployment. Data of Dalits' land owners 23 percent are landless, 48.7 percent own less than 5 ropanies, 15.6 percent own 6 to 10 ropanies, and 9.6 percent own 10 to 20 ropanies and 3.1 own more than 21 ropanies of land. If we mix up data of the Dalits and some selected indigenous peoples as done by Shiva Sharma (1999:11), about 60 percent and if we analyze the data of the Dalits only then about 88 percent families are unable to make a living from their land. Thus they are forced to find employment in agriculture or non-agriculture sectors but employment in these sectors are simply not available. Lack of land ownership and denial of purchasing milk produced by Dalits by the diary industries have made it impossible for the Dalits to engage in animal husbandry.

Activities Required for the Socio-Economic Upliftment of Dalit Women

To uplift the socio-economic condition of the Dalit women, His Majesty's Government of Nepal (HMG-Nepal), donors, women's rights activists and Dalits should do the following activities:

1. While preparing long-term and short-term plans and budgets Dalits should also be allowed to participate in the decision making process. In the case of plan and programs for Dalit women, Dalit women also should be allowed to make decisions while preparing such plans and programs. The continuing practices of for or to the Dalit women and men should be abandoned.
2. HMG-N should identify the Dalits and list in the Nepal Gazette.
3. All government documents should include issues and problems of and policies, strategies, and programs for the Dalits in general and Dalit women in particular.
4. Both HMG-N and all international donors, including multilateral, bio-lateral and INGOs should make sure that Dalits participate in the decision making process concerning planning, designing and implementing programs or projects. If Dalit organizations need capacity building, such programs should also be implemented.
5. HMG-N should formulate and implement positive discrimination of affirmative action for the Dalits in general

and Dalit women in particular. Also, Dalit Women's department and Dalit Women's Cell should be established in the Ministry of Women, including ministries of education, health, agriculture and forest.

6. Both HMG-N and the donors should accept the fact that the battle against poverty, illiteracy and socio-cultural discrimination can not be fought if the plans and programs are not Dalit-centred. It must be realized that the development of Dalit women and men means the development of Nepal as well. Without their development, particularly of the Dalit women, development of Nepal would be a mirage.
7. Dalit women should claim and find their due space in the "main stream" women's movement. Also, Dalit women should be organized in such a way that they themselves should be able to launch a strong movement even at the streets. The "main stream" women's movement also thinks seriously to give due space to Dalit women without whose support women's movement would never achieve its mission and goals.
8. Each Dalit caste should get organized at the national level and all such castes should be federated into a Dalit Federation. All Dalit caste organizations should work together for the common causes and issues to fight against the continuing Brahmanism. Each Dalit caste should form its own women's organization.
9. Dalit women (and also men) should form and alliance with other victims of Brahmanism (Bahunbad) and seek their help and support for their liberation. The most natural allies of the Dalits are indigenous people. In any case, Dalit movement should be intensified (Bhattachan 2056).
10. The human rights organizations and human rights activists of Nepal should take up the issue of untouchability and plight of the Dalits very seriously. Effective implementation of the convention on All Forms of Discrimination Against Women (CEDAW) and the Convention Against All Forms Racism and racial Discrimination are important for the upliftment of Dalit women.

Dalit Fishing Women, Struggling Women

We met some 150 of the Dalit women from this village, in a community visit organized by Tamil Nadu Women's Movement. We were welcomed with so much energy and excitement-lots of drum playing, flowers and warm embraces. Heavy garlands were put around our necks; tikka, tumeric powder made into paste, was put on our forehead; and misri which were sugar crystals were placed on our tongue. While we were all standing there, with amazement and anticipation, two women came in front of us-one holding a brass bowl, the other a coconut husk, each with flames inside.

Both women raised the bowl and husk, and moved them in circular motion around us-to welcome us, and to drive away evil spirits. And that was how we started our gathering-with a lot of good will, sisterhood, and laughter in our hearts. Throughout the sharing, one would see that it is with the same level of energy, and more, and with strong spirit that they confront and fight against those who come and threaten their survival as a community. The Chinnu Aqua Farm Private Limited which was established in Chennai and started operating three years ago would definitely know how it is to be on the other side of this-how the Dalit women can make someone feel oh so unwelcome.

Umapathy

She is part of the sixth generation who has lived in Kolathur, and has been living and working on lands which were never put in their names. Umapathy and her husband would work on these farms owned by the upper caste men. She would grow and take care of the fruit trees surrounding her house, but were never allowed to touch any of the mangoes, jack fruits and coconut from these trees without the permission of the owners. The other families in her community would be working on agricultural lands of the upper caste men where they would cultivate paddy, ragi and groundnuts.

Umapathy, along with the other Dalit women in the village, used to spend hours in the backwater to gather prawns and fish with her hands. After selling them, she would earn 100Rps/150 Rps at the end of the day. This would be enough for food for her family. Today, she could not spend that long in the water, which meant lesser catch, and lesser food for her family. On the other hand, the agricultural lands were sold by the upper caste men to Chinnu Aqua Farm. This meant no more paddy, ragi and groundnuts to grow on. Umapathy of course has no input whatsoever in the decision of the upper caste men. She and the other members of the Dalit community were simply workers on these lands.

Kalpana

Just 25 years old, one would think Kalpana had lived her life three times over, for how else would she gain so much courage and determination to fight the aqua farm, the uppercaste men supporting it, and the Indian bureaucracy who make it almost impossible for the Dalit community to legally and peacefully challenge its operations. Perhaps it's giving birth on top of a hill after running away from the tsunami waves. Or simply being a Dalit mother who knows that fighting is the only way to survive. Kalpana tells us about the public distribution system in Tamil Nadu. It is a fairpriced shop of basic products-rice, oil, soap, sugar. There used to be a 3 Rp subsidy from the government for all products, then was reduced to 2 Rp subsidy. However, she could not avail of these subsidized products as much as she needs to. As a Dalit woman, she could not stand in line to cue along with non-Dalit, upper caste people. Thus, she had to wait when she could fall in line. By that time, all the basic products she needed would be all gone.

Most of the time, she would go after fishing, and by that time, the shop is already closed. Fishing in the backwaters now takes longer, as the prawns, crabs and other fish are harder to find. They are dying, and disappearing. "Where can we go for food? Where can we go to fish?" asked Kalpana. "The shrimp farm has taken over." Kalpana is one of the more active Dalit women who organizes community actions for their voices to be heard, and to campaign against the aqua farm.

Shanti

"I used to catch enough prawns to earn decent living for my 4 children," Shanti said. "Then came Chinnu Aqua Farm." The prawns and other living organisms in the backwater were found dying, in the increasingly polluted backwaters. Now, they can catch worth 30-40 Rp a day, less than a US dollar. Then the tsunami came in 2004.

Their area is part of the badly hit area in the Indian coast. Though not as bad as the other villages in Indonesia, Sri Lanka and Thailand, for Shanti and her family, the impact was bad enough to make their lives more difficult. Their house was heavily damaged, and lost most of whatever they had. However, they received no compensation from the government as they were not considered affected, being on the side of the backwaters. The relief packages never reached their villages, as these were handled by upper caste people. "Life as Dalit is hard enough. The Chinnu Aqua Farm is making our lives even more so."

Rajam

Rajam was supposed to be one of our resource persons in a workshop on tsunami and women's rights that APWLD organized last year in Aceh. But she wasn't able to process the necessary documents for her to travel abroad. She has a police record. She was one of the 33 Dalit women who were beaten up and arrested by the police men two years ago.

Rajam and some 2,000 other villagers blocked the road to the shrimp farm, as one of their acts of resistance. Rajam is one of the more vocal and active in resisting the shrimp farm, making her more vulnerable to harassment and violence. One of the women stood up while Rajam was telling her story. She said that when police came, the men ran away and left the women. This drew laughter among the women who were all in agreement with the remark; even among the few men who were standing nearby. But while that lightened the mood a bit, the intensity of the anger and frustration was determined to be felt. Rajam went on to talk about the different ways and actions the communities are taking to reclaim their source of livelihood and their way of living-peaceful protest actions, dialogues with the officials, asking the help of the media people to expose what's happening in their villages. There was one attempt by some unknown people to poison the aqua farm. As a consequence, the security in the premises was tightened; ferocious dogs are now milling around the farm. There was one incident when one of the dogs bit one of the farmers who was passing through. When we were there, a fact-finding mission has just been conducted; and a legal suit was filed against the aqua farm.

Kaliyammal

She came to me after we all had our lunch. We sat away from the big group as she wanted to show me something. She showed me her arms, where her skin was intensely dry. She lifted her sari to show her skin below her breasts, in her midrib, inner thighs, legs-scaly whitish skin. These were Kaliyammal's body parts which were regularly immersed in the backwaters, as she would go fishing.

Wading through the waters until chest level, Kaliyammal and other Dalit women would stay there and catch prawns, crabs, lobsters with their bare hands for hours. She has been doing this since her younger years. But lately, the itchiness on her arms and everywhere else has become unbearable. She stopped fishing. Her other companions had similar health problems, and more-some are suffering with white discharge and urinary infection. Kaliyammal had to rely now on her children who are working in salt marsh for support. The other Dalit women are now relying on the produce of their fishing husbands. The fisher men who use boats and large nets, go further and deeper for fishing, for bigger catch.

Chinnu Aqua Tech Private Limited

When the Chinnu Aqua Tech fenced off the shrimp farm and started their operations, other major changes started to happen. As the barbed wire fences were to prevent the villagers to come inside the shrimp farm and cause problems, these fences were not enough to contain the problems within it. The effects of the shrimp farm go well beyond double its size; and profit from this for one corporation, outweighs the number of lives it has destroyed. But the company flatly denied they were causing these problems. When faced with the protests and criticisms, they would simply brandish the permit they have acquired from the pollution board. Indeed, they have a permit.

So what does the permit cover? Basically, the permit issued by the pollution board meant that the company has met the anti-pollution standards and that therefore, the Chinnu Aqua Tech can operate. What does this exactly allow the company to do? The permit practically allows the Chinnu Aqua Tech to suck large amount of water from the backwater and fresh groundwater to recreate the environment that shrimps thrive in. To keep the shrimp pond clean, water has to be changed daily. The shrimp ponds are stocked with shrimp larvae, usually not of the endemic specie of the local area. To prevent then the shrimp population from getting sick as it is not adjusted to the local environment, the ponds are pumped with pesticides and antibiotics. So when they clean the pond, the water flushed out from these ponds is filled with chemicals. And this goes to the river, or sea. In Kolathur's case, the polluted water goes to the backwaters, where Kaliyammal and the other Dalit women fish. This permit then, is a permit to cause health problems to fisherwomen such as skin, eye and cervical infections. The permit, further, allows the Chinnu Aqua Tech to poison, and so, eliminate the shrimps, lobsters, crabs, mussels that the Kolathur fisherwomen have been living on for generations. The permit, basically, is a permit to eliminate the Kolathur villagers.

Resistance

The songs, dances and drum beating which followed the story-telling were equally passionate. If only these would be enough to lure the shrimp farm businessmen into the circle of the Dalit women and realize that this spirit is what the shrimps in their ponds are destroying. But that would be too naive of me to think. The lure of profit is too strong. Profit has destroyed nations, and peoples. For them, what is one poor village to dispense with. Laughter, they say, is the best medicine-too bad laughter is not enough to cure the skin peeling off, nor the cervical infections; the mirth in our conversations which enthralled me and my companions who came all the way from Kyrgyzstan, the hills of Chittagong and Nepal, from the plains of Philippines, Burma, Thailand, and the shores of Sri Lanka, will not be enough to bring back the shrimps and crabs into the backwaters of Kolathur to once again bring livelihood to its women. But is the courage and determination of the Dalit women to fight their ground, and their waters, which will bring changes in the Bay of Bengal. It is with the solidarity of women across seas and mountains which will ensure that the voices of Kaliyammal and Umapathy will be heard, and the struggle of Shanti and Rajam will be duplicated, inspiring other women to resist and defend their songs, their laughter, their lives.

CHAPTER

2 Dalit Women and Reservation Policy

Introduction

Of Nepal's total population, the share of the Dalits is 13%. Dalit women constitute about 15% of total Nepalese women (who constitute over fifty percent of Nepal's total population). Generally, women in Nepal have been discriminated on the basis of gender for centuries because of the defective value based society, which regards woman as second and low class human and make the subject of the exploitation and suppression. Such discrimination has lead women to their subordinate status in the society and deprived of equal participation in all governance process. Only a small group of women from elite class and caste have access to power-playing centres. The Dalit women are nowhere in the race or are far behind in the race. Dalit women are discriminated due to a patriarchic dominated social structure on the one hand and humiliation within them duc to caste ridden social system on the other. As such, they have virtually very low access to resources, power and control over their lives than Dalit men and other women in Nepal. Dalit women's families are ultra poor and represent about 80% of the ultra poor in Nepal The situation of the Dalit women is worse even among the general women whose status is very low. They face triple discrimination, because they are women, so-called low caste and discriminated by their male from their own caste groups. Due to triple oppression of class, caste and gender, Dalit women have least of access to opportunities for social and economic nobilities. Their liberation does not lie purely in economic or political terms. The social and cultural liberation is the determining factor for their lives.

Situation of Dalit Women

The ignorance to the Dalit women by the Government is the common case. On top of that, the political parties and the international aid agencies have ignored them. They are similarly neglected by Nepalese women's movement. Women activists in Nepal never tried to merge Dalit women in their movement. They hardly pay attention towards Dalit women. They advocate for the women in general in their manifestoes and constitutions. But, while the question on Dalit woman is raised, they stay with folding hands. Voiceless Dalit women, therefore, are deprived of their rightful place in the governance process. It is an irony that even the Dalit activists raise the issue of Dalit males and largely overlook the case of Dalit women. It is a fact that no political parties have supported Dalit women by way of associating them at different levels. In the Nepalese context, gender, caste and ethnicity are the three interlocking institutions or critical fault lines defining social identity.

The constitution has enshrined for equality and equal opportunity before the law. But these three groups and communities are subject to exploitation, discrimination and unfair treatment. One Human development and welfare indicators states: Nepali women are almost invisible in the civil service making up only 8% of overall staff and 4% of officers. There is hardly any representation of Dalit women in public services. Dalit women's literacy rate account for 9% compared to 42.9% on national average (CBS, 2001). Their life expectancy remains the lowest among Nepalese women: 42 years (Mushar women) while national average stands for 59.8 years. High rate of infant mortality, child mortality and maternal death amongst the Dalit women are serious problems. A small tribe namely the Badi women are still forced to continue the traditional prostitution. They suffer from trafficking and prostitution due to their poverty and ignorance. Similarly, the Dalits are highly disadvantaged groups. Dalit females have one of the lowest levels of literacy of all groups in Nepal. Their low level of literacy is due to three interrelated factors:

- Continued monopolization of so-called high caste women and men,
- The stronger influence of casteism in rural areas on Dalit females, and

- The control of Dalit males over Dalit women and girls.

As a consequence, Dalit females' access to even basic literacy education is limited. As mentioned above, Dalit women's literacy rate accounts for 9% compared to 42.9% on national average (CBS, 2001). Close to 95% of Dalit women are rural; most are landless or marginal farmers who live in subject of poverty with grinding labour. Many work as day-to-day manual workers. Wage of the women is less than that of men. Their economic situation has worsened due to the overall deteriorating rural economic conditions over the centuries. In all cases of caste conflict, the Dalit women are first victims.

They are raped, gang raped and even made pregnant showing the temptation of marriage and finally left. Even though these incidences of violence against women are extreme, nevertheless, some of these caste biases exist in schools among Hindu teachers. In addition, Dalit females are invisible in school curriculums and textbooks.

There are still various words and sentences hostile to the dignity of Dalit and women. Malnutrition among Dalit women is high. Controls by men over women starts as a girl child where infant mortality due to neglect and malnutrition is very high.

Many Dalit girls and women are used and abused by drunken male relatives. The sexual division of labour, child marriage and restricted mobility also limit Dalit females' access to education. Most importantly, it must address issues important to Dalit women and be accompanied by other social and economic reforms such as the following; sanitation, health, childcare, credit and loans, land reform, conservation, reservation and scholarship for Dalit women.

Existing Positive Actions for Women and Dalits and Impact upon Dalit Women

There are about 150 existing positive legal provisions and policies for the substantial change of women at large Though, in general, these provisions were made intentionally to upgrade the status of women, only few from so called high caste and class women have benefited to a larger extent only. No impact on the Dalit women is seen so far.

Actions for Women

- Reservation of Women in National Assembly: There is also a provision in the constitution for three seats in the National Assembly of the Parliament. Only the women from so called high caste have got the advantage by this provision. There is not any instance of the Dalit woman as beneficiary of this provision.
- 5% candidacy from women for House of Representatives is mandatory to all political parties. But the practice has shown that only elite women have succeeded and benefited by this provision. Since personal identity of a candidate rather than of political parties is the attraction, the political parties fear to put candidature from Dalit community.
- Reservation in Local bodies: In the Local Self-governance Act, there is a provision of the reservation to women for at least one seat in ward Committee. But no Dalit woman benefited by this provision. Similarly there is a provision for the participation of women in the Development Council. Nominal Dalit women have got chance to participate in the Local Councils at the Municipal, Village Development Committee and District levels.
- Free Education: The education act obliged all state schools for free education to women. However, Dalit women are not able to have such access due to early marriage and low economic status.
- Mandatory Provision for Inclusion of Women: For the compulsory participation of women in all committees, this provision has been made in various laws i.e. consumer law, local motion pictures, central children welfare, steering committee of local development, breast feeding protection and promotion committee.
- Scholarship: The scholarship rule has mandated for 20% reservation in scholarship. But none from among the Dalit girls could benefit from this arrangement. Every seat is provided to the so-called higher castes girls and the girls of high economic profile.
- Women's Bodies to be searched by Women Police: If the body of woman has to be searched in connection with

investigation of a crime, the search has to be conducted by women police without insulting her. Under the existing arrangement, the body of a Badi woman is searched by male police even without prior notice, which is not only objectionable but an insult to the pride of the women folk.

- Relaxation in Age for Civil Service: The civil service rule (amendment) has relaxed the age limitation for the enrolment for public services to women. Maximum age limit for women to join civil service is 40 years, whereas it is only 35 in case of men. But, there lacks the record of the beneficiary from Dalit women by this provision. Major beneficiaries of this provision of reservation are women from the forward castes.
- National Commission for Women: The Commission is established with a view to protecting and promoting the women's rights. But, the composition of this Commission lacks any representation form Dalit women. As such, the Dalit women have not got any positive feeling towards this institution.

Actions for Dalits

- Deprived, Depressed and Dalit Community: His Majesty's Government has established this community with a view to planning and executing the welfare policies for Dalit, but there is no any woman's representation in the composition. The males dominate the committee. This situation is self-defeating as the women from Dalit community have no control over the policy and programmes executed through this body.
- Committee for Formulating Reservation Policy: The Government has formulated a main committee under the chairmanship of Finance Minister and several sub-committees with a view to formulating the model of reservation policy to women, Dalit and Janajati. But apparently, there lacks representation of Dalit women in any committees.
- National Dalit Commission: A single Dalit woman was appointed in the commission out of ten members from the Dalit community. There were several claims that there existed potential candidates from the Dalit women for this august body.

Though the government has taken several positive actions for the gender justice Dalit women are considered neither at the time of planning nor in the executing of the policies.

Affirmative Action Elsewhere

With the transformation of the nature of state structure, it becomes the liability of all state to initiate the welfare programs for the marginalized communities. The motto of democracy itself advocates for the rule of law and wide participation. Wide participation and rule of law will not be meaningful, without giving due respect to the empowerment of all backward and marginalized communities. Various states have included the reservation policy for women, backwards and handicapped. Few examples are: In South Africa, an Employment Equity Act was promulgated with a view to empowering the blacks. This Act has come for promoting equal opportunity, implementing affirmative action measures to redress disadvantaged in employment experienced by designated groups to ensure their equitable representation in all occupational categories. The Act goes also to elaborate measures that constitute affirmative actions.

These measures are to be taken by employers to ensure that members of designated groups are adequately represented in the workforce and equal opportunity to compete for and advance in jobs. In India serious efforts are being made towards the enhancement of their participation as well as imparting training to the elected women representatives. The members of women elected to the rural and urban bodies in Karnataka exceed the mandatory reserved for them. Districts are selected as the population of Dalit women in the constituency. Under the 1983 Karnataka Act, 25% seats were reserved for women. The reservation for the SC and ST was in the proportion to their population. The new law of 1993 reserves one-third seats for women (from all caste categories) and one-third for backward classes. The amended 1995 Act provides for reservation of seats for the SCs and STs and the OBCs and women on rotation basis. There is a provision for not less than one third of the total no. of seats to be reserved for women, which includes not less than one third of the seats reserved for SCs and STs belonging to these respective categories.

Demand for Pro Dalit Women Measures

Time has come to execute the affirmative action policies and implementation as well. Realizing the need of the reservation for bringing the disadvantaged community into the mainstream of the governance process, the government has called for formulation of the reservation policy to the marginalized communities namely; women, Janajati and Dalit. Affirmative policy is generally perceived as steps taken to correct historical disadvantages and unfair discrimination by enabling access to full opportunities and benefits.

Therefore, the Dalit women should be given specific focus. There should be 10% reservation in Dalit reservation and 10% in reservation for Dalit women. Otherwise only the creamy layer or the forward women will be benefited and rest of the real oppressed women will not be benefited which is not real objective of the reservation policy. Within the women and Dalits, there should specific provision for Dalit women and ensure their participation in policy formulation positions as well.

Other Program oriented activities to be focused are:

- Revise the civil service curriculums and make it Dalit women friendly,
- Create one contact officer in all ministries,
- Family friendly provision should be made for public services like day care, husband and wife in same district, increased maternity mourning leave and paternity protection,
- Gender audit specific reference with Dalit women,
- Dalit women should be given information about the positive policies and provisions and their impact,
- Programs should be framed for the voters' education and for their encouragement in the contest of election.

Following measures are recommended in the plan on reservation:

- Specific land reform and allocation programs should be implemented where the population of Dalit women is high. Allocation of state resources for the advancement of women's equality is essential for the fulfilment of the state parties obligations under the ratified international human rights instruments also,

- Skill providing program should be launched and provide them the job as per their skill for their economic survival.
- Specific programs should be planned for exemption of loans to Dalit women.
- There should be provision for compulsory and free education. Mere free education is not enough. The school-going children, particularly from the Dalit communities, should be provided necessary books, bags and school materials as per their needs free-of-cost.
- For the participation in civil service, the curriculum for examination should be made Dalit women friendly. These women should be provided travel cost, relaxation in fees and extra costs. Provision should be made for preferences to Dalit women in coaching classes. Separate merit list system should be made for encouraging them to be participated in public services.
- Seats should be separated for Dalit women in gazetted class.
- Participation in political and public life has traditionally been regarded as a male dominated sector in Nepal. However, women have been active in various political movements and benefited. But Dalit women are not included within the ambit of political beneficiaries. The factors behind this are their illiteracy, lack of resources and support for their mobility. So, for their political participation, there should be specific provision in the constitution and other laws for the reservation for women. In them Dalit women also should be given special preferences.
- Dalit women are in a disadvantaged position in every sphere of political life. Therefore, 10% seats in constitutional bodies, commissions, committees and mission should be separated from the quotas visualized for women in general.

Conclusion

Unity among diversity is a constitutional motto, but the integration is not an easy task to maintain it. For this, the government will have to go forward with specific programs for marginalized and poor communities. Until and unless, Dalit community, so-called untouchables are not brought into the governance process and can not give the due respect to the Dalit women for participation, national integrity will remain confined to the constitution only. Though the Government has planned various gender friendly programs for women in general, it is an irony that the Dalit women have not been beneficiaries from these all. Still they are deprived of participating in the committees for planning the policies for women and forgotten to have the accessibility in the welfare programs. Women from so-called higher caste family have grasped all the welfare programs and plans.

The government does not care for them. Not only the government, even the political parties do not voice for the Dalit women. Political parties have frequently fashioned their campaigns slogans around the need for uplifting the marginalized sectors, while political leaders, mostly drawn from higher castes offer the promise of equal status and equal rights. But, the political condition of Dalit women is highly determined by the caste and gender discrimination. For the overall development of the country as a whole, there should be a plural participation from all castes, classes, communities and groups from all sectors. Dalit community, which has not any representation in any state level, has to push for representation. Since the Dalit women are triple victims from society, males, and economic and social condition, they should be given specific focus. Government while formulating and executing the programs should not forget to include Dalit women while planning for the reservation policy to women in general. Government should separately determine the quotas for Dalit women and encourage for their education, political participation, representation in public administration and employment. Even there should be clear-cut provision for the representation if any committee is framed. Otherwise, the issue regarding Dalit women will not come into account.

Dalit Women put up a Brave Show to Secure Land Rights

It all began in 2006 with a foot march organised by the APVVU Mandal Union to unite Dalit women in southern India. Since then, displaying a relentless spirit against upper caste oppression, they have overcome all hurdles in seeking land allotments in their names.

Andhra Pradesh, India: Forty landless Dalit families live in Marthuvari Palli Dalitawada, a hamlet in Jogivari Palli Panchayat of Sadum Mandal located at a distance of 65 km from the district head quarters. All the agricultural lands are in the hands of 20 Reddy families of landlords of the same village. The Reddys are the dominant caste of this village.

While the landlords own large chunks of land (both dry & irrigated Lands), dalits earn their bread as agricultural labourers. The wages are low and also unequal between men (Rs.30/-per day) and women(Rs.25/-per day) labourers, while the minimum wages according to the Act should be Rs.60. Due to agriculture crises, the dalits do not get employment for more than 75 days in a year. Therefore, they have to depend on the landlords for food grains during emergency situations and in lean season. Taking advantage of this, landlords offer hand loans with an exorbitant rate of interest of 60% to 100% per annum. Most of the time the landlords offer loans with the condition that the borrower must work for the farmer until the debt is repaid. Further, distress migration has become inevitable for at least 50% of the Dalit families.

To survive in the lean season, they go to Bangalore (about 250 km away) to work as construction workers for six months. As a result, child labour, early marriages for girl children and illiteracy have become the reality of their lives. Added to this misery for women, are desertion and bigamy. APVVU Mandal Union organised a foot march during February 2006 in Sadum Mandal to strengthen the unionisation in the Mandal after identifying the most backward villages. The women have formed a separate unit within the village as they have recognised the need to be together to discuss their own issues Six Dalit women from Marthuvari Palli participated throughout the 5-day *padayatra* and since then the union membership is increased to 77 members in their village.

The women have formed a separate union unit within the village as they have recognised the need to be together to discuss their own issues. While the men continued to migrate and also work in submission to the landlords with low wages, the women decided to make use of the provisions of the National Rural Employment Guarantee Act (NREGA) to get employment. It is in this context that all 40 Dalit families were motivated to obtain Job cards.

Knowing their Rights

The dalits were completely ignorant of the availability of government lands in their village. Therefore, without probing too deeply into this, they applied under the NREGA (which ensures 100 days employment for rural workers) for working on a road to the hillocks near their village. While many people started working on the road, the union leader Chendramma continued investigating the various legal spaces available to dalits to occupy the government land which is illegally under the control of landlords. Hence she applied for the status of land under the RTI and finally realised that the land was noted as government waste land not allotted to any body on records. But in the reality they were in the hands of the landlords as grazing lands. After several rounds of discussions among the dalits in the village, the women decided to take up the task of land appropriation. As usual the men did not show interest because they were afraid of the backlash from the dominant caste landlords.

Strategically it was decided collectively by the women to take over the land, while the men stayed behind, extending support. The women-led collective action not only strengthened the women's unity, it also developed the positive feelings of the dalits The entire village staged a *dharna* (demonstration) on May 19, 2008 in front of the Mandal Development Office for taking the side of the landlords.

The media also exposed this issue in the newspapers. One of the demands of the demonstration was that the Grama Sabha meeting should be attended by the District Panchyat Officer and that meeting should be organised with proper advance information to every one in the village. Subsequently, on June 16, a Gram Sabha meeting was organised in which dalits succeeded getting approval for NREGA work on the 32 acres of land, after proving with the factual data collected through RTI, that the land was not reserved for grazing purposes. A lot of preparatory meetings had taken place for building the unity of dalits and also to equip them to participate in the Grama Sabha meetings.

All the strenuous efforts of landlords to stop the participation o: dalits in Grama Sabha failed despite their arranging liquor and Rs.100/-for every family to visit their relatives outside the village. People took the money and the liquor but still participated in the Grama Sabha meeting! This was the first victory of their collective effort against the landlords and unhelpful bureaucracy. Further, the women-led collective action not only strengthened the women's unity, it also developed the positive feelings of the dalits.

Fighting Against all Odds

The general saying in Telugu among the poor about the law is "Chattlanni vunoodiki chuttale" (Laws and Legal systems work as relatives to rich people.) Similarly another saying about the legal system is "courtuku poyinavadu, katiki poyinavadito samanam" (stepping inside the court is equal to entering in the graveyard as dead body). These two sayings have emerged from the experiences of rural poor as all the laws have adequate loopholes to support the rich people. Hence, the poor are always reluctant of going to courts, while the rich take advantage of this and exploit the judicial system for their own selfish reasons.

APVVU has more than two decades experience in using the law and courts as tools for asserting Dalit rights. Therefore, it decided to play a key role in building the case of Maruthuvari Palli at the District Court in Chittoor by filing a caveat to prevent the landlords from getting any injunction orders to prevent Dalits' entry into the disputed land. As per the legal procedures with regard to the government land, the person asking for land ownership should cultivate the land at least for a year. Therefore, in all cases of land appropriation the union's strategy is to occupy the land and cultivate it collectively, so that the cultivation status can be entered in the government records. To till the land, dalits do not own cultivation animals as they can not afford them. Hence, the land can be cultivated only by tractors. Therefore, SAHANIVASA sent a tractor to assist them. Around 700 people from four neighboring villages joined the Maruthuvaripalli dalits in order to support the land appropriation.

The landlords sent their women with chilly powder to attack the tractor driver and also the people. All the Dalit women gathered around him in a human chain to physically block the entry of upper caste women on land. Both sides lodged complaints against each other with the local police. The dalits demanded that the landlords withdraw from the land after which they would withdraw the case. After a long debate finally landlords withdrew their case and also agreed to stop further interference on the land. But they have not stood by their promise after the court cases were withdrawn. Though they don't come directly they have supported a backward caste community (Yadavas), to enter on the land.

A Remarkable Feat

As a general decision in the union, Maruthuvari Palli dalits have agreed and also stand by the pre-condition of land appropriation "to assign the land in the names of women". In this case woman led the movement for land and also took all risks of divisions, pressures from their men and landlords, and the non-cooperation of the bureaucracy. Dalit women of Maruthuvari Palli stood boldly against all pressures and put up the application to the district collector on August 15 demanding the government to issue the titles on verification of cultivation status. Followed by the District Collector's promise, the government has appointed a surveyor to measure the land and prepare the documents for titles. A demonstration was organised again on October 17, 2008 in front of Mandal Revenue Office in the context of Stand up and Take Action Campaign demanding for the immediate allotment of the land titles in the names of women. Traditional way of pest management is practiced and no chemical manure is applied Land ownership for women not only gives economic security it also gives space for decision-making process in the family. In Maruthuvari Palli the women took the decision to go for bio-diversity agriculture where every family is going to harvest food crops which will give them at least four months' food in the families. They have grown 12 varieties of mixed crop which is to be harvested in a month from now. Traditional way of pest management is practiced and no chemical manure is applied. As Dalits fight for their social dignity and equality, women will also continue to fight to restore their rights and equal opportunities in the society

Dalit Women's Leadership

Before sharing my views on the Dalit women's leadership I would like to focus on the basic objectives behind the need for leadership of Dalit women

- The issues of Dalit women have remained sidelined in the women's movement

- Dalit women have been suffering from Caste based systemic violence and atrocities. They have been subjugated to various forms of discriminatory practices. Therefore there is no doubt that the leadership coming from these experiences is more powerful and committed.
- Dalit women's leadership is not being much recognised in the Dalit movement.

Therefore there is a need to bring visibility to the core issues of Dalit women, which have been discussed as below:

1. Existence and Survival: The need for existence and survival is the prime concern for all human beings. But the Dalit women are never treated as human beings. Therefore their need for self-respect and dignity is much higher as they are treated as lesser humans. There is also false perception generated that the Dalit women are weak and vulnerable.
2. Atrocities and Violence: Caste based atrocities and violence has increased. The Dalit are targets of atrocities like mass attack, gang rape, naked parading, etc. The society can see the grievousness of the atrocities but cannot see the cruelty and mental sickness of the so-called upper castes. However, the Dalit women do not get adequate protection and legal aid from the state implementing agencies like police, judiciary etc.
3. Dependence on Agricultural Labour: Nearly 75-80 % of Dalit women work as agricultural labourers. There are no fixed hours for work. They are not paid wages as per prescribed wage rate. Most of the girls working in the tobacco or cotton units are between the ages of 12 to 25 years. They are forced to work in the night shifts. They are sexually abused and raped by the employers. The local police never report these cases. In village Ajarpura of Anand District in Gujarat a girl aged 12-13 years was gang raped by the upper castes. She was then put in to a tractor and pushed from it. The wheels of the tractor went over her and she died. The local police filed an accident case and after postmortem her body was buried. The case was reported to us. We filed a petition in the High Court for repost mortem. In the repost mortem it was found that she was gang raped.

4. Forced labour: The Dalit Women are the victims of caste based forced occupation. The scavenger women are forced to do the inhuman practice of cleaning filth and human excreta with bare hands. In return they get stale or left over food from the upper castes. They are paid monthly wages between Rs. 25 to Rs. 125. The worst impact is on the Scavenger girls. The teachers and children discriminate them in the schools. Unable to bear this, they dropout from the schools and join with their mothers as scavengers. Another kind of inhuman practice is the Devdasi system i.e. "temple prostitution". In the Southern part of India, around 5000 to 15000 Dalit girls between 6 and 8 years of age are forced to become maidens of God. Once dedicated, the girls are unable to marry and are raped by temple priests and upper caste men, eventually auctioned secretly into urban brothels and ultimately die of AIDS. Unable to repay their debt taken from the landlords the Dalit families become Bonded Labour. The wives of the bonded labour is forced by the landlords to become their "Paniharis" i.e. house servants. They do all the domestic chores of the landlord like cleaning the cattle shed, bringing fodder for the cattle, cleaning and sweeping the house, making bed for the landlord etc. The wages they earn for this is between Rs. 25 to Rs. 75. Many times they are not even paid. The Landlords sexually abuse them.
5. Migration: Nearly 70% of Dalit families are landless agricultural labourers. As wages are not paid to them adequately, they are forced to migrate for 6-8 months a year. The labour of women who also migrate is never recognized. The children are forced to drop out from their schools. The women have to stay at most of the times in open fields with no space for privacy. They suffer with health hazards like premature pregnancy and miscarriage. They suffer from respiratory and skin diseases. They also become victims of sexual abuse.

This is an overview of the situation of Dalit women. The complexities and its severity can only be realized or understood if we go in depth. What has happened because of this that I would like to reflect upon:

a) Lack of Education: The patriarchal and casteist structure has left very few opportunities for Dalit women. As per the National Commission for SC/ST report, 1996-97 & 1997-98, 12 states in India have less Dalit female literacy rate as compared to total Dalit female literacy rate of 39.29 %. The same commission also highlights that the drop out rate of Dalit girls is 53.86 % as compared to the general girls drop out rate, which is 45.97 %.

b) Lack of employment opportunities: Lack of education has generated lack of employment opportunities for the Dalit women. The other reason is caste-based mindset of the society. This does not allow the educated and trained Dalit women to join in the competitive world. Hence they are forced to work as unskilled labourers in the unorganised sector. Even in the factories, they are underpaid, no fixed hours, forced to work at nights and sexually abused by the employers.

c) Insecurity in the Dalit community: The vulnerability of Dalit women has generated tremendous insecurity in the minds of the Dalit community. There has been generational transfer of fear. One of the indicators for this can be the low birth rate of Dalit females. As per the UNDP-India's report, 1997, in comparison to 1000 males the sex ratio of Dalit females is 922 while that of general females is 944.

d) Atrocities and violence within the family: The atrocities on Dalits are correlated with awareness. Whenever they ask for land rights, minimum wages, access to public services, etc. they are atrocised by the dominants. The implementing agencies also cooperate with the dominants, which further perpetrates the violence. This generates frustration in the Dalits. Unable to bear this, they pour it on their wives and children.

The other form of violence by the family is the observance of the traditions and customs like purdah (veil) system, dowry system, special rituals to be observed by women after the death of their husbands, etc. The Dalit communities had never practised these rituals in the past. But the same has come through the dominant castes who call themselves very progressive. This observance is based on the graded inequality in the social structure where each caste wants to follow the norms and conditions of those who are above them in the caste hierarchy. Hence there have been cases of dowry deaths in Dalit communities.

Given all the issues and challenges stated above leadership of Dalit women is emerging in Gujarat. I have witnessed strong Dalit women fighting for their rights themselves. No doubt their struggle has shown that the leadership, which comes out of experience of this kind of situation, tends to be stronger and committed for the cause. Their leadership is worth recognition and admiration. I would like to highlight Some of these Dalit women's stories:

1. In another case a Dalit widow named Valiben's son was badly beaten up in the police custody. They suspected him of stealing a bicycle. Later on he died in mysterious circumstances. An atrocity complaint was filed. The police tried to bribe the old widow. They tried to offer her Rs. 5,00,000. The widow said, "I want justice not money".
2. In another incident a Dalit woman named Kashiben aged around 60 years took leadership in the agricultural labourers rally. Having seen this, she was socially boycotted by the non dalits in her village. Kashiben took a stand that if the landlords do not pay her minimum wages, then she would not work there. At the present, Kashiben walks for 4-5 kms everyday. She works in the brick kiln and earn Rs. 50-60 every day. Kashiben is now president of the Agricultural Labourers Union in Vadodara district.
3. In Gujarat, the village council on false charges suspended a Dalit woman named Shakriben who was the village head. Her husband was attacked and brutally injured with sharp weapons. She filed an atrocity complaint. She also went for an appeal against the suspension order. Few months back she was reinstated as Village Head. Last year she won the legal battle. The Sessions court sentenced three of the accused for 7 years imprisonment each. This incident is worth noting because for the first time in Gujarat the Dalits boycotted the Non Dalits by not selling milk to them. They stopped carrying dead animals in the village. They also wrote on the walls of their houses "Rabaris i.e. Shepherds

are not allowed to enter their locality" Through this fight Shakriben has proven her courage to fight for self-respect and justice. She has also established her leadership in the area.

4. The Dalit women many times fight without their struggle being very much visible, village Golana in Anand District was one of the incidents where four of our colleagues were shot dead in 1986. It were the women who became witnesses and fought the case. 13 of the accused were sentenced for life imprisonment. This became a historical judgement for Gujarat and brought lot of impact in the State. This also reduced the extent of atrocities in that area.
5. In another case a Dalit Lady teacher fired a non Dalit student in village school. The father of the student slapped her on the face. She filed an atrocity complaint. The father was sentenced for 3 years imprisonment by the session's court.

These are some of the examples signifying the importance of Dalit women's contribution in Dalit movement. This always builds up the confidence and moral of the community. But there is no doubt that the Dalit women take added risk and many times face more isolation and suppression by their own community as well as by the society. The women who show tremendous courage to fight, do they get enough space and promotion?

What needs to be done in the women's movement?

The women's movement has been perceived as a fight between women and men. This struggle has become so much prominent that there is very less space available for the issues of Dalit and tribal women. Hence there is a need for programme-based action, which provides space and visibility to these issues. What should be done?

a. A detailed study on the issues of Dalit and Tribal women should be taken up by the Women's movement to bring visibility to their issues.
b. Awareness and education about the caste-based discrimination should come in the agenda of the NGOS who believe in the ideology of equality and fight against caste based discrimination.
c. Dalit women should be provided space and training to establish and build up their leadership.

d. NGOs should develop an agenda and program to address the issues like Manual scavenging, Devadasi system, atrocities on Dalits.

e. NGOs should also monitor the role of various governmental agencies mainly the education, social welfare and Labour welfare departments. It should also study in depth about the implementation the various laws and acts.

OBC Reservation in Higher Education and Protests

Are Reservations Necessary?

While it may be true that some sections of the Dalit society have managed to move away from their poverty-ridden past in rather spectacular fashion, it is a fact that large numbers of them continue to languish in the same abject conditions. It is a group that comprises a significant percentage of the country's population-a huge number. Who is responsible for this sorry state of affairs? Is it completely the fault of the Dalit millions? Have they not been able to exploit opportunities that are supposedly open to all? Is social change in this context all about bringing in reforms in the way the education system is approached, financed and administered by the Centre? Will this path work better than direct reservations in centrally-funded institutes? Is reservation needed at all? Let's explore all these questions a little further.

The Random House Dictionary defines reservation as 'an exception or qualification made expressly or tacitly'. This definition seems to justify the action of different governments in keeping aside a specific number of seats for a community that has suffered from being ostracized socially for centuries. That they've been ostracized for ages is an undeniable fact. What is less certain is the politician's motive in facilitating the reservation policy. Leaving the motive aside for a while, it's not difficult to see that reservations are just one more way of ensuring that a hitherto oppressed community finally gets an opportunity to leave its past behind and find a place for itself socially and economically. At this point, some may argue that there are other ways of ensuring the same outcome-by making the playing field level for all. Some of the more commonly listed ways are:

- to provide improved primary/secondary education so that the Dalits can match steps with the others.
- to offer quotas to the economically-deprived across all communities.
- to increase the slice of the educational pie by creating more seats in the open category.

All these solutions neglect crucial facts.

The first completely fails to consider the gestation period for improving education across the country. At the very least, several years will pass before we begin to see any marked difference in the quality of education provided to Dalits and its impact on them. In the meantime, are they expected to remain satisfied with the indifferent teaching staff and sub-standard infrastructure that passes off as their education today? A Dalit student with a dream of becoming a doctor may not be willing to see the long-term view and with good reason. In 59 years, our nation has not managed to provide all its citizens with the same quality of education. Let's say that aloud this time-FIFTY-NINE YEARS! Can it suddenly be trusted to fulfil this promise? Who in their right minds would wait for this promised change to be brought in eventually, that too when governments change at the drop of a hat, and with them, sometimes their policies too? Would you?

The second solution is one that can very easily be sabotaged. When exam papers, college degrees and yes, OBC certificates too can be purchased illegally and used for admissions to higher courses and for jobs, how difficult would it be to bypass this clause? Public corruption ensures that a degree or an exam paper can be easily bought and sold. What is to stop human greed from benefiting from this policy as well? Before we know it, corrupt officials from the administration, who are meant to protect the rights of the underprivileged, will be selling official certificates that prove your status as economically deprived!

And the third ignores the ground reality that adding the kind of numbers (of seats) required to really benefit students in the open categories would need drastic revisions in infrastructure and facilities, teaching staff, budgets, etc. Not all of this is easily achieved. For example, where would institutes find the extra space required, especially since the government envisages that this increase in physical infrastructure (new buildings, classrooms) and in teaching and administrative staff would happen over the next one year before the proposed increase happens next year. Is this realistic? In any case, the government's face-saving measure of making a provision for more open category seats or jobs is not a long-term answer to deeply entrenched attitudes of discrimination in the minds of many upper-caste people in such cases. This, like the quota system, is yet another way that doesn't address the real issue of an unequal playing field. The government's move to impose a further education cess (we already pay 2% along with our income tax) to finance this move will also cost the taxpayer dearly.

The Common Arguments Against Reservation

Many OBCs, women, ethnic and religious minorities continue to experience deliberate discrimination socially, professionally and otherwise, even today. All these groups, in spite of their large numbers, are often disproportionately represented in the negative in both government and in private sector jobs. For reasons of relevance, let us talk only about OBCs here. What could be the reasons? These are some of the more commonly held perceptions.

Merit should be the Deciding Factor

Talk of merit has increased exponentially because that seems like a safe position to take. Who could really argue against that? But a closer look reveals some serious flaws in the way India has treated the idea of merit for some time now. Isn't it at all possible that many from the backward classes are losing out on seats and jobs simply because the interviewer is not objective? Are we to believe that those in positions of authority in India have achieved the pinnacle of impartiality when it comes to perceptions based on gender, caste, community, skin colour and religion among other identifiers? A casual look at any newspaper will unmistakably show this belief up to be a delusion. Take marriage for example. The senseless desire for fair skinned brides screams at you from the matrimonial columns. Where is the merit in being fair-skinned? And statistics on Dalit literacy, enrolment in schools and dropout rates, for example plainly indicate where we as a people stand when it comes to being impartial.

Maybe we could go all out for privatization then, perhaps that will solve all our problems! We would all have to be objective then because privatization demands excellence and does not pay homage at the altar of appeasement. However, many in the socially and economically privileged carry deep-rooted and potentially damaging perceptions about 'backward' castes. It seems very unlikely, however, that these perceptions based on centuries of collective conditioning will be abandoned hastily in the interests of the organization. If it were that easy, then the US, a nation that has enshrined equality of the sexes in its constitution (as has India), wouldn't have had any issues over the glass ceiling at work. But the glass ceiling, while it definitely seems to be on the decline, continues to exist, despite the fact that private companies have been around for a very long time. So privatization cannot be the simple counter to deeply entrenched perceptions in the minds of the elite. These practices help perpetuate the domination, intended or not, of the elite. Discrimination based on subjective behaviours such as these is clearly very difficult to eradicate in a hurry no matter how good the intention. Is it helpful to argue that reservations haven't helped the position of Dalits in the last 50 years because discrimination against them hasn't gone anywhere in that time either!

Incompetence

This adjective is now quickly gaining credibility as an argument against the increase (or even provision) of quotas. Apparently, reservations lead to increasing incompetence in the system. Which basically means that the country is being flooded with doctors, engineers and other professionals who are a menace to society. This could well be true since we periodically hear of patients dying because of mistakes on the operating table, buildings collapsing because they were badly built and so on. On the other hand, claims abound that beneficiaries of the quota system are often so incompetent that they drop out of their courses midway. Or they fail their exams. The system has therefore succeeded in weeding them out. This would mean that the higher education system produces largely competent professionals. And that these competent professionals are the ones we are entrusting our lives to when it comes to say, medical help. Yet we continue to hear of patients being misdiagnosed, treated wrongly or even dying due to doctors' negligence. Where are we going wrong? Who are these doctors and where did they get their education? They can't all be Dalits. And if they largely are, then who is giving them these jobs and why? Similarly, they can't all be incompetent since it's the same foolproof system from above that has created them. But wait a minute-does this foolproof system actually weed out the incompetents? Here's where we come up against another interesting phenomenon-non-caste based quota.

Are Non-caste Based Quotas Okay?

An interesting question to ask is 'Are people against reservations generally, or are they against caste-based reservations alone?' Reservations based on economic criteria (especially in private institutions), such as NRI/ Management quotas and payment seats, are as strongly against the idea of a 'meritocracy', a term that is being bandied about rather loosely by those opposing reservations. Do the rich, who can afford to pay for their seats, have a gene that ensures automatic 'competence'? How does having pots of money make you more intelligent than being from a 'backward' caste? By that logic, Paris Hilton should be an intellectual giant! And for many of us, our entire academic life has been in private schools and colleges run by trusts established to cater to different communities/ minorities. Those are also reservations-and based just as much on lowered standards as the caste-based ones. And maybe, just maybe, this is where some of those incompetents floating around causing untold damage are coming from!

Reservations are meant to give a push to SC/STs and OBCs to get into institutes. To obtain the relevant qualifications and come out of these same institutes, they have to write and pass the same exams that others have to without any consideration for their caste. So, in fact, when you see a professional from the 'backward' classes who has passed out from a reputed institute, chances are s/he has gone through a lot more than other students who have led a far more privileged life in terms of economic, social, cultural and historical backgrounds. Far from being incompetent, these select few have proved their mettle as they have had to compete with the academic cream of Indian society that comprises the student body of most IITs and IIMs despite most of them carrying the load of their historical baggage of alienation, exclusion and disentitlement and very importantly, their lack of fluency in English, the language of the elite in India. To make an example of the Dalit who has managed to succeed without any reservations is to ignore the harsh social and economic realities of the rest.

Is this the new face of Indian caste politics?

The real deal may be this. The anti-quota stir is not about incompetence or the unfairness of reservations at all. If they were really about these, why do our masses choose to remain silent when incompetence is exhibited consistently even when the complicity relationship between a conscienceless buyer and a greedy seller of professional degrees has been established time and again by the national media? No, it cannot be about incompetence. And is our anti-quota protester indignant and outraged when he sees seats being earmarked for the moneyed? Isn't this the kind of reservation that deprives the middle class student of his open category seat? No-it cannot be about the inherent unfairness of reservations, for they should have been out on the streets when management quota seats were sold to the rich, irrespective of their eligibility.

What is it about then?

Chances are the world is good to you if you happen to be born in an upper-caste family. This, of course, doesn't automatically ensure financial soundness, but in most parts of the country, it does bestow certain unspoken advantages upon you. To start with, you are not considered inferior in any way. While urban areas may be somewhat progressive in this, rural India is not exactly a bed of roses for the oppressed classes who largely populate those regions. They have been branded as 'inferior' and are often treated as such. This branding scars the Dalit for life-she is not allowed to define her identity. That privilege is hijacked by those who see themselves as God's chosen ones-the upper castes. Even the nomenclature is inherently biased against Dalits. They are rarely the 'oppressed', more, the 'lower' and the 'backward'. So, the Dalit by virtue of being lower or backward gets to clean out our excreta, our garbage, our cities and our villages. And he is tolerated, as long as he doesn't harbour dreams of transforming himself into the 'upper' or the 'forward' classes.

Much has been made of the acceptance of Dalits in the higher echelons of mainstream society. But let us be brutally honest with ourselves-just how many of them are there? And are they there because of us-or despite us-regardless of the conscious and unconscious attempts by the elite at excluding them from the benefits of being a part of the privileged? Tolerance of the other sets a limit, acceptance does not. In fact, it asks the privileged to let go of some of their privileges so that the other has an opportunity to rise up to the same level. A very good question to ask ourselves is, 'Is India accepting its oppressed or simply tolerating them?'

Valid Points of Anti-quote Protesters

Some points that the anti-quota protesters have brought up are extremely valid and need to be debated thoroughly. For example, in many reputed institutions, reserved seats are often not filled at all. These are not opened up to the general category students and are therefore wasted. Data from IIT Mumbai supports this claim. Apparently, nearly 50% of the reserved seats in IIT Mumbai are not filled up thereby denying an opportunity for the open category student to get in inspite of having scored higher than the Dalit student. Another question being asked is "why are there reservations at the post-graduate level especially since quotas already exist at the graduate level?". The answer to this question probably lies in the politician's efforts to portray himself as the messiah of the oppressed. This needs to be challenged. Also, what is the government doing about providing a high standard of primary education to the poor in our villages? Why has there been little or no improvement in the last 60 years? Why does the government legislate without a national debate to further controversial policies such as these?

All these are extremely compelling questions brought up by the anti-reservation protesters and need to be addressed squarely by the government. But the anti-reservation protesters are doing the oppressed a great disservice by linking blanket labels such as incompetent and undeserving with terribly divisive and badly implemented administrative measures like the quota system. Questioning the efficacy of these half-baked measures and focused protests against them will also help in other ways. It will help Dalits see that India is not against them for being Dalit, that they are not alone, that people do care about them. The value of such a perception in the minds of the oppressed cannot be underestimated for openness and understanding flower where every voice is heard, no matter how insignificant.

Does it have to be an either/or situation?

This raging issue has clearly shown that a democracy works well only when there is sustained public participation in influencing policy in issues, directly and indirectly relevant to them. When this is absent, elected representatives find themselves in a position where they have to debate and decide policy based either on their own attraction for a particular viewpoint OR the tendency many of them have, to manipulate policy in order to benefit from vote bank politics. Given this, it is vital that the process of dialogue take centrestage rather than confrontation, fault-finding and issuing ultimatums. So much energy and time is being invested in reinforcing ideas that are at best serving any one of the two parties in the conflict.

When such debates go on for years altogether, we may urgently need to stop in our tracks and ask the all-important question-are there only two positions that we can take as a people? The dominance of the 'either/or' perspective is a clear indication that we are fast turning into a creatively bankrupt society. Perhaps the time has come for the two groups to shed their positions and come together to fight the real enemy-no, not the government, but caste-based discrimination! Far-reaching reforms, such as increased government spending and more seats in institutes offering primary and secondary education are a must. But of what use are such progressive ideas and laws when people are inflexible when it comes to jettisoning their own outdated perspectives?

The anti-quota protesters are asking, 'why are we unfairly being made to pay the price for the oppression of the 'backward' castes that were committed in the past?'. The mistakes may largely have been committed in the past by an unaware and uncaring people, but their debilitating effects continue to surge relentlessly forward into each new generation of SC/STs and OBCs till today. Maybe the protesters should instead be asking: "Why were we not on the streets protesting vehemently when the Dalit faced severe violence because of his caste, when he was displaced from his home for 'the greater common good', when public money earmarked for his welfare was swallowed by an apathetic administration, when he was denied a job because he is Dalit? Where were we?"

Protect Unity with Social Justice

A decade after its submission, a part of the recommendations of the Mandal Commission report has been implemented by the announcement of 27 per cent reservation for the Other Backward Classes in jobs in Central Services and public sector undertakings. While there were periodic agitations for and against implementation of the Mandal report after 1981, now the decision of the National Front Government has sparked off widespread student protests against it in different States. They have the backing of a considerable section of the intelligentsia and practically the entire media controlled by big business.

Retrograde Opposition

The vociferous protest against reservation for Other Backward Classes (OBCs) and the growing unease about reservations for scheduled castes and scheduled tribes reflects the sharp conflicts which are erupting in Indian society over the distribution of a limited number of Government jobs and educational resources. It should be noted that the vocal opposition to the reservations for OBCs goes hand in hand with a more disguised resentment against reservation for the scheduled castes and tribes. One has only to recall to the Gujarat anti-reservation movement of 1981 and the recent December, 1989 U.P. agitation against the Parliament extending the reservation of seats in legislatures for the scheduled castes and scheduled tribes for another ten years.

The movement against reservations in the present Indian context is definitely retrograde and objectively serves the interests of those who seek to preserve the dominance of the upper castes. The plea against reservations is advanced on the basis of equality of opportunity and merit. In an unequal society like India, where scheduled castes, tribes and shudras (the bulk of whom are the OBCs) have been discriminated against in choice of occupation, social mobility and control over the means of production, all talk of equality, without taking into account this reality, reduces equality to the concept of formal equality.

As for merit, it is perfectly possible in India to discriminate in recruitment and promotions, on the basis of caste prejudices or preferences, militating against merit. Further, merit, as the Mandal Commission and a host of other commissions and Supreme Court judgements have pointed out, must be seen in the context of achieving real equality of opportunities, social environment and compensatory discrimination to ensure social justice.

Reservation for SCs & STs

The CPI(M) has viewed reservations for scheduled castes and scheduled tribes as the minimum relief extended by the Indian State to those sections of society who have historically and socially suffered the worst oppression over the centuries. While supporting this reservation (totalling 22.5 per cent at the Centre and varying in States according to the proportion of population of SCs and STs), the CPI(M) has also held that this is limited concession which does not tackle the roots of the problem necessary for their social and economic emancipation. The history of four decades of reservations for SCs and STs amply confirms this fact. Only a thin stratum (not more than five to ten per cent) of the SC population has benefitted from the reservations. Even in education, they are unable to fully utilise the quotas allotted to them.

The untouchables are still not "touchable" despite the four decades of constitutional sanction against this evil practice. They are subject to lynchings, rape of women and arson when they seek to stand up for their rights. Altogether 28,736 cases of atrocities against scheduled castes were reported in 1987 and 1988.

The reason for this is the lack of change in the material conditions of the vast mass of the scheduled castes people living in the rural areas. Land, the main means of production, is outside their control. The failure of the Indian bourgeoisie to complete the democratic tasks of the first stage of our revolution due to their compromise with landlordism, has led to the landless scheduled castes and tribals remaining not only at the bottom of the social ladder but also at the bottom of the economic ladder. That is why the CPI(M), while firmly supporting reservations in jobs and education for the SCs and STs as offering some openings, consistently demands radical land reforms and building of the unity of agricultural labourers and poor peasants of all sections to provide the basis for a powerful agrarian movement to achieve the same. The Mandal Commission report itself recognises this basic truth and notes: "unless these production relations are radically altered through structural changes and progressive land reforms implemented rigorously all over the country, OBCs will never become truly independent. In view of this, highest priority should be given to radical land reforms by all the States.

The Question of OBCs

Reservation for the OBCs has existed in many States for a long time. In the four southern States there has been some form of reservations from the pre-independence period. The other States where reservations exist in varying degrees are: Gujarat, Maharashtra, Bihar, U.P., Punjab and Himachal Pradesh. In West Bengal, Orissa, Assam and most of the north-eastern States, such reservations do not exist due to the nature of the historical evolution of the caste pattern, and in West Bengal due to the major socio-economic changes which were brought about through prolonged struggles.

It is a fact that the bulk of those who are categorised as OBCs in the States belong to the rural poor. They are sharecroppers, small tenants or poor peasants with small holdings. Further, in the rural areas the OBCs are in occupations which are still based on the traditional caste hierarchy such as dhobis, barbers, cattlerearers and artisans. Their lowly caste status prevents their entry into education and new occupations. These are the facts confirmed by detailed studies conducted by the Havanur Commission in Karnataka (1975); the Backward Classes Commission in Tamil Nadu (1971); the Backward Classes Reservation Commission in Kerala (1971); the Socially and Educationally Backward Classes Commission in Gujarat (1976) and the Backward Classes Commission in Andhra Pradesh (1970); that within OBCs there are many sub-castes which are educationally and economically backward judged by a number of socio-economic indicators.

Support for OBC Quotas

Therefore, where the caste status contributes to the backwardness of communities under the OBC category, and where anti-caste movements have not been able to cut across caste barriers and build powerful class-based mass organisations, there is a justification for providing reservations to such communities. This is the basis on which the CPI(M) supported the implementation of the Mandal Commission report since 1981-82 and earlier in States where due to prolonged movements the OBCs were accorded reservations.

Need for Economic Criterion

The CPI(M) has, however, qualified this support on two counts. Firstly, it has argued for an economic criterion within the reservation for OBCs. This is a demand distinct from the blanket reservation for the SCs and STs for whom no economic criterion is necessary. Four decades of socio-economic developments and growth of capitalism have led to class differentiation within the caste structure. In the case of OBCs, it is well known that there are a few castes in different States which contain influential strata who own land and other means of production. They are well represented in the political power structure also. The complexity of the OBC problem lies, thus, in the fact that within some communities of the OBCs there is a great economic (inter-caste) differentiation and also there is inter-caste differentiation, i.e., compared to a few better-off communities there are a number of more backward communities.

In order to see that the landless as compared to the richer landed, the poor as compared to the affluent, the more backward as distinct from the strata of the developed — i.e. the majority of the poor and deprived of these communities — benefit from reservation, the CPI(M) wants an economic criterion. This criterion need not necessarily be just an income ceiling, but can be a package in which income tax assessments, extent of landholding, professional status of parents, etc., can be taken into consideration.

Experience of States

The concept of an economic criterion is not a new proposal. As early as 1958, the Administrative Reforms Committee in Kerala headed by E.M.S. Namboodiripad, Chief Minister, suggested such a criterion for backward classes reservation. The Nettoor Damodaran Commission report of 1971 also made a similar suggestion. The Justice Chinnappa Reddy Commission report, the most recent in Karnataka, has recommended that from the OBC reservations those whose parents are income tax or sales tax assesses, hold land upto eight acres or are Class I officers can be excluded. In Kerala reservation in admissions to medical colleges is governed by an income criterion. Only those whose parents draw less than Rs, 20,000 per year are entitled to benefit from OBC reservation. In some other States like Tamil Nadu and Karnataka, there are two or three categories of backward classes, with the more backward either getting more fee concessions and other facilities or getting a greater quantum of reservations. The difficulty is that wherever OBC reservations already exist, the introduction of an economic criterion meets with strong resistance. Only when a broad consensus is reached can it be implemented. In Kerala, it has not been implemented so far as there is no such agreement. In the case of Bihar, when OBC reservations were being introduced for the first time in 1978, it was possible, after a destructive anti-reservation movement, to arrive at a formula which has been working since then. The 26 per cent reservation consists of 12 per cent of the most backward category listed in Annexure 1; eight per cent for other backward classes listed in Annexure II with an income ceiling of Rs 12,000 per annum; three per cent for women and three per cent for the poor of the forward castes. The National Front Government at the Centre should consider the Bihar Experience which brought about some stability in the tense caste situation. In this connection, the proposal of the Prime Minister for additional reservation of five to ten per cent for those economically backward can be accepted provided that this is allotted to those who do not fall within the reserved categories. This may help in alleviating the fears of those economically deprived amongst the forward castes.

Need for Consensus and Review

There is a second qualification with respect to OBC reservations. While the CPI(M) has been supporting the demand for the implementation of the Mandal Commission report, it has also been asking for a consensus to be evolved on the sensitive question. Only by taking care to see that substantial sections are convinced on the justification and reasonableness of the scope of reservations can be divisive anti-reservation movement be avoided or limited. That is why the Party criticised the sudden announcement without proper consultations. That an all-party meeting has now been proposed to held on September 3, shows how such an exercise earlier could have been helpful. Anyway, after the rich and varied experience of OBC reservations in the States, it is clear that there has to be periodic reviews of the status of those on the reserved lists and for identification of those who continue to remain backward. Here a good example is the Chinnappa Reddy Commission (the third in Karnataka in the space of 15 years(which has further defined the identification of backward status apart from keeping in mind the caste factor and computing other criteria along with it such as access to education, economic status, occupation and employment pattern.

History of Anti-caste Movements

But reservations for the OBCs have come to stay. Unlike the superficial portrayal which depicts V.P. Singh as the villain who has suddenly opened the Pandora's box of reservation for the OBCs, the social and political implications of the aspirations of those downtrodden in Indian society, has been with us before independence and during the past four decades. These facts of history are deliberately suppressed by the likes of Arun Shourie who have railed against reservations. He is only being consistent in his Hindu upper-casteist outlook. Advocating the "shifting" of Babri Masjid from its site in Ayodhya and pouring scorn over the aspirations of the lower castes, are both of one piece.

An aspect of the prolonged struggle against upper-caste domination was the non-Brahmin movements in the south and in Maharashtra for well over a century. In the north, the anti-caste social reform movements had a belated start. Bihar saw this phenomenon earlier than in other north-Indian States. In the pre-independence period, these anti-caste movements spearheaded the fight against the upper caste domination. Their main weakness lay in their alienation from the anti-imperialist movement a feature due also to the approach of the Congress party. It sought to fight caste-domination not by advocating a thorough-going agrarian revolution which could have altered the relations of production in agriculture, but by an upper-caste approach of reformism which was exemplified by Gandhism, both before and after independence, with its reliance on preaching against untouchability by inter-caste dining, inter-caste marriages, and of course reservations.

Need of Agrarian Revolution

The Marxist analysis of contemporary reality holds that the anti-caste movement, if it is to be successful in eliminating caste domination, requires linking the anti-caste movements with the movement for agrarian revolution, for building the unity of the working people, and advancing the democratic movement. Where this task remain unaccomplished, or where this impulse is weak, the consciousness of the oppressed mass within the lower caste considers reservations as the only safeguard for their advancement. The working class party, therefore, while supporting reservations, seeks to strengthen its links with the rural mass which will be a main force of the agrarian revolution. At the same time, it also considers the building of unity of the toiling people of all castes to be the crucial question. Unfortunately, some sections of the intelligentsia with democratic inclinations are opposing reservations for the OBCs on the plea that it perpetuates casteism and fragments society. This is to ignore the fact that it is the casteism of the upper-castes attendant with the monopoly of the means of production, which has perpetuated backwardness. If with capitalist development, class and caste alignments are getting redefined and divergent, the end to casteism and building class-based movements requires a dual approach.

The CPI(M) recognises that a big section of the working people come from castes and communities who, though not belonging to the SCs or OBCs, are economically exploited and suffer from social deprivation. They constitute an important and advanced section of the democratic movement. The modern working class and the organised movement of the working people can advance only the basis of the unity of both sections of the working people — the advanced sections of the urban working people and rural mass who suffer from both caste and economic oppression. Those who advocate reservations without any restrain and recklessly compete to hike up quotas for the backward classes and scheduled castes are not mindful of the vital need for unity. Their stand mirrors the approach of those upper caste sections who seek to oppose any increase in reservations as a threat to their interests. Both the pro-reservationist and the anti-reservationist leaders work within the bourgeois mould and foster the illusion that the distribution of the limited number of jobs at stake is a life and death question for the advancement of their communities. Both these approaches have to be countered and the working people of both sections mobilised on a common platform. Let it be emphasised that reservations alone cannot solve any of the basic problems facing the socially and economically oppressed.

Protect Unity

The CPI(M) attitude to OBC reservation stems from its class standpoint. It seeks the unity of the toiling people, of all castes, both urban and rural, against the main exploiters who perpetuate a social system which is retrogressive. This unity is necessary to fight monopoly capital and concentration of wealth which should unite both the forwards and backwards who comprise the working class. It is necessary to fight landlordism, for which the entire rural poor has to be mobilised breaking caste oppression and divisions. The democratic sections amongst the toilers not covered by reservations, both working class and peasantry, have to accept the necessity for reservations, so that overall unity can be cemented.

Call of the 13th Party Congress

Unlike the past, the CPI(M) cannot see the anti-caste struggles as only a sphere for social reform. The Left has to channelise this anti-feudal current into its agrarian movement. The Thirteenth Congress of the CPI(M), in its Political Resolution, addressed itself to the situation of the masses belonging to these downtrodden castes and state: "Large sections from these masses often stand alienated from the democratic and working class movement, and are swayed by sectional leadership which diverts their discontent and anger into narrow channels. The period since our last Congress has witnessed a new militant awakening among these sections — the adivasis, harijans and backward classes. It is necessary to make all efforts to draw this new awakening to the common struggle developing a correct attitude and tactics towards their organisation".

The resolution proceeds to point out that the successive Congress Governments have attempted to rally these sections, tempting them with the promise of reservation of jobs in Government service. "This was also a device to bypass the question of land reforms and redistribution of land". Since reservations cater only to a small minority amongst them, "the growing misery of the uneducated mass is bursting forth in militant protest and action. These protests against social discrimination, caste tyranny, police repression, are at present carried out under the leadership of their caste leaders. They represent the anti-feudal, anti-landlord discontent of these agrarian masses."

The resolution exhorts: "The Party, the democratic movement

and class organisations should led support to their struggle against caste tyranny and repression, and enable them and their organisations to join the common struggle." This applies to the SC and ST, toiling sections as well to the oppressed in the OBCs.

BJP's, Cong(I)'s Double Standards

The RSS has come out openly against the declared reservations for the OBCs. Denouncing V.P. Singh, the Organiser stated: "He wants to undo the great task of uniting Hindu society from the days of Vivekananda, Dayanand Saraswati, Mahatma Gandhi and Dr Hedgewar." The RSS view, not surprisingly, is governed by its Hindu chauvinist upper-caste bias. Notwithstanding the official position of the BJP leadership, that reservation should be there with an economic criterion, its ranks are active in the student agitation. One of its M.P.s, Dr. J.K. Jain, went on a hunger strike against the announcement. Both the BJP and Congress(I) activists are actively competing to lead the anti-reservation agitation. Their representatives in the executive of the Delhi University Teachers Association have ganged up to try and pass a resolution condemning the implementation of the OBC reservations. From these activities it seems that for these parties, (unlike the CPI(M), the demand for an economic criterion is not meant to improve the scheme of reservations, it is a ploy to try and scuttle its implementation.

Responsibility of Democratic Forces

One has to condemn the manoeuvrings of bourgeois political leaders who seek to make reservation a device for consolidating their influence and thereby fan caste divisions and divide the people. This is a cynical manipulation of the aspirations of the most oppressed sections in the downtrodden castes. At the same time, the advanced democratic movement, the fighting organisations of the different sections of the people have a heavy responsibility before them:

1. To oppose movements against reservations.
2. At the same time, explain to the democratic sections not entitled to reservations, the necessity to accept this limited concession to those deprived of the capacity for equal competition due to historical-social conditions.
3. Counter caste-exclusive movements which stress only reservations and seek to keep the SC or reserved categories

of employees and workers away from the common movement. This requires championing their special demands and problems.

Strengthen the United Fight

All efforts must be made to see that people do not get divided on the reservation question. For this, it is essential that the struggle to change the present direction of policies is stepped up. The National Front Government has promised the right to work in the Constitution; it is yet to be implemented. The struggle to expand employment and ensure the right to work can be the basis of the broadest unity encompassing the crores of the unemployed. In the sphere of land reforms, the fight to distribute land already identified as surplus (63 million acres) but not taken over the distributed by the Government (58.5 million acres), provides the basis for uniting the rural poor. The right to education and expansion of education facilities to make them accessible to all is vital in view of the continuing trend to restrict higher education and neglect the primary school sector. If increased reservations in educational institutions are there, it must go hand in hand with compensatory increases in seats in higher education, so that no one deserving is deprived of higher education.

The National Front Government has been unable to make a radical break with the old economic policies of the Congress. It has no plan to revive the over two lakh sick units which are closed in the industrial sector; its industrial policy pronouncements with a bias to foreign capital and privatisation will restrict the scope of employment. It has not withdrawn the ban on recruitment in Government services and public sector undertakings. Many State Governments do not want to proceed of land reforms on the specious plea that its implementation is completed. All these policies have to be reversed, and this requires the broadest unity of all sections of the people.

The stand taken by the CPI(M) Politbureau and Central Committee on the OBC reservations, in practice, is the way the unity of the people, the toiling sections can be maintained and strengthened to see that the main struggle against the bourgeois-landlord system further advances.

CHAPTER 3

Problem of Gender Inequality and Expansion of Women's Education

The pace of social change in West Bengal has accelerated in recent years because of the globalisation trends. But the problem of gender inequality in West Bengal has revealed as a new dimension. Despite the land of various political, social, economic and cultural movements, the State has failed to organize a movement for development and upliftment of women as an entire class. Even after entering the new millenium the popular saying frequently heard from the men and even the women 'Sonar Aantir Abar Banka Na Soja' (The golden ring is free from crooked or straight) upholding their male counterparts. This little example clearly explains the degree of prevailing gender inequality in once Renaissance enlightened Bengal. The project will evaluate how such gender inequalities have been created and reproduced in the households, markets and societies in West Bengal. The factors that underlie gender inequality will be thoroughly examined. Women in West Bengal are commonly portrayed as among the most oppressed and majority of them are grounded in both poverty and patriarchy.

Patriarchy limits women's ownership and control of property and other economic resources including the products of their own labour. Women's mobility in West Bengal is constrained and their access to education and information hindered. The clearest example of gender inequality are the various forms of violence systematically meted out against women. They are practically excluded from decision making. Preventable diseases and unequal access to health care still affect women and girls, especially those in rural sector. HIV infection among women continues to increase. Incidents of physical violence against women in West Bengal are increasingly mentioned in the media but rarely within the context of longer processes of gender discrimination. In this research project we will investigate the opportunities and constraints that women face in and outside the home. West Bengal is an unusual, unique state in the country.

It is the only one of the states in our country to have been ruled continuously (since 1977) by a progressive, coalition government for about three decades. This government in turn has been motivated by a different vision of political, social, economic cultural change. The pace of social changes in West Bengal has accelerated in recent years but the problem of gender inequality in the state has revealed as a new dimension. Despite the land of various political, social, economic and cultural movements, the state has failed to organize a movement for development and upliftment of women as an entire class. Even after entering the new millennium the popular saying frequently heard from the men and even the women "Sonar Aantir Abar Banka Na Soja" (The golden ring is free from crooked or straight) upholding their male counterparts. The little example clearly explains the degree of prevailing gender inequality in once renaissance enlightened Bengal. Women in West Bengal are commonly portrayed as among the most oppressed and majority of them are grounded in both poverty and patriarchy. Patriarchy limits women's ownership and control over property and other economic resources including the products of their own labour. Women's mobility in West Bengal is constrained and their access to education and information hindered. The clearest examples of gender inequality are the various forms of violence systematically meted out against women. They are practically excluded from decision making. Preventable diseases and unequal access to health care still affect women and girls, especially those in rural sector. HIV infection among women continues to increase. Incidents of physical violence against women in West Bengal are increasingly mentioned in the media but rarely within the context of longer processes of gender discrimination.

Objective of the Study

The project has tried to evaluate how much gender inequalities have been created and reproduced in the households, markets and societies in the state. The factors that underlie gender inequality have been tried to examine. The research project has tried to investigate the opportunities and constraints that women face in and outside the home. This work has tried to study how far the problem of gender inequality has been solved by the expansion of education of women in West Bengal. The rate of infancy marriage in Kerala is only 7%. In comparison in this state the rate is higher. 53.3% women are illiterate among the women secretly removed. The age of 40% of them is less than 18 years. The secretly removal of women has increased 45% in last few years. 65% of the women less than 18 years have attained early marriage. Oppression on women, dowry system, still exist in the society. Early motherhood, ill health due to malnutrition, concept of male and female child in obtaining higher education have worried the government, administration and social scientists. According to census, 2001 the gender development index in West Bengal is 0.549. Districts like Howrah, North 24 Parganas, Burdwan and Cooch, Behar obtain gender inequality as an alarming situation. The reservation for women has already been put in place in Panchayats and local bodies and experience of its working can only be described as encouraging.

Research Methodology

Observation, Documentation and Analytical Research

The research work has followed the guideline with the help of discussions, seminars, symposia, sharing views, exchanges dialogue with common mass, rural and urban women, reports of Women Commission, Administration, Human Development, conversation with Women Activists, Social Workers and also with the help of opinion surveys. The project has interacted with different groups of people including students, house wives and non-government organizations.

Case Study: The method has provided a host of observations, ideas, insights to and several aspects of a single case. Gender discrimination has been an important feature of economic and social processes in the state. It has declined in some respects in the areas of the State. But it is more evident in economic variables and in literacy rate that indicate improving health position of women in comparison with their male counterparts. This comes out very clearly in the calculations of the Gender Development Index (G.D.I.) which are presented here:-

Table 1:-Gender Development Indices by District

District	Health	Income	Education Index	GDI Index	Rank Index
Darjeeling	0.731	0.356	0.714	0.600	2
Jalpaiguri	0.614	0.281	0.581	0.492	11
Cooch Behar	0.497	0.287	0.628	0.471	13
Dinajpur	0.616	0.291	0.527	0.478	12
Bardhman	0.740	0.270	0.669	0.560	7
Naida	0.649	0.215	0.653	0.506	9
Malda	0.491	0.291	0.465	0.416	17
Murshidabad	0.566	0.176	0.527	0.423	16
Birbhum	0.533	0.178	0.595	0.435	14
Purulia	0.606	0.161	0.506	0.424	15
Midnapore	0.683	0.323	0.728	0.578	4
North 24 Pargnas	0.721	0.219	0.752	0.564	6
Hooghly	0.764	0.259	0.720	0.581	3
Bankura	0.662	0.215	0.605	0.494	10
Howrah	0.773	0.194	0.742	0.570	5
Kolkata	0.824	0.320	0.783	0.642	1
South 24 Parganas	0.705	0.192	0.666	0.521	8
West Bengal	0.697	0.270	0.681	0.549	

Source:-West Bengal Human Development Report, 2004.

From the table mentioned above, it is observed-that the rankings of the GDI broadly follow the same pattern as the HDI rankings., The districts having low HDI also tend to have low GDI. Some districts like Howrah, North 24 Parganas, Bardhaman and CoochBehar tend to have worse ranking in term of GDI than HDI indicating especially acute gender discrimination. The very low "income Index" component of the GDI esssentially reflect, the low workforce participation of women in West Bengal, which in turn suggests a combination of greater restrictions on women's economic agency as well as social look of recognition of women's unpaid work.

Both of these striking features suggest a considerable undercurrent of gender inequality ad discrimination in the society. The problem of gender inequality and discrimination is interlinked with the differential rates of literacy of a particular locality, access to primary and basic education, health and nutrition indicators. The policy interventions of the West Bengal Government have had mixed effects in this regard. The beneficiaries of policy of land reform tended to aggravate gender discrimination. Women's participation in Panchayat, has been greater and much significant effect than in many other states and there are some regions within the state where this has had very striking positive social impact. It upholds the very notion empowerment of women in more diverse form. With respect to human security issues, women in West Bengal are in relatively better position than in other states of the country. Economic exclusion appears as one of the most significant problems for women in the state, which tends to have spill-over effects in other aspects of life. However, the trends in all of these variables are broadly in a positive direction, although the pace of change is not as rapid as could be desired.

Gender Inequality & Discrimination

There is a perception in society even urban also that girls are more homely and are better at taking care of things. That is why arts, fashion, designing and drama are generally fields reserved for women. Engineering and other related fields are considered hardcore; so more men than women enroll in these programmes. This perception is however, gradually changing. Women students have family affairs to attend to. Some students say they are better at attending to these jobs. Studying social sciences gives them this kind of freedom and flexibility.

For instance, the teaching profession, which appears to have been completely taken over by women. Even today, we find more women than men in this profession both at the school and college level, as they find it relatively easy to juggle home and career. A majority of women are still being "pushed" into disciplines, which have traditionally been called "soft". It is just the reverse for male students. The so called " soft" disciplines are Education and Social Sciences, while the "core male" disciplines are Engineering and IT. A few women's college do offer science course, the majority do not and this pushes more women into taking "softer" options. That is how we have scores of all women's colleges running Social Sciences, Humanities and Mass Media progreammes. Again, while Business/ commerce and Science disciplines are (to an extend) skewed in favour of men, Medicine and Social Sciences are singularly dominated by women.

Expansion of Education

In West Bengal, in the decades of fifties, sixties and mid-seventies the question emerged gradually was why women should join the mahila mandal or attend the functional literacy session. Almost three decades later, concrete and tangible achievements have paved the path of women's participation, giving them their right to association and opportunity to exercise their choices due to expansion of education in West Bengal. The articulate presentations by women on their real life experiences as elected representatives in Panchayat and other local bodies or forums are really encouraging. In the light of education the shyness of a woman gradually disappears and there is a tendency of pervasive boldness and enthusiasm in 'queuing up' to speak from the podium. The directness of communication is astounding. It is equally amazing that the spontaneous interventions from the floor from women without distinction of class, location, religion, caste or literacy.

In the rural Bengal a woman is able to identify the levels and locus of her needs and objectives. She clearly explains why girls' schools should have lavatories. Is that not women empowerment? The women representatives plead for direct dispensation of funds to the gram panchayat without intermediaries. Is that not a visible milestone for devolution of power? Due to the gradual expansion of basic or primary education, women representatives express their desired role in rural development planning and agree to assume responsibility for pure water facilities, set up village school and the anganwadi. So, there is no scope of disillusionment about the capacity of rural women to assert their rights for equal participation in local governance. When and how did this change happen? The women's political activism, the strength of their intellectual analysis and discourse, their boldness to break barriers of male dominated institutions and the solidarity of their network made irreversible dents in the policy and administrative fabric of the state. The openness of the few but influential male allies to join the struggle and steer the change from within the system is a major support and cannot go unrecognized. The facilitating factors have been the increasing participation of women in public and private spheres, the equalizing of salary for equal work, targeted credit and economic assistance and incentive linked girls' education.

Mainstream Media and Gender Issues

Perception about women seem to be one of the few things constant in this fast changing world. Or so it appears from a study conducted by researchers at the School of Women's Studies (SWS), Jadavpur University, which analyzed the representation of women in the media and how it is changing with time. The Director, SWS Samita Sen said "We discovered that although there is an apparent change, the basic roles and presumptions about women's worlds remain the same." According to Prof Sen, the depiction of women in television serials showed a distinct binary between the good woman and the vamp. The regional channels and the Bengali serials, however, had greater diversity while the so called K-soaps mainly concentrated on interiorzed, Hindu upper caste women. A narrowing down of diversity in women's representation has also noticed in some of the newspapers analyzed during the information gathering process. It is evident that though some of the newspapers have done away with pages devoted exclusively for women. There is a tendency of increasing preoccupation with celebrities and glamorous women.

Stereotype Representation

There is no better metaphor for how tragically trapped in polarizations the modern gender debate has become. If we go through the mainstream media apparently we see there only two kinds of women in India. Type A is draped in gold and gaudiness, she is devoted to Duty. She is selfless and servile. And she is usually fat. Type B is draped in barely anything. She has a perfectly toned body and slithers like a snake to the beat of her own sensuality. And she usually does not eat.

Efficiency Dimensions of Gender Budgeting

Gender budgeting means the entire budge via a gender lens to identity differential gender impacts and translate gender commitments into budgetary ones. The real challenge lies in the analysis of mainstream, 'non-rival', public expenditure whose benefits all get to enjoy, irrespective of caste, creed or sex. Gender budgeting enhance the transparency of and accountability for public expenditure and revenue and examines the gender disaggregated incidence of benefits of budgetary policies for effective public expenditure targeting. It stresses reprioritization. A key thrust is to lift the veil of statistical invisibility of the unpaid 'care economy' and incorporate it in fiscal policy. It is also a people-centred initiative can redress capability deprivation across genders and accords with the last decade's UN conferences. It has yet to percolate to state and local governments. Tax benefits extended to women workers are expected to reduce the double burden that they face at home and the work place – the gains, for example, can be utilized to appoint domestic help. But can't the working husbands of working women pay for them too? If the husbands are dependents, this move would be seen as a positive one for women's welfare. Women continue to bear the double burden and the state ends up paying for the domestic help. Isn't that a subsidy to the married working male?

Gender sensitive budget is a gender sensitive approach if a chunk of development outlay is specifically spent on women's health, education and employment generation. This can help them overcome household inequalities and negative development outcomer (like environmental degradation) that affect women more. An important and better way of empowering the women in West Bengal would be to upgrade their skills and spread education inexpensively; that can yield them better access to earning opportunities. That holds also for the enforcement of equal wages in the unorganized sector; that is urgently needed and the requisite incentive structures should be speedily devised. Finally, the nutritional status, education and overall well-being of the girl child depends largely on her mother's earning and particularly so within low-income households. Despite that, a gender differential in wages in the unorganized sector cannot be treated as an excuse to artificially like women's net incomes in the organized sector. Real legal reform in West Bengal can only follow vital social reform. The idea of gender equality needs to be implemented first within the deep recesses of our society through liberal education, increased cultural socialization between the minority and the majority communities. It is only when the basic power relationships in our society – between men and women are also debated, analyzed and critiqued within the civil society will it be possible to translate the new law against domestic violence into practice.

Violence against Women

Violence against women remains a constant practice across societies. Crawling under the umbrella of violence is an array of horrifying acts – female foeticide, trafficking, workplace harassment, domestic torture and rape. When women defy societal norms and prejudices to report criminal action they are confronted by unequal laws that refuse to give them redressal. The UN says that violence against women is a major cause of death and disability for women 16 to 44 years of age. Crimes against women are committed with impunity in the absence of any meaningful punishment or deterrent for their perpetrators legal luminaries and citizens' groups engage in lofty debates on the merits of current punishment patterns, yet verdicts that may qualify as justice done are few and far between. Whether it is female foeticide or trafficking of girl children, domestic rape or harassment at workplace, there seems to be an unhappy acceptance that these 'wrongs' will continue. Little progress can be made if the roots of such violence are not needed out. Expressions of violence against women reflect a society's values, law and order responses act only as deterrents. Yet, the scale of the challenge should not deter us from pressing on in this battle, on all fronts – community education, better law enforcement and deterrent punishment.

Gender Discrimination and the Protection of Women

No one speaks of its. Women suffer it in silence. They are schooled to believe that ultimately it is their fault. Women are abused physically, emotionally, verbally. But these stories rarely make it to the public domain because the victims themselves will not speak. Women think there is no option but keep quiet and accept. Domestic violence is a violation of the human right of women. The Protection of Women from Domestic Violence Act, 2005 which was notified on October 25, 2006. Accordingly to this Act, all forms of physical, sexual, verbal, emotional or economic abuse are defined as "domestic violence". It offers women victims of such violence civil remedies of a kind not available to them earlier. Some critics argue that a poor uneducated woman would be unaware of her rights or would not know how to turn to the Law. The paper raises a question why do so many educated middle class women also tolerate abuse? Women have to be made aware that such an act exists. The research paper expresses its concern at the lack of knowledge on women's legal rights even amongst educated young women studying in some of our renowned educational Institutions. These are the very same middle class women.? Despite their education, these women act also like the women of lower class believing that they have to tolerate abuse because they have no option. So, public information and education of the kind that has taken on the Right to Information Act is essential on this. The Protection of Women from Domestic Violence Act, 2005 came into force from October 26. State Government officials are now formulating the government's charter of demands to the centre including more funds and recruitment of additional hands for implementation of the Act. Government orders are being issued for appointment of District Social Welfare Officers as Protection Officers (POs) with immediate effect. The POs would have to investigate each case of domestic violence reported in the areas under his/her jurisdiction. To educate the POs about the aspects of the Act and their duties, a brainstorming session has been organized in Kolkata on November 11. The Additional District Magistrates overseeing various programmes and schemes for women and child development attended the session. The POs and other district officials have been asked to involve NGOs and voluntary agencies in acting as "service providers" in compliance with the provisions of the new Act. The opinion that men and women are not equal is derived from the view that gender follows naturally from sex. In other words, a man is biologically masculine by birth and a woman is feminine. There is need for much greater gender equality and sexual liberalization. Every person should have equal rights to education regardless of whether they are male or female or for that matter, rich or poor, Dalit or Brahmin. Similarly, every person should have equal freedom to pursue a career or hold a job. In West Bengal the rate of women is higher than the national rate but the situation of Kolkata is not so good. The number of women is 828 in per thousand man. The statistics and information say that female foeticide is increasing in well to do families than down trodden.

Role of Media in Gender Discrimination

Politics apart, there are other sectors where women allege gender bias. Media studies, time and again, emphasize that men restrict women. At a recent round table conference on the role of the media in projecting development needs of women, male editors were blamed for keeping women reporters out. In a government sponsored study, media were criticized for not reporting on women's issues Women journalists are invited to discuss the report expressed helplessness at the apathy of news managers in projecting women's issues. If a good story deals with women, it is not spiked. It finds space in the media not because it deals with women but because it is a good story. By the same standard, an average story will not command attention, even it is gender based.

Combat against Oppression

Combat against oppression of women will be initiated from all corners of the society. Domestic violence will be closed if the male members of the home become careful. Women are verbally, emotionally, psychologically abused since the teen age. Women face sexual harassment at their work place. Many of them have been forced to enter the business of flesh trade. Widows, unmarried or lonely women are oppressed physically, psychologically or sexually. Oppression free life is the fundamental right of women. Eradication of the gender biasness can only save the right of women. We have to implement such value system oriented education that will provide a boy and a girl equal benefits and opportunities.

Real Condition of Women

Some critics advocate that all women are terminal in the male dominating society. Women are the worst sufferer of destruction and sexual harassment. Women of lower class are compelled to accept it. They do not know how to protect it. 25th November and 10th December are observed each year as "International Women Oppression Day" and "International Human Rights Day." But the morning newspapers cover the incidents of sexual harassment, rape, wife oppression, female foeticide, Removal of women secretly on a daily basis. Effect of gender biasness directly fall on the women. Imbalance deprives women from education, health, physical and economic resources etc. They are deprived in the field of politics, economics, social and culture even. Rural women do not work by laptop but in the cropfield. They have to be understood about their rights. Urban women know the language of protest. They have achieved freedom in a considerable degree. But the rural women are still in the climate of darkness. Child marriage, dowry system and female foeticide are still happening even in the progressive state like West Bengal are treated since their childhood as "Your are a woman" not "You are a human being". Boys are still at the top of the priority list than girls. They are fed by nutrious food. The village women do not know about women freedom, women liberty, women emancipation etc. Light of education can only provide the necessary awareness amongst the victimized poor women.

Come Forward Men

An ideal family always exhibit the equal dignity of men and women. Men should not take upper hand in the family due to their masculinity. Men have to protest in streets, markets, work places, shopping malls, tramcars, buses, trains or hotels, restaurants against any sort of abuse of women. It is essential to treat the matter as a social issue. Men should forward their hands towards oppressed women as a real friend. Protest against dowry system should be initiated from the corner of men. Women deserve equal share and status in a family and men have to accept it. Virginia Woolf once commented that there were two wants in woman's life-self income and self residence. Women now uphold their voices. They form associations. They unitedly try to change the existing situation.

Case Studies

Namita Das is a member of a downtrodden family. Her husband is a rickshaw puller. Namita's son Mukai fell ill one day. Namita had no money to bring her son to a medical practitioner. Namita borrowed Rs.200 from a self dependent group and made necessary arrangements for her son's treatment. Chhabi Kundu and her husband are rice dealers.

But the majority share of their profit was consumed to meet the interest of the money lender. The want of the family went on.

Chhabi became the member of "Surabhi" – a self dependent group. Now, she has achieved the provision of loan. Now their profit increased. Her economic stability and social establishment have enhanced. Arati Mandal lives in Bankura. Majority of her land was sterile. Her husband was daily wage worker. On day he passed away. There was no option infront of Arati than went to city for searching a new job. But the other members of self dependent group helped her to stay in village. The villages of West Bengal have gradually changed.

Village does not mean the story of grief and failure. Namita, Chhabi, Arati arre indentified with their stories of success. They form self help and self dependent group to stand firm on their own feet. Distant villages of West Bengal exhibit two features. Self dependent groups and deposit loan and insurance. These groups being changes in the life of backward women especially in the remote villages in the state. Infact, self dependent group means association of 10-15 socially and economically backward women having equal status. This association is area based. Deposit of money and loan help them to form the group. As the group strengthens, the women become self confident. The expansion of primary and basic education help them to give more attention on the education of their children, nurturing of the little girls. The exploitation of women, oppression on women become decreased. Women are now eager to know the functions and activities of Panchayats. They are participating in the session of Gram Sansad. Group formation, financial management, groupbased organization formation, relation with bank-these are some developments in the rural sector of this state. The role of self dependent group may be important in the Gram Unnayan Samity in West Bengal. At present, there are about 3 lakh groups in the state. 36 lakh families are involved with it. 1 crore 80 lakh people are attached with this activities.

Besides NGOs, the State Government has extended its hands for the development of rural women. Swarnajayanti Gram Swarojgar Yojana (1 lakh 40 thsandsand groups) of Deptt. of Panchayat and Rural Development, Swayangsiddha Project (6,000 groups) of West Bengal Women Development Corporation. NABARD, CO-operative banks, Samabaya Krishi Unnayan Samity have helped a lot. SIDBI and Rashtriya Mahila Kosh have worked well. Cash project of care and its associated organization (11,000 group) have done well in this sector. Self Help Group Promotional Forum has arranged with the association of State Panchayat and Rural Development Organization. They have arranged Annual Conferences every year. Women participated in this conference coming from Kalchini to Kakdwip, Basirhat to Bandoan and from all districts of the state. They attend, participate in the discussion and ultimately frame the future plan of action. The fifth Conference was held at Bagnan in Howrah district during 10-12 February 2006. As a consequence, gender discrimination, educational discrimination have decreased. Though in a slow rate but decreasing.

Central Government's Stand

National Common Minimum Programme (NCMP) of United Progressive Alliance (UPA) was a commitment to empower women politically, educationally and legally. Further, the NCMP promised to take the lead in introducing legislation to reserve for women one-third of the seats in the State Assemblies and in the Lok Sabha and address the issues of domestic violence, gender discrimination and discriminatory legislation. While many of these promises have remained on paper, the overall intent of the government on women's issues presented in the draft approach paper (DAP) to the Eleventh Five-Year Plan (2007-2012) has installed new fears among women's organizations. In the DAP, titled "Towards Faster and More Inclusive Growth: An Approach to the 11th Five Year Plan", gender discrimination is confined to a few paragraphs under the sub-heading "Gender Balancing". Even if the restricted nature of the content can be overlooked, the lack of perspective and strategy has disappointed women activities. The paper states: "The 11th Plan strategy for gender balancing must take care of the special needs of women such as clean cooking fuels, care for pregnant and nursing women, etc..Gender balancing would require appropriate provisions in government policies/schemes across Ministries/departments and sectors."

While it says "special measures for gender empowerment and equity should be an essential element of the 11th Plan". The link between patriarchy, caste and religion, all three of which have serious implications for the status of women. It says that "while women's needs will be specially tackled across all sectors, the Plan will particularly focus on three aspects – violence against women (VAW), economic empowerment and women's health" and will seek to check violence, ranging from domestic violence to foeticide and sexual assault, through effective policies and legislation. It says that "effect will be made to ensure that towns and cities under the NURM (National Urban Renewal Mission) are made women friendly." Women's groups see VAW occurring in a socio-economic and political context and as such feel the need to change this particular context.

Indira Hirway, Professor of Economics and director of the Ahmedabad-based Centre for Development Alternatives said that with the onset of globalization, there had been a declaration of employment in general and a decline in the quality and extent of employment of women in particular. A qualitative shift in the nature of women's work, a shift from regular to irregular forms of work, had taken place. Vina Mazumdar, national research professor in social sciences, said, admitted that a "nation cannot be healthy unless its women are healthy". But as a remedy it suggests steps to reduce anemia and malnutrition but only among "adolescent girls" to eliminate "maternal and infant mortality". A huge chunk of women in the reproductive age group has been left out. According to the National Sample Survey 55th Round, July 1999-June 2000, of the around 106 million women in the workforce 40-45 per cent were in the reproductive age group. The Mid –Term-Appraisal (MTA) had underscored issues such a adverse sex ratios, high infant and maternal mortality, wide gaps in the rates of literacy and wages of men and women, feminization of poverty and the exploitation of women in the unorganized sector and in the export processing or special economic zones. It recognized that women were both productive workers contributing to the economy and mothers and home-makers. C.P. Sujaya, vesting Fellow at the Centre for Women's Development Studies, said: "Women's productive and non-productive roles and functions are both equally important and this should be a non-negotiable premise to the Eleventh Plan."

Women's Participation

There has been substantial representation of the rural women who are social deprived in the elected bodies. This has helped to change the power equations in rural society and encourage the social and political empowerment of women. West Bengal has a history of substantial representation of women in Panchayats well before the 73rd and 74th amendments passed by Parliament. In 1980s and 1990s more than one-third of Panchayat members were women. Even Zilla Parishads exhibited women representation. The Panchayat Elections in 2003 have created even more gender balance because of the active policy of the ruling party and its partners in terms of fielding more women candidates, and now the Sabhadhipatis of several districts are women. Active women's participation due to expansion of education improves the local enforcement of the requirement of people. Special meals for girls students, nutrition programme for pregnant and lactating mothers, public health campaigns have been implemented more effectively due to greater participation of women workers. The significant increase in the proportion of girls in education, the better performance of girls in school and strong the motivation of schooling even among girls in low income or socially deprived groups can be partly attributed to the influence of women Panchayats members in raising consciousness and gender awareness in the local communities. Even in the backward district like Purulia, young women Panchayat members from poor and socially disadvantaged backgrounds are increasingly more articulate and empower able to express the concerns of women in public forums and conscious of the need to influence policy making.

Expansion of Education of Women

The literacy rate is generally considered as one of the important indicators of the development of a population, and the educational level of a population is seen as an important determinant of its quality of life. In addition, of course, education interacts with other human development variables in crucial ways. For example, universal education and special attention to the education of women are critical in improving the health practices of a community. Universal education is also likely to be necessary for meaningful and effective decentralization, especially in the coming phase when panchayats are being given greater responsibility for a very wide range of activities.

The literacy rate in West Bengal has always been higher than the all-India average, and West Bengal ranks sixth among the major states in this regard. But until the last decade, the improvement in literacy has been relatively slow in the state, especially for women. However, in the past decade, the state government has been making concentrated efforts through various special schemes such as 'total literacy campaigns,', 'non-formal education', etc. apart from formal schooling for children to achieve the goal of 'education for all' as soon as possible. As a result, according to the Census, the literacy rate in West Bengal has increased from 48.6 per cent in 1981 to 57.7 per cent in 1991 and to 69.2 per cent in 2001. While rural literacy is predictably lower than in urban areas, it has improved more rapidly in the recent past. Furthermore, as can be seen from Figure 7.1, while literacy among rural females is still low compared to other groups, it has increased more rapidly in the recent past, going up by nearly 16 percentage points in the last decade. It is encouraging that the largest improvements in literacy in the past decade have been in some of what were the most "backward" districts, and especially among females. Increases in the female literacy rate have been in excess of 20 percentage points in Dakshin Dinajpur and Koch behar, and more than 15 percentage points in Jalpaiguri, Murshidabad, Malda, Darjeeling, Nadia and Birbhum, in the period between 1991 and 2001. So there is substantial improvement in literacy – and especially female literacy – in the recent period.

By 1998-99, 48 per cent of rural males and 27 per cent of rural females in the age group 15 years and above were estimated to have completed at least primary education, and around one-third of these had completed secondary education or above. In the urban areas, 79 per cent of adult males and 62 per cent of adult females were found by the NFHS-2 to be literate at least up to primary level or above. The variations in literacy rates across occupational groups in rural West Bengal for all the population above 7 years, and separately for females above 7 years.

The relatively most deprived occupation group appears to be that of agricultural labour households, of whom more than half of all such population, and nearly two-thirds of the females, are non-literate. Households consisting of the self-employed in agriculture show the highest rates of literacy, for men and women in rural parts of the state. Gender gaps remain substantial, and women of rural labour households (both in agriculture and non-agriculture) are the worst off among the rural population in terms of illiteracy. Interestingly, gender gaps in literacy appear to be slightly less marked in urban parts of the state. Casual labour households are the worst off, and nearly half the women in such households are illiterate. In urban areas, those households where the main source of income is from regular wages, as well as "other" households, show the lowest rates of illiteracy. Quite obviously, females in the ST households in the rural areas of West Bengal need special attention to improve the education levels in the rural West Bengal.

Next come SC households, where more than half of the women are illiterate. The gender gap seems to be approximately equal across caste category, indicating that gender discrimination is not more marked among any particular caste group, but is shared across all castes. Nor is the gender gap among Muslims higher than it is among Hindus, indicating that the general perception that Muslim women are less likely to be educated than their Hindu counterparts, is not borne out by the data. However, attendance rates for girls aged 6-10 years in rural West Bengal were generally better than the all-India average, although in urban areas the rare in West Bengal was slightly lower. For girls aged 11-13, attendance rates were higher or the same as the all-India average. Increasing the efforts for resource mobilization to enable more state government spending in necessary areas; and innovating and strengthening institutions and mechanisms to ensure the better delivery of public services. Such a strategy would help to generate a virtuous cycle of human development and economic growth positively reinforcing each other.

Last Few Words

There are particular areas that require specific intervention which are mentioned very briefly here. The reversal of employment generation for urban women, and the large male-female wage-gap in urban work, both point to the need for focused intervention. The low nutritional status of women and young children require urgent attention. Areas of public intervention that can be usefully pursued in this regard include the provision of sanitary facilities and campaigns to improve food consumption practices to ensure adequate nutrition. Targeted interventions in terms of provision, access and raising public consciousness about desirable food intake patterns are especially necessary, given the large production of vegetables, which do not appear to be consumed within the state. In education, certain spatial and social pockets of illiteracy need to be addressed. In occupational terms, agricultural labour households (and especially females in such households) require special policy attention.

Scheduled Tribe households (especially females) also require a focused drive to increase literacy. The Constitutional provisions of social equality and justice need to be strengthened by the efforts of common people in our villages and cities. Efforts to end gender based discrimination should be implemented aggressively. Expansion of education of women in West Bengal should be aimed at ending injustice and enhancing the individual potential as well as social contribution of those member of society who have limited opportunities. The year 2005 marks the 10th Anniversary of the Beijing Declaration and Platform for Action – the world's first truly comprehensive plan in the areas of critical concern to women's advancement. The Govt. of West Bengal should ratify the United Nations Convention on the Elimination of All Forms of Discrimination Against Women (1979). Gender equality can only be achieved truly if alongwith observation of International Women's Day (8th March) people around the State rededicate themselves to provide women their due in social safety nets, in decision making, development of the State and most importantly in the home.

CHAPTER 4

The Triple Oppression of Dalit Women

Background

Nepal is a country characterised not only by biodiversity but also by socio-cultural diversity. Meanwhile, Nepalese political and social life is primarily dominated by the Hindu religion, which divides Hindu society into four varnas, namely, Brahmins, Kshatriyas, Vaishyas and Sudras. Over a period of time, casteism developed a rigid hierarchical society with the purity and pollution of castes. In this manufactured caste hierarchy, Brahmins lie at the top, and Sudras, or Dalits, lie at the bottom of society. The word Dalit literally means "a person immersed in a swamp." Traditionally, Dalits have been treated inhumanely as "Untouchables."

Although untouchability was abolished by the New National Code of Nepal in 1963, its practice still continues. The people belonging to this community are living in a swamp of illiteracy, exploitation, marginalisation, absolute poverty and, above all, caste discrimination. Dalit women, however, are triply oppressed: (1) oppressed by the so-called high caste people, which equally affects both male and female Dalits, (2) oppressed by the design of the Hindu patriarchal system and (3) oppressed by Dalit males. It is estimated that the Dalit community constitutes 20 percent of the total population of the country, or four million people, and that the population of Dalit women is half of this figure, i.e., two million people.

In general, Dalits are characterised as being illiterate, unemployed, landless, poor, ignorant, exploited, docile, unhygienic, dirty, sick and ignored by the rest of society. The Dalit community has lost its self-respect and dignity as a result of centuries of social discrimination, oppression, exploitation and suppression. Despite being marginalised, Dalits are skilled artisans. However, statistics have revealed that Dalits are far behind in the development process compared to other caste groups. Unlike other ethnic groups, Dalits are scattered throughout the country. In today's context of the globalisation of women's issues, Nepalese women from different segments of society are also raising their voices against discrimination and exploitation.

The government has already established the Women Development Ministry to monitor national and international women's issues, which can be viewed as a good initiative. Unfortunately, the Dalit women's issue has not been recognised yet as a national issue. In addition, the so-called "mainstream" women's movement, led by high caste women, ignore Dalit women and their concerns. In general, the status of women in Nepal is very low, like in other South Asian countries. Among them though, Dalit women face the worst conditions and oppression. Dalit women are living a history of pain, agony, sorrow, misconduct, maltreatment and suffering. They are not only the victim of gender discrimination but also the victim of casteism. Moreover, the lives of Dalit women are spiralling downward from bad to worse. There is no controversy among development planners and workers that there has been very little impact on raising the status of Dalit women from the development initiatives implemented thus far in Nepal.

The Condition of Dalit Women

The difficult lives of Dalit women are perhaps best revealed by studying the social, economic, educational, health and political conditions of Dalit women, which are outlined below.

Social Condition: Untouchability

Though outlawed since 1963 and made punishable by the Constitution of the Kingdom of Nepal in 1990, untouchability is still practised. Thus, Dalits are treated as socially untouchable even in a democracy. This can be observed around the periphery of the Kathmandu Valley and in the rural areas. Even in public places, such as schools, Dalit students face discrimination. The entire Dalit community is exploited and discriminated on the grounds of caste, but women, as noted earlier, are further victimised. Untouchability related to women is practised in many ways that affect all Dalit women every day.

For example, when Dalit women fetch water from public water taps, wells, etc., they suffer from mental as well as physical assaults. Moreover, by traditional cultural practise, women usually are the member of the family that worships in the temple; but in Nepal, Dalit women are not allowed to enter the temples nor are they allowed to enter the house of upper caste people. Meanwhile, intercaste marriage is socially disapproved, and Dalit women are the principal victims of this system. If a girl from an upper caste family marries a lower caste boy, for instance, then she is accepted by the boy's family. However, when a marriage takes place between an upper caste boy and a lower caste girl, problems occur as she is not accepted by her husband's family. Subsequently, she is mentally and physically abused and abandoned in many cases.

Economic Condition: Exploitation

Most Dalits have their own traditional occupation, but they are economically exploited. It is estimated that more than 50 percent of the total population of the country lives below the absolute poverty line. Dalits, due to their history of discrimination, exploitation and abuse, constitute a large proportion of this number-approximately 90 percent of the total Dalit population of four million people. Since women have no economic power in the family, it clearly indicates the economic condition of Dalit women. These women have to work hard as labourers to earn a living, but they receive very little in return. Moreover, payment is mostly in kind, and their pay does not justify the intensity of the work. There is no doubt that Dalit women are more economically exploited than their upper caste women counterparts.

Education Condition: Illiteracy

The literacy rate of Dalit women is very low in comparison with high caste women. The present literacy rate of men is 66 percent, and the education rate for women is 30 percent. However, the literacy rate of the Dalit community is 16 percent; and for Dalit women, the literacy rate is only 7 percent. Among two million Dalit women, there are hardly 10 to 15 graduates and postgraduates. Ignorance, absolute poverty, caste and gender discrimination can be considered as the explanation for such statistics.

Health Condition: Lowest Life Expectancy

In Nepal, the life expectancy of women is lower than that of men (Nepal is one of the three countries in the world where women live less than men). Compared though to the so-called "upper caste people," the health condition of Dalits is very miserable. For example, a very backward Dalit caste-the Mushar of Terai-has a life span of 42 years against the national average of 55 years. Moreover, gynecological diseases, like a prolapsed uterus, are very common among Dalit women. They do not know much about birth control and spacing and become pregnant every year. Furthermore, because of illiteracy and ignorance, they live in filthy and unhygienic conditions which further deteriorates their health. The children of Dalits are also severely malnourished. As Dalits do not have easy access to clean drinking water in most places, they are compelled to drink polluted water and thus suffer from various gastrointestinal diseases. In this environment, both the mortality and fertility rates are high.

Political Condition: Non-Representation

Nepalese society is patriarchal, and the involvement of women in public life is not encouraged. This social prohibition applies to politics too. Thus, although Nepali women comprise 52 percent of the country's population, their representation in politics is among the lowest in Asia, i.e., as low as 5 percent. This is in spite of the 1990 Nepalese Constitution in which there is a mandatory provision that 5 percent of all candidates put forward by the country's national parties should be women. However, there were no mandatory rules for women to be represented in local government. In 1997 though, 5 percent of the seats were reserved for women in local government, and yet this rule cannot embrace Dalit women. Dalits are about 20 percent of the total population, but Dalits are not represented in national-level politics. Presently, there are four nominated parliamentarians in the National Assembly, but there is none that have been elected to the Lower House of Parliament. If the representation of men is so negligible, then one can easily imagine the political participation of Dalit women.

Sexual Exploitation: Trafficking

Because of poverty, ignorance and illiteracy, Dalit women and young girls are compelled to be involved in prostitution. One of the Dalit castes-Badi-is regarded as the prostitute caste. In addition, there is the trafficking of girls. Most of the Dalit girls taken by the brokers are trafficked to Indian brothels. In addition, many women working in carpet factories, hotels and government and private offices are sexually harassed and exploited. Because of the untouchability problem related to caste, Dalit women are deprived of the opportunity of working in the moneymaking professions, i.e., opening teashops and restaurants. Their time is spent on earning subsistence wages, and they do not have time to think about improving their condition.

Solutions

We feel very uncomfortable in reporting that very few efforts have been made by the government of Nepal to eradicate the problems of Dalits in general and of Dalit women in particular. In recent years, particularly after the restoration of multiparty democracy, the women's movement has gained momentum with the emergence of many women's organisations and leaders. Unfortunately, none of these women's organisations have taken the issues and plight of two million Dalit women seriously.

This is why we established an organisation dedicated to the rights and emancipation of Dalit women. As mentioned above, there is a serious lack of consciousness among the entire Dalit community about their fundamental human rights. Therefore, they accept all forms of discrimination and exploitation as God's grace to them. Meanwhile, the outside world has been silent about caste exploitation and discrimination.

In recent years, we, a few educated Dalit women, have come forward to move the issue forward. We intend to influence the government, donor agencies and international non-governmental organisations (NGOs), enabling them to realise the harsh reality of Dalit women and to direct resources for the upliftment of these downtrodden women. We also plan to agitate at the local level against caste discrimination and violence and to join hands with other like-minded organisations. The vast problems of Dalits and

Dalit women cannot be solved through the efforts of one or two organisations though. Therefore, we strongly feel that all national forces should join hands together. In this spirit, we would like to offer the recommendations below.

(1) Various programmes should be launched to uplift the living conditions of two million Dalit women.

(2) Scholarships should be provided from primary to higher education to all Dalit girls.

(3) The practice of untouchability in all public places, like schools, water sources and teashops, should be punished with immediate effect.

(4) All laws and acts which discriminate against Dalits and Dalit women should be rescinded immediately, and a law should be formulated and enforced to discourage the practice of untouchability.

(5) Intercaste marriage between Dalits and non-Dalits should be promoted and protected.

(6) There should be reserved seats for Dalit women in appropriate constitutional bodies, and these seats should be reserved for Dalit women in elections from the local to the national level.

(7) The government should abide by the U.N. International Convention on the Elimination of All Forms of Racial Discrimination.

(8) Dalits and Dalit women should be represented in the National Human Rights Commission.

(9) A separate commission at the national and the international level should be formed to identify the problems of Dalit women and to make recommendations to resolve these issues.

As for national and international NGOs, it is recommended that they consider the steps that follow.

(1) A series of in-depth studies should be undertaken about Dalit women.

(2) All NGOs should declare Dalits as one of their target groups of development and should formulate specific programmes to improve their lives.

(3) All human rights organisations should network with Dalit organisations and expose the human rights problems of Dalit women at the national and international level.

(4) The government of Nepal should be pressured to implement all of the U.N. conventions on human rights.

(5) International NGOs especially should give priority to Dalits and Dalit women in employment and involve them in the formulation of plans and programmes for the Dalit community.

Struggles and Challenges of Dalit Women

India has celebrated its 62th year of Independence. The country is now recording 2-digit economic growth every year and successfully takes quite an important and dominant position in international politics and in the economic arena. The success of India is built up with the international reputation of well-educated human resources, "democratic and stabled" political circumstances, and promises of land, benefits and other resources to the foreign and national investors-which are all based on exploitation of Dalit women. In reality India remains the world leader in maternal mortality, female infanticide and foeticide, deaths due to preventative disease, and other indicators of human development. Even in 2007, in Raitara village of Vanarasi in Uttar Pradesh, a five-year-old Dalit girl is facing imminent death from starvation as the family being slaved in a farm for free labour. Likewise, vulnerable villagers, namely, rural women, meanwhile, get a lot of impacts in the gap between two faces of the country.

Those bad indicators are always appeared in Dalit women. The Dalits and the marginalised are still colonised by the feudal lords the Elites without freedom from caste discrimination. Indians have driven out the colonizers but not the one who are discriminating Dalits. For Dalit women, they are also coerced to be victimised in the patriarchy. Dalit women are bearing the burden of double day caste and sexual division of labour. Dalit women are demeaned and degraded and their body is a free terrain of colonization by men from other community. Dalit women are a deprived section and at the lowest level of economic and educational structures. They are poor, illiterate, sexually harassed, faces state, caste violence and exploited. Doubly, triply or multiply discriminated, Dalit women face a lot of struggles in daily bases otherwise just being overwhelmed with those surges of discrimination up to them. Without being struggling, Dalit women would be just left in despair. This paper, therefore, focuses on struggles of Dalit women.

The paper, firstly, sees Dalit women's struggles. The struggles, however, spread out to wide area of Dalit women's life-too broad to cover just with a paper. The paper, therefore, tries to show a piece of dimensions of the struggle-which helps the readers to understand the overall background of the exclusion of Dalit women-anti-Dalit women's tendency in historical context as well as in cultural context. Secondly, it would be taken up the violation against Dalit women in the culture of globalisation with detailed analysis on their socio economic including rights to livelihood. The violation is now intensifying and internationalised. And lastly, the paper would suggest people's movement based methodology to tackle with multiple discrimination against Dalit women, which can alternated with the course which was set by the top or the others. Also, in throughout the paper, many cases would be presented including nation-wide known incidents as well as local problems of Dalit women.

Dalit Women-their Pathway of Struggles

Discrimination against Dalit Women

Although it is now in modern world, caste discrimination, an age-old practice that dehumanizes and perpetuates a cruel form of discrimination continues to be practiced. India where the practice is rampant despite the existence of a legislation to stop this, 160 million Dalits of which 49.96% are women continue to suffer discrimination. The discrimination that Dalit women are subjected to is similar to racial discrimination, where the former is discriminated and treated as untouchable due to descent, for being born into a particular community, while, the latter face discrimination due to colour. The caste system declares Dalit women as 'impure' and therefore untouchable and hence socially excluded. This is a complete negation and violation of women's human rights. Dalit women are thrice discriminated, treated as untouchables and as outcastes, due to their caste, face gender discrimination being women and finally economic impoverishment due to unequal wage disparity, with low or underpaid labour. According to the Hindu caste hierarchy, there are four castes namely the Brahmins (priestly caste), the Kshatriya (warriors), the Vaishyas (traders) and the Shudras (menial task workers).

Below this four-tier caste ladder there is another rung of peoples, who are called the untouchables (Panchamas). Among the untouchables, the status of women is further eroded and closely linked to the concept of purity. This is what the rigid, fundamentalist Hindu promotes through continuation of caste system, imposing the Brahminical values to maintain the caste system. The creation of a number of Hindu religious books including the *Manusmriti, Atharva Vedas, Vishnu smriti*, and many others like these and their strict compliance by the Brahmans (upper priestly Hindu caste), led to a society in which equality between men and women was far from existent (Agarwal: 1999). Dr. B.R. Ambedkar, an architect of the Indian constitution, also makes it very clear in his article titled "The rise and fall of Hindu woman" that the root cause of suffering for women in India are these so called Hindu religious books. Books like the Manusmriti divide people into a stratified caste system and promote inequality between men and women. According to the *Manusmriti*, women have no right to education, independence, or wealth. It not only justifies the treatment of Dalit women as a sex object and promotes child marriage, but also justifies a number of violent atrocities on women as can be seen in the following verses: A man, aged thirty years, shall marry a maiden of twelve who pleases him. Or a man of twenty-four a girl of eight years of age.

If (the performance of) his duties would otherwise be impeded, he must marry sooner. (*Manusmitri* IX.94) By a girl, by a young woman, or even by an aged one, nothing must be done independently, even in her own house." (*Manusmriti* V.147) Her father protects (her) in childhood, her husband protects (her) in youth, and her sons protect (her) in old age; a woman is never fit for independence. (*Manusmriti* IX.3) Even the killing of a Dalit woman is explicitly justified as a minor offence for the Brahmins: equal to the killing of an animal (*Manusmitri*). If the killing of an untouchable was justified as a minor offence, you can imagine the treatment they received throughout their lives. In a male dominated society, Dalit women suffered unimaginable oppression, not only through caste, but gender too, from which there was no escape.

The laws in the *Manusmriti* and other Vedic scriptures close all economic, political, social, educational, and personal channels through which Dalit women could be uplifted. The horrendous Laws in the *Manusmriti* were incorporated into Hinduism because they were favourable only to the Upper castes, which form the majority of India. Even today, in modern times, we see the severe oppression and exploitation of Dalit women. The Laws of the *Manusmriti* have a devastating effect on the level of education reached by Dalit women. The caste discrimination inherited by birth leaves Dalit women facing multiple oppressions that violate their economic, political, social and cultural rights. The most deprived section of the society comprises of Dalit women who are the poorest, illiterate and easy targets for sexual harassment. The women face not just caste violence inflicted on them by the dominant castes, but also state violence.

Dalit Women's Struggle in Hindu Culture

Culture, meanwhile, regardless of its history-traditional culture or modern culture-reflects positionality of peoples collectively with rules, values and norms. Culture is dynamic changes never static with identities and shared experiences. Family, religion, and education system used to be the main elements of culture. Culture is influenced by media. Rituals are always carried out by people, which are reinforcing the meanings of life. The traditional culture which is locally interacting, reconstitutes against this the cultural imperialism which is institutionalized which is the identity of cultural power. Culture of the Oppressed is to resist the culture of the dominant to bring freedom. Traditional culture has continuity of people's lives and respects moral codes adopted by people. The stories of the oppressed revealed through symbols and practices. People's culture is a culture of multiplicity which is dominant over other culture. This involves a political structure which is decentralized sensitive to local culture. The alternative cultural politics leads to cultural and social change. India is, essentially, home for many cultures mutually enriching contact with each other. Indian culture has come from Dravidian culture.

Indian culture is a living force. It has a significant role in moulding the culture of Asia. The Hinduism History which has continued degrading Dalit women through dogmas and concept of purity, then, affects culture which can work as a catalyst for progress of Dalit women's living environment. With Sanskritization which is hinduization a dominant model, the ideals and beliefs of the Brahminic practices are imposed on Dalits to adopt a life style with untouchablility practices. Sanskritization is an alien faith to Dalits, the spirituality of Dalits is replaced by Sanskritic spirituality. The Dalit life is incontinuation, that is, of dead and living are the integral spirituality of Dalit culture. Brahminical culture endangers Dalits' identity and integrity. It enhances and annihilates Dalit culture instead of enriching the culture.

The culture is reflection of resistance from the past to the present and moves to shape a blueprint for the future life which becomes a flowing stream. There is continuity of collective life in Dalit culture. In addition, modernization introduced consumerism and market economy which has destroyed ethos, value system, celebration, and affirmation of the culture of the people, particularly the culture of Rural Dalits. Traditional culture is a way of living and producing for life, to sustain life. But through imperialistic modern culture, the mode of production is set only for consumption. It is called as neo-colonization of traditional culture which is not the people's culture. Meanwhile, what would be the question of duties of a wife? Who is the head of the family? Wives are devoted to their husbands and afraid of even mentioning the name of their husband. Barren woman considered to be "*amangalam*", bad omen and inferior to others, to be a curse to the society. Puberty is viewed as 'flowering' stage in a girl's life, as pleasurable. Fertility, women are referred to mud waiting to receive seed. Woman in marriage are framed to be obedient and submissive wives. Motherhood is expected to be nurturing, fearful, good wives and bearers of worthy sons. Sexuality of fertility is socially permissible and sexual acts such as homosexual, lesbian behaviours are considered to be deviant, perverse and abnormal. Society allows multiple forms of sexual behaviour to co-exist practically but not socially. Erotic literature such as Kamasutra hints at the existence of homosexual desire and love.

Hindu Temple Sculpture

Diverse sexualities are present and celebrated in Hindu temple sculpture. Pro-life existence of non-normative sexual culture is significant. They reveal the norms that a society lives by, to be constructed rather than given, clearly authorized by systems of patriarchal power. Madurai Meenakshi, Queen of the city, becomes bride given away every year in marriage. Marriage ceremony is the history of female domestication and husbandry authority. Although it has been praised diverse of sexuality of the "human beings" at the one side of Hindu concept, Fundamentalist, Hinduism excludes plurality of the people even in sexuality.

Particularly, lower caste, labouring women, who are Dalit women-are treated as the sexual "property" of the men of the all caste. The other caste women are treated as good and lower caste Dalit women as bad women because of Dalit women social status is low, subordinated that is why they are made to be sexually available to other caste. Dalit women are marked as natural and fit victims of violation, contrast to upper caste women who are considered to be pure and custodians of chastity. Chastity of upper caste women could be taken up as big issue in their "culture" because of being submissive wives who is called *pativiratas*. The lower caste women are considered not to be chaste. Sexual purity is anticipated caste purity which is honoured by the society. Dalit women follow the Rituals more than the Dalit men. Dalit women associate with earth. They put the earth on the forehead, the mixture of water and mud strained that water is given to babies. They are related directly with the earth which is the life source. Worshiping the trees, decorating trees with *Kungumam,* turmeric that is worshiping old trees and rocks with the decoration. Cultural programme of festivals is only moment for the Dalit women who get into trance (or being "possessed" so to say). It is the only time they express their inner feelings and speak against other caste men, husbands, and demanding arak the local alcohol, chicken, good food, and behave like goddess. Before transplanting, the seeds are germinated in pots and Dalit women carry them by singing songs. Dalit women worship the nature for better and more food to be produced. Dalit women's dances are *Kummi*, and following to them they have *Kulavai*-wherever they work they sing. To show the closeness with the nature, they sing songs about their forefathers, mothers, the children and they abuse the landlords through their songs. After the hard work in the day during the night they sit together and chat with each other.

They use lot of proverbs while talking and fighting. They tease each other and their blood related men from their kin who are about to be married with them. They relate with each other, and while calling the person they will not use the name but the relationship. They sing when a baby is born, when a girl attains puberty and also *Oppari* death. These practices we never find with women of other caste. Dalit women are very strong and they give birth to more children. Dalit women work equally with the men, that is, why they oppose male domination and prove that they are stronger than the men.

Dalit women work hard to survive. They are very open-minded, innocent, and not exploiting others but exploited by others. They have good characters. Dalit women, everyday, relate themselves with people in four ways. 1) With their family members, children, husband, 2) With the traders who buy their products, 3) The other caste landlords who give them work, and 4) Relate with distant relatives during marriages, deaths. Now beyond this the new effort is that Dalit women attend conferences, meetings, workshops and training programs which allowed them to meet with many Dalit women. Dalit women are illiterates. They know only work related to land. They have not achieved even as one persent politically. They remain only us voters. They have no chance of learning about the country, the other ethnic groups and languages. Not all the Dalit women are member of the movement as well as in the political party.

They are not involved in politics. Dalit women leadership is also controlled by the men. Dalit women have their own language. They preserve their language of their land. They have their own justice that is they do not have permanent enemies amongst themselves. For many years they follow the Rituals of the land. They are different from other caste women because they do not depend on their men like others. They work equally with men. When the men were taking the spade, Dalit women are ready with their basket to take mud. Every work it is both Dalit men and women work equally. Dalit women are workers, and they are not slaves to their husbands. Dalit women have very strong resistance power which has to be sustained. Dalit culture was destroyed after the invasion of Aryans. Dalits lived through the dominant Brahminical culture. Sanskritization of Dalit culture, based on pure and impure concept was thrust on the oppressed, downtrodden communities especially on Dalit women. Dalit culture was silenced and destroyed. Dalits through a war, resistance gave life to the culture that faced the death by the dominant culture. Dalit culture is liberation, freedom, solidarity, equality, a culture of resistance towards freedom. Dalit culture is preserved through various forms of theatre which is revolutionary, disturbs and leads to action which is political action.

Perform Dance of Dalit Women

Dalit women perform dance which is devoted to Mathamma the Kulathaivam. The dancer is, however, almost exploited as being expected to dance in an erotic way. This is religious sanctioned prostitution. The month of June (*Anni Matham* in Tamil Calendar) is the temple festival for five days. The temple is built, festival conducted, the 'Car' is held in front all by the other caste. Out of five days the Mathammas, Dalit girl children are given to the goddess believing those children will be cured by the healing power of goddess. Once the child is cured, she is married to the goddess and named after her. She becomes a powerful replica of Mathamma. Later on she is mocked and treated as a public property. In public places she is teased and her children born are face lot of humiliation in the school by other children.

Mathammas socially and economically exploited by the community. She lives on her own without the support of families. A Dalit woman, becomes a dancer, then sexually exploited ends her life with nothing but left out with diseases. The dominant brahminical culture from which the Devadasi system is extended to Dalit community is prevailing Dalit women. Tamil Nadu Dalit Women's Movement (TNDWM), meanwhile, faced harassment even from Dalit men in the community for exposing the issue of Mathamma. The Dalit movement with patriarchal norms started publicly attacking leaders from TNDWM "individually". They are accused, through wall posters, public meetings and black mailings. TNDWM faced harassment confronting the caste and patriarchal nature of the communities which is also influenced by Hindutva ideology. Hindutva Ideology perpetuates hatred towards other religion and maintains the culture, the exploitative dominant culture through caste.

Contemporary Oppression against Dalit Women

At Special Economic Zones (SEZs)

At present, 134,000 hectors of lands are set 67 multi-product SEZs in India (Financial Express, 30 Aug 2006). Although the land owner might receive the compensation for the land acquisition as the SEZs, the peasant Dalit women are facing the peril of the livelihoods by losing their job as well as being evicted from the land. For Dalit women, "trickle-down effect" theory, in which people can expect "trickled" benefits dropped down from the country or big companies' economic growth, is just a mirage, not a reality at all. The alienation is creating widespread discontent amongst farmers and common people all over India. The state, meanwhile, behaves as an agent of the corporation. The state government, which is essentially responsible to the citizen not only becomes advocates of the corporations but also acts as corporations. The state government itself takes away the land, especially agricultural lands, coastal lands with the coastal regulation zones, salt pans, and forest lands for SEZs.

The land taken for SEZs, meanwhile, only 35% is used for industry and the rest for non-industrial purposes: recreation centre- and housing. Although people are raising their voice, the oppression from the state government is intensified. In Nandigram, West Bengal, 17 villagers were shot to death with the protest against government taking away lands for corporation; chemical hubs of Salim group. Out of 17 killed 12 are Dalits. The people of Nandigram have lived in daily fear of retaliation when the Citizen's Committee entered to the district. The mission found that women were extremely apprehensive, begging the mission to spend the night with them. The state, however, is not restoring land rights and titles to landless Dalit women.

Land given to SEZs promoters is more than 1000 hectors which obviously violates Land Reform Act. SEZs will not create employment for local Dalit women but it will push away Dalit women because SEZs employs skilled and educated workers. Communities, especially Dalit women in unorganised sectors, will not be employed in SEZs. In Tuticorin, Tamil Nadu, for example, another Nandigram is about to be occurred. Even though there are vociferous protests against the Tata's titanium dioxide plant to be situated at Sathankulam of the district, there are a lot of oppressions from the ruling party to the pantchayat leaders to urge them to accept the project. Also, even before the pantchayat leaders accept the project, the state government made an agreement with the company for establishing the Rs 2,500-crore titanium dioxide project. Negligence of local people voices in the politics and economy in SEZs definitely erodes the livelihood of the most vulnerable groups in the region, the Dalit Women. Besides of land conflict occurred by SEZs, the insecurity of women is intensified. Those who work as manual labourer in big factories are mostly poor women, such as Dalit women. When returning from the factory to their home late at night, women need to worry about their safety. In Ulundurpettai taluk of Villupuram district, there were 3 rapes – one was Dalit woman, and other women were from other community.

All are workers in big factories, and attacked on the way to go home from their workplace. SEZs are not only taking away the land, political rights, and dignity, but also depriving of Dalit women's opportunities for self-improvements, such as educations. In northern Tamil Nadu, where Society for Rural Education and Development (SRED) develops various community-based activities, it has been introduced between Chennai and Kancheepuram. From all over India and foreign countries-e.g. Reliance Group which runs many business all over India, Nokia, Hyundai, and Samsung-have invested to the zones and established huge factories along with the super highway which connects Chennai, Kancheepuram, and Bangalore. The establishment of SEZs firstly affects peasant landless Dalit women by displacing them from the lands without any compensation. They employ not only skilled workers, but also manual labourers from Dalit villages, mostly young women for manual works. Buses with the company logo are waiting for Dalit young girls early in the morning in front of the Dalit villages. Dalit girls are encouraged to go for work with SEZs than continuing for higher education. Dalit girls cannot have opportunities to learn any skills, even as "on the job trainings", and would face the unemployment as "uneducated woman" when the economy goes bad. Very recently, the Swiss based international lingerie company-Triumph has decided to invest to the area in order to establish key factory for underwear business throughout of the Subcontinent. The key of the final decision of investment was the quality of traditional technology in Garment industry, which Rural Dalit Women have conserved for many years in order to sustain their rural life (The Indian Express). Meanwhile, they are planning to sell those women's underwear for 400-1000 Rupees which is almost impossible price for local Dalit women, whereas the provider of the skills would face of insecurity.

At Dalit Women's Workplace

The political economy of globalisation erodes livelihoods of Rural Dalit women, who even luckily live far away from the Special Economic Zones. The agriculture sector has been transformed into the easier money making industry, such as floriculture and horticulture. Agriculture is turned into floriculture where small farmers would be eager to see cash everyday. Dalit women and school-going Dalit girl children are employed to pluck flowers for extremely low wages. Dalit Women and Dalit children are working in the fields where hazardous agro chemicals and pesticides are sprayed which affected the health of the Dalit women and Dalit children. The studies conducted on the impact of floriculture on the health of Dalit women in Santana Gopalapuram were on half an acre of land there are 10 workers: both men and women.

According to the villagers, floriculture has been around for last 20 years, but in the last 5 years, it has intensified and more farmers are moving to floriculture. Earlier they used to grow groundnut and rice. Women specifically mentioned that they have to get up early and finish household work before going to pluck flowers. They work from 6am in the farm and they can eat only after 10 am at the earliest. Also, due to constantly bending and plucking of flowers for almost 6 hours for low wages, at a stretch, there is chest, back and leg pain. Pesticides are sprayed almost when they are on the field, and smell persists for 3 days or more. Women are suffering from excessive white discharge, rolling feeling in the stomach, hysterectomy, and even tumour in uterus. Floriculture affects also the rights to education of Dalit girl children.

Dalit girl children are employed in order to pluck the flower before going to school and after the school. Dalit girl children are not able to recheck what they have learnt in the school and this turns into potential factor of drop-out. Of course with the health problem with pesticide, Dalit girls are failed to access to the school as well. Even some of the family members fell down with diseases caused by the pesticide this affects children's rights to go to school. In Kollathur where the agricultural lands were taken away for aqua farm for exportation which is located by the Buckingham Canal, at the backwater area of east-coast of Kancheepuram District, Tamil Nadu, is a Dalit village. Dalits have worked for cultivation of cashew nuts, prawn and fish catching in the backwater. In 2004, a Chennai based entrepreneur, F. Bartholome has obtained the license from the Aquaculture Authority and opened an industrial prawn farm called Chinna Aqua Farm. The farm came up on agricultural land, right alongside backwaters. The farm discharges untreated effluences from the farm which salinated agricultural lands and the backwaters. The Aqua farming in India was promoted by the government in 90's for one of the international business strategies of the country without thinking about the environmental impacts.

Soon after, in 1996, the Indian Supreme Court has regulated the use of coastal area for environmental reason, including creeks and backwaters which polluted water bodies. Running the farm without registration and permission shall be a criminal offence, but in practice, Bartholome's farm, for example, successfully got the license although it violates the regulation which stated in the law due to the lack of seriousness in the implementation of the law and due to corruption. Kollathur aqua farm is located on agricultural land whereas agricultural land should not be used for Aqua farming. Bartholome himself is also connected strongly with politicians. Ironically even after the inclusion of regulations, the production of prawns in the area for the exportation is increasing. The land has been transformed from traditional agricultural lands for people's food to money making products for exportation.

And now, with the toxic waste the Aqua farm cause loss of agricultural production which affects directly the daily food production of the Dalit villagers. Also, prawn catching and mussels collection by the Dalit women was totally affected with the pollution. This causes food insecurity as well as livelihood insecurity to Dalit women. The toxic waste polluted not only plants and animals but also human beings, mostly Dalit women who work in the field and with the toxic polluted back waters directly. Women got itching, skin disease and dimming of eyesight. Ground water has been salinated, and Dalit women lost adequate water for agriculture as well as for drinking. Not only endangered the livelihood by losing their work, but also women had to suffer from the physical pain by the disease, and from no money for the medical cost for treatment. The Dalits of Kollathur village are suffering from impacts of the pollution directly and indirectly due to the false cases many villagers who struggled against the farm were beaten up and charged.

Just in the last two years, more than 40 young men from this village of 4000 attend court cases four times in a month; need to pay a lot of cost for legal procedure; cost for advocates as well as transportation cost to the court. The increasing vulnerability in rural traditional life encourages not only industrial transformation but also migration. At Thirumalpur of Vellore district of Tamil Nadu where women earn only Rs.12.50 as wage for half-a-day's labour for agriculture work forced them to migrate to neighbouring State to earn more than Rs.50 per day. The Dalit women leave their children with their elders. Both men and women migrate they are made to stay in big halls or in schools. The women migrant workers sleep in one corner and their husbands as well as other men in other side vice-a-versa. They have no privacy they rely on near by pump sheds, lakes and ponds to bathing and washing their clothes, which are very insecure places. Every time they migrate from their village for a maximum of 20 days. The contractor employs them with an assignment to carry out harvest in 20 acres of land. After taking his commission of 30%, the contractors pay the rest to the workers. Women lose freedom and dignity in bad working conditions when they migrate.

Sustain Dalit Women's Struggles

Civil Society's Challenge?

Having faced the deprivation of human rights of Dalit Women, what kinds of actions have been taken by the civil society? In order to achieving "uplifting" or "development" of peoples in disadvantage class, Development NGOs as well as international institutions emphasize recently "rights based approach". The United Nations Development Programme has set so-called Millennium Development Goals in order to "monitor" the implementation of the goal for human development. But those are neither our approach nor our goals. As it can be seen in Dalit women's situation, people are struggling for their livelihood, and the movement should reject those meaningless mercies from the top. The movement, in fact, pursues "struggle based approach" and "People's Goals". The "Right based approach" is a language of donors. This makes movements isolated in each cells. People's movements are compromising not confronting. We should rather keep up the "Struggle based approach", which leads movements to bring changes in people's lives. The peoples around so-called 'civil society', therefore, do not share the problem with Dalit women. The civil society is narrowing down by becoming fundamentalists under the name of "rights based approach". At the citizens' forum for celebrating 60th years of independence, which was taken place at Bangalore, for example, there are a lot of oppositions to serve beef cutlet as a choice of the meal service. As the reality, however, there are people who have beef. Inclusiveness is important and not to exclude efforts of various initiatives. There is a need to join hands to stay with the people in multiple struggles against multiple discriminations and exploitations.

Dominant Culture

Supporting of Dalit women by providing services: children's day care centre, and urgent scholarship is of course one of our struggle against dominant culture of globalisation. Likewise, SRED and TNDWM also directly support the struggles for the victims of culture of casteism and patriarchy: such as Mathammas. Our approach to Mathamma begins with their name and status. Mathammas refused to be called as Mathammas. The first change with in them is to have new names, and to remove the 'Sacred Pottu Thali'. The movement of Mathammas: Mathamma Liberation Movement was formed primarily to stop the practice of giving the Dalit girls to Mathammas. During the festivals, Mathammas from the movement were vigilant that no woman, no Mathamma dancing is taking place publicly. Now the temple festivals dress up men as women and the dance continues. In Kaverirajapuram during temple festival the leaders stopped Mathamma dance with the help of police.

But the movement found that it was the wrong strategy as it created incredible views from the villagers from other movements. The Mathamma movement is, now, visiting villages where Mathamma temples are, and conducting meetings, cultural programs, explaining the hurdles they went through by themselves. They keep persuading by saying that 'Stop the practice of Mathammas'. Mathamma leaders from the movement contested in election with many threats and boycotts. They, however, claimed equal status, and went through all the procedure of the election which itself is an empowering process challenged the system, the community and the men in the villages. Devi, the leader of the movement who was contested, explains her experience in the election as follows;

During the election campaign, those who are against me strongly said: "why do you nominate yourself for the election? You are Mathamma and who will vote for you?" But I didn't accept any words in the remarks. I did not win this time, but it was brilliant experience. There are a lot of problems that Mathammas are facing. If I become a ward member, I will give the rights for the mathammas and totally I would like to stop this practice. I will make employment, education and housing, and all basic needs-I will try to get them through government.

They stopped dancing of exploitation but started to dance to liberate others because she is to be liberated. Now, some of them have leadership and empowerment training with the support of Yasuda literacy foundation of Buraku Liberation and Human Rights Research Institution. With the training, the women gains more force to struggle against the dominant culture.

Kollathur women are also challenging to the huge dominant entity by empowering themselves in the movement. They organised Kollathur Dalit Women's Sangam, and are fighting in the struggles in legal process as well as in their livelihoods. They keep embracing a slogan: "Close the Aqua Farm". Globalisation emphasises efficiency and competitive culture. Thus it appears that for the majority of Dalits and poor, globalisation has meant further deprivation. The struggles against globalised economy are also, for Dalit women, struggle against culture of dominant casteism and patriarchy.

Dalit Women's Challenge

SRED, thus, extends the area of activities in various levels: from local to international level. For local level, if there are caste based oppression against Dalit women, immediately stay at the side of the people to protest against the oppression. In Rangapuram village, Dalit children are not allowed to go to school because the Non-Dalits blocked the way to go to school. SRED immediately sent fact finding mission of people's movement, such as Tamil Nadu Dalit Women's Movement, and made a petition to make a safe road to school-going children. When making a petition, police forces was sent from many place to the district educational office of Kancheepuram, and they immediately arrested unlawfully activists of Dalit women. This year, at last, the new road for children was successfully launched at the village. In Anandapuram, village, without the bridge over the river, Dalit children are not able to cross the river in rainy season to go to the school.

Dalit mothers, meanwhile, who work in the field, definitely need the place to send children whilst they are working. Since 2004, SRED launched Dalit day care centres, to provide space for children to play, to sing, to paint, to learn and to prepare for the formal school. Primarily the centres are used for day care centre, which enable Dalit women who have to go to the field to leave the children at safer place. After this day care centre, they will go to primary school. The centres are, however, used for multi-purpose.

Working children can get education after work in evening class. The centres are playing crucial role for school going children as the safer place after school for doing further learning. Some times the centres are used for meeting purposes. At Anandapuram, with the warm support from Nagano branch of Buraku Liberation League, successfully established a centre. But meanwhile, have limitation of the budget to launching the centre for many villages, therefore re-arrange meeting room to Day care centre. Actually Sred staff members are doing secretary work just by hearing children's voice, and also frequently have a discussion where there are a lot of paintings and learning materials for children. In the community based work, found out that the similar situation to other children, namely, Irulas, Tribal people as well as quarry workers. When families remain as bonded labourers, when parents have to take children to quarry work place because of lack of finance to prepare for their study, families migrate seeking for their work. Children's rights to education are denied. The centres and the programmes in the centres are particularly designed by paying attention with caste-free environment, and children are ensured to be away from any discriminated thoughts, practices, and behaviours. Dalit communities, particularly girl children, face difficulty also in higher educations.

Just only with falling to financial difficulty affected by Tsunami, Dalit girl students were sent back to their home without continuing the second year of the course whilst they managed for the first year of the course. Even getting the best scores at the twelfth grade, Bharati, a Dalit girl faced difficulties to find appropriate scholarship schemes and resulted to give up their education (nursing course). SRED collects supports for those Dalit girls and help them to continue their higher education.

Asian Rural Women's Conference

Apart from the community and grassroots based challenge for overcoming the difficulty surged up to Dalit women, the SRED and Tamil Nadu Dalit Women's Movement are trying to organising forums on rural women. Amongst Dalit women 81.45% lives in rural area. The globalisation, meanwhile, affects firstly the vulnerable sectors in rural area, where, obviously, Dalit women are working. But also, the rural women in other community, such as Irulas Tribes, Narikuravars, Dhobis, and fisherfolks are suffering in the similar situation. Not only in India, but also, there are many rural women who are struggling in current political economy of globalisation. The concerns on international trade, international agro-business, and patents to traditional seeds are all rural Dalit women's agenda as well as women from other community. Actually, Dalit women flew to Hong Kong to take an action at the 6 ministerial meeting of WTO to protest against promotion of pesticides and genetically modified foods. The forum, Asian Rural Women's Conference, which is taking place on 6-8th March, 2008 in Arakkonam/ Chennai, India, is putting together marginalised women in the region who are against imperialist oppression. By asserting dignity of rural women, which cannot be seen in any other rights-based documents, many marginalised women in the region create the power to struggle.

The conference will develop a unity of analysis from the experiences of rural women and the situation of women in the context of a globalised world. Last July, some Indian women's organisations gathered at our office, and conducted National consultation on rural women, which of course include latest developments on rural Dalit women. On 31 July to 2 Aug, presenters from some Asian countries gathered in Manila, and have issued rural women's declaration. Of course caste based discrimination was clearly mentioned in the context of the struggle against patriarchal globalisation. Meanwhile, the Manila conference did not have any Japanese participants, particularly from Buraku community. It would be grateful for Dalit women to share the issue with Buraku women in March for "Rights, Empowerment and Liberation", which is the main slogan of the conference. Asian Rural Women's Conference would also be the occasion for cultural expression of oppressed rural women.

Dalit women are using '*Thappu*', the drums, to show that drums can be beaten up by women not only by men. Drum beatings are to give life to the Dalit culture which was killed by the Brahminical culture. There are Dalit women's dances as well, such as *Kolatam*, *Oyilatam*, *Karagattam*, *Thappatam*, *Paraiyattam*, which all accompany with the drum music. The drums have languages that the Dalit women beat all rituals. *Parai* the drum is beaten by *Paraiyer* is the myth and the *parai* was treated like the Dalits as 'untouchable' by the dominant culture. The Dalit women revived the beating of *parai* and revolted against the dominant culture by giving new, revolving meaning to *Parai*. Dalit women beat drum to oppose the domination which is systematic, structural and multiple. Beating drum is to destroy the ideology of domination. Beating drum is to beat up the monoculture and to bring inter-culture of the oppressed, downtrodden, the broken, people together towards liberating humanity, transformation to achieve Equality, Freedom, Justice for a 'Humane' society through cultural and social society. Dalit women in Tamil Nadu are ready to drum out the globalised patriarchal fundamentalism, which produces casteism and gender discrimination, with the solidarity of other minority women.

CHAPTER 5

Power and Representation: Reservation for Women in India

Introduction

Political under-representation of women has emerged as one of the key concerns for women's movements in the nineties. Arguments relating to it revolve around two broad issues: the representative character of democratic institutions and their public accountability on women's issues. Recent developments in feminist politics in India not only indicate growing concern with under-representation of women in elected and decision-making bodies, but also with arguments for some form of reservation or affirmative action to redress existing gender imbalances. These arguments are advanced precisely because gender balanced representation is expected to alter development priorities, perspectives, and concerns and thereby increase accountability. The notion of affirmative action has always been contested both in terms of its meaning and the goals and practices it encompasses.

The term had its genesis *in* the United States and includes a range of policy measures and programs (Bacchi, 1996). In India, the term reservation is commonly used to denote similar state sponsored initiative. Reservation policy, therefore, seeks to redress inequalities in labor force representation, in political parties, educational institutions and public committees. The understanding of affirmative action or, in the Indian case, reservation, includes notions such as equality of opportunity, social justice, positive or protective discrimination, compensatory discrimination, and so on. In addition, several other subsidiary questions such as concession versus right and compensatory justice versus meritocracy have also been debated, In the Indian context, the terms 'reservation' or 'quotas' have been used and apply to "socially and educationally backward classes of citizens and scheduled castes and scheduled tribes," ever since the framing of the Indian Constitution in 1950. It is significant to note that the egalitarian framework of the Constitution had to be altered in order to accommodate non-discrimination.

Articles 14 and 15 of the Constitution, prohibiting discrimination on grounds of religion race, caste, sex, and language, had to be amended to give powers to the state to make *spedai provisions* for the advancement of socially and educationally backward classes. This followed the judicial verdict in Champakam Dorairajan's case in 1951 that characterized any preferential treatment to socially and economically weaker sections as discriminatory, leading to the first constitutional amendments to Articles 15 and 16 of the Constitution. This empowered the state to make reservation in favor of any disadvantaged group, without being challenged on grounds of discrimination. Thus, as Justice P. S. Poti, in his Foreword to *Dynamics of Reservation Policy* noted, this amendment made reservation a non-issue. Instead, the question that continues to persist in the debate relates to who are the disadvantaged groups? Article 15 (4) brought in by the Constitution (first Amendment) Act in 1951 enabled the state to make special provisions for the advancement of any "socially and educationally backward classes of citizens." Similar provision was made in Article 16 (4) for reservation of posts in favor of any backward class of citizens, who in the opinion of the state, are not adequately represented in the services under the state. Significantly, both these clauses refer to 'classes of citizens' and not to individuals. The persistent paradox of liberal democracy has been the tension between the notion of political equality and pre-existing social and economic inequalities.

Thus, while introducing and justifying the first constitutional amendment, Nehru said: we come up against the difficulty that on the one hand, in our Directive Principles of State Policy, we talk of removing inequalities, of raising the people in every way—socially, educationally and economically, of reducing the distances which separate the groups or classes of individuals from one another, on the other hand we find ourselves handicapped by certain provisions of the Constitution.... We cannot have equality because we cannot have non-discrimination, for if you are thinking of raising those who are down, you are somehow affecting the status quo, undoubtedly. You are thus said to be discriminating because you are affecting the status quo. If this argument is correct then we cannot make any major changes in the status quo whether in the economic or any other sphere. Clearly whatever law you may make you have to make some change somewhere. Thus, the greatest appeal of liberal democracy was the promise of equality of status and opportunity.

However, the biggest challenge to the stated goals has come from the social and political elite and other hegemonic forces in the multicultural and stratified society of India. A strong sentiment was expressed at the time by Ambedkar, the architect of the Indian Constitution, in his address to the Constituent Assembly debates, preceding the framing of the Indian Constitution: he saw Indian society based on privilege and inequality, and at the same time, entering a public life of contradictions. The political system, he noted, would recognise equality, insofar as it would be based on the individual right to vote but in social and economic life, inequality would continue to prevail. Thereafter, it is seen that the inverted pyramid that became the basis of India's planning and development administration, resulted not only in uneven growth but reinforced the class, caste, and gender hierarchies of an unequal society. The criteria for deciding 'backwardness' or who are the disadvantaged groups, have dogged reservation policies in India. Even during the Constituent Assembly debates, the policies of preferential treatment for the disadvantaged Scheduled Castes (SCs) and Scheduled Tribes (STs) were criticized on the grounds that they placed a premium on backwardness and inefficiency. The Kalelkar Commission, appointed in 1953, submitted its report in 1955 and recommended that the social position of a community in the caste hierarchy should be used as the criterion to determine backwardness (Backward Classes Commission, 1955). No action was taken on this report as the criterion of caste was viewed as promoting the dangers of separatism. The second Backward Classes Commission was appointed in 1978 under the chairmanship of B. P. Mandai to determine the criteria and examine the condition of "socially and educationally backward classes." The Commission identified 11 indicators and 3,743 castes as backward, constituting 52 per cent of India's population. The belief that certain sections have suffered historic injustices and need special safeguards and affirmative action to realize their constitutional rights, has formed the basis for reservation policy in India. This, however, has been strongly opposed by entrenched class interests. For example, the V. P. Singh Government that sought to implement the Mandai Commission recommendations in 1990 met with fierce opposition and agitation by the educated middle class, as is well-known.

A series of writ petitions were also made against it in the Supreme Court, challenging caste as a criterion for determining backwardness. Several political thinkers, social scientists, and activists are of the view that the issue of reservation should be seen in the wider perspective of social change in a hierarchical caste-ridden society. Arguments in favor of reservation place emphasis on the case for equality of opportunity as well as for social justice. In the case of scheduled castes and scheduled tribes, the Indian Constitution recognizes that the unequal status of these sections has to be dealt with on a preferential basis. The programs envisaged for them are of three types: reservation of seats in legislatures, reserved posts in the public sector, and quotas for seats in educational institutions. The package evolved, thereby, was one of social justice, intended for the advancement of "socially and educationally backward classes of citizens" (Constitution of India: Article 15 (4) and 16 (4)). According to Marc Callantar, reservation as proactive or compensatory discrimination is envisaged only for the purpose of mitigating inequalities. He sees the role of reservation for its instrumental qualities. According to him, these policies show a sense of connection and shared destiny, while this compensatory discrimination embodied the brave new hopes of India that animated the freedom movement and crystallized in the Indian Constitution (Gallantar, 1984).

Both arguments, for social justice and for equality of opportunity, assume that systematic inequality and discrimination prevent certain groups, such as women, from playing equal roles. There is considerable ambiguity, however, over how representation of gender, ethnic, or minority groups can serve the cause of social justice. Accordingly, the Beijing Platform for Action states that "women's equal participation is not only a demand for simple justice or democracy but a necessary condition for women's interest to be taken into account." It further adds that "women in politics and decision-making positions in governments and legislative bodies contribute to redefining political priorities, placing new items on the political agenda that reflect and address women's gender specific concerns, values and experiences and provide new perspectives on mainstream political issues". However, the paradox of reservation is that the claim of certain groups for equality, as a matter of constitutional right, is forgotten and it is mainly viewed as protective or compensatory, whereby discrimination can be reduced through preferential treatment for certain sections of the population. In a limited sense, the concept of social justice has been carved out from a number of other rights and presupposes protection of the under privileged sections of society.

Equality implies creation of favourable conditions and equal opportunities to all, for transforming the position of those sections that are victims of existing social arrangements and inequality of status, power, and knowledge. The laissez faire liberal democratic paradigm propagates that it is the business of the state to provide a level playing field and the state is seen as an agent that promotes equality of opportunity. The notion of equality, which implies competition based on merit, ignores political and social arrangements that invidiously discriminate against certain groups. The idea of compensatory justice or preferential treatment, through a series of actions by the state, has given impetus to movements for people's rights and the demand for pro-portionate representation in decision-making structures. People's movements have thus constituted a critical arena for debates on democratization and representative democracy.

However, they have also generated tensions due to conflicting demands being made by different interest groups. Within democracy there are disagreements over development priorities and goals and whose interests are being served through political and economic processes. These differences go on to arouse mobilization of group interests around shared ideals and experiences. The principles of the liberal democratic framework are being questioned by the debate on political processes, democracy, and the perspectives of different movements engaged in trans-forming institutions and systems of governance. People's movements—for instance, of civil rights activists, women's groups, and ethnic groups—representing the interests of disadvantaged groups, have tried to forge a unity and collective identity around shared experiences. The current demand by the women's movement in India for reservation of seats in the Parliament and State Assemblies has partly arisen in the wake of the experience of women in *panchayati raj* institutions (institutions of local self-government), following the 73rd and 74th Constitutional Amendment that provides one-third reservation for women in these bodies. This chapter is primarily concerned with the debate on political representation of women and reservation of seats in elected bodies. Increasingly, the concern with the under-representation of women in political institutions is seen as a by-product of gendered spaces and opportunity structures. A world-wide comparative survey on parliamentary representation of women also suggests a corollary between the degrees of democratization in a country and the extent of women's participation in political life (IPU, 1997: 11).

Women's participation is seen not only as central to the functioning of democracy but also for their ability in struggling for their rights and challenging the ideologies and hierarchies that keep women in subordinate positions. In the 1990s, the demand for Indian women's political representation in legislative bodies has been raised with renewed vigour, not only by the women's movement but also by elected women representatives across all party lines. The arguments in defense of political reservation are tied to an understanding of the historical legacy of women's oppression and disadvantage, the nature of gender inequality, male dominance in political institutions, gender insensitivity in systems of governance, the nature of electoral politics, and so on.

Political Reservation for Women

The current debate on political reservation or quotas for women in parliament and in state assemblies in India has to be seen in its historical context, as it is more than seventy years old. The early phase of the women's movement began with the emergence of three women's organizations: the All India Women's Conference (AIWC) in 1927, Women's India Association (WIA) in 1917, and the National Council of Women in India (NCWI) in 1925. Several local and provincial women's associations had started after 1910 but later merged to form these national organizations. The battle for the vote began in 1917 when Sarojini Naidu led an all India women's deputation to Montague, the Secretary of State for India, who had arrived to discuss India's demands for political representation. The memorandum said that when franchise was extended to the people of India, women must be recognized as "people." When Montague's scheme of reforms for India was published, however, women were completely left out. The 1919 Government of India Act enfranchised a mere three per cent of Indian adults for the provincial assemblies, based on qualifications of education and property. It excluded women from the vote but allowed provincial assemblies to drop the exclusion clause of property and educational qualification if they wished. Indian nationalist leaders, however, were sympathetic to the cause of women's suffrage, for example, in his Presidential Address delivered at the thirty-fourth Annual Session of the Indian National Congress on 27 December 1919, Motilal Nehru brought attention to this failure in providing for the political rights of women. In the light of the demonstrable lessons of the women's suffrage agitation in England, he expressed the hope that Indian men would come to the rescue of their sisters. Subsequently, in 1924 a Reforms Enquiry Committee started recording evidence and views on whether Indian women really desired membership of the Legislatures. With the removal of the ban in 1927, the Madras State Provincial legislature threw open its membership to women, just a few weeks before the elections. Jana Everett has argued that the campaign of the Indian women's movement for political representation had two phases: in the first phase (1917-1928) the issue was female enfranchisement and eligibility for the legislature; in the second phase (1928-1937) its focus was on liberalization of the terms of enfranchisement and increasing female representation in the legislatures.

In both phases, the extent to which the interests of the women's movement and those of the political authorities coincided, was the main factor determining the outcome of the demands of the women's movement. In 1928 the Simon Commission came to India to discuss the issue of franchise and political representation. At the time, many women leaders, the Congress and other nationalist parties boycotted the Commission. However, one faction of the women's movement appeared before the Commission and argued for extension of female suffrage and reservation of four seats for women in the legislatures in order to encourage women to take part in political affairs and to represent their interests in education and social welfare. The Simon Commission did not recommend reservation of seats for women in the legislatures, but left it to the provincial governments to nominate women if none were elected. The Commission also rejected the system of separate electorates for minority groups, nonetheless recommended reservation of seats for the depressed classes. Everett has called this group of women representatives the "women's uplift faction." Their approach to encouraging women's enfranchisement was in line with the government's position as they supported the idea of wife-hood qualifications and reservation of seats for women in legislatures. At the first conference, which was boycotted by the Congress, the British Government appointed two women, Radabhai Subbarayan and Begum Shah Nawaz.

These representatives supported the idea of wife-hood qualifications and seats reserved for women in legislatures, though not on a communal basis. The memorandum they presented was on the lines of the British women's memorandum and was presented on behalf of the three all-India women's organizations. Furthermore, it demanded the principle of equality. Everett (1981) argues that a split developed within the women's movement between those who aligned themselves with the Congress and those women who were not involved in nationalist activities. In 1931, when a new Constitution for India was being discussed in the British Parliament, the three major organizations.

Women's India Association (WIA), All India Women's Conference (AIWC) and National Council for Women in India (NCWI), met and drafted a joint memorandum supporting adult suffrage. They, however, rejected special measures to ensure women's representation in legislatures. The AIWC, along with NCWI, organized a meeting of women representatives in Bombay, where a Drafting Committee of eight women was elected to prepare a Memorandum for submission to the Franchise Committee of the so-called Second Round Table

Conference. Their main demands were for universal adult suffrage and mixed general electorates, but not for reservation, nomination, or co-option of women. Thus, while Sarojini Naidu during her Congress Presidential address in 1925, had pleaded for a women's section of the Congress, reservation was rejected by women leaders as a retrograde step after the acceptance of political equality in the Fundamental Rights Resolution of the Indian National Congress in 1931. In her presidential address to the All India Women's Conference, Sarojini Naidu said:

We are not weak, timid, meek women. We hold the courageous Savitri as our ideal, we know how Sita defied those who entertained suspicion of her ability to keep her chastity. We possess the spirit of creative energy to legislate for the morale of the world. I think this conference is writing the history of women of the world. I will, however, confess to you one thing. I will whisper it into this loud-speaker. I am not a feminist. To be a feminist is to acknowledge that one's life has been repressed. The demand for granting preferential treatment to women is an admission on her part of her inferiority and there has been no need for such a thing in India as the women have always been by the side of men in Council and in the fields of batde.... We must have no mutual conflict in our homes or abroad. We must transcend differences. We must rise above nationalism, above religion, above sex. In the same Session, one of the members, Lady Tata, lamented the absence of women members in the Legislative Assembly as a great drawback as women could have voiced the feelings of their sisters with greater directness and force than men. In their letter to the Premier and Chairman of the Minorities Committee, the three organizations (AIWC, WIA and NCWI) jointly issued a memorandum on the status of Indian women in the proposed new Constitution and demanded immediate and complete recognition of women's equal political status in theory and practice. They further stated that they did not wish to seek any form of preferential treatment as that would violate the integrity of the universal demand of Indian women for absolute equality of political status (AIWC, 1931a).

In 1932, the AIWC and WIA met to draft a declaration and send representatives before the India Franchise Committee (1932), also known as the Lothian Committee. Nine members gave evidence before this Committee and they opposed the reservation of seats for women as it may have created "a spirit of communalism against women." The Lothian Committee's Report stated that women should be treated as one of the main sections of the community and be represented in a manner similar to the Muslims, Sikhs and depressed classes. It recommended that 2 to 5 per cent of the seats in provincial legislatures be reserved for women for the first ten years, but did not elaborate on any particular method of selection. The India Franchise Committee took the view that unless special provision is made for women, it was improbable that many women would be able to fight or win elections, considering the existing prejudice against women entering public life in India.

Recognizing the fact that the AIWC was opposed to the granting of any special facilities, as they wished to be returned by the open door of competition, the Committee pointed out that a very large number of witnesses, both men and women, who gave evidence individually or as representatives of associations, felt strongly that some minimum representation should be secured for the first ten years (Reddy, 1930). The report further stated that under a system of responsible government, nomination is ruled out. The Communal Award (1932) specifically mentioned that in the provincial legislatures, all seats, including those reserved for women, would be allocated to members of specific communities and the electorate for each seat would consist of members of a single community. The Congress and the women's organizations continued to oppose communal electorates first established in the so-called Morley-Minto reforms of 1909.

In the seventh session of the AIWC at Lucknow (AIWC, 1932-1933), a resolution was moved and unanimously adopted to reiterate the demand for "universal franchise in all its bearings." One of the members pointed out that women do not want favours, but wish to resist reservation of seats or anything that may tend to perpetuate their inferiority. It was Rajkumari Amrit Kaur, an important woman leader of the Congress Party, who, while supporting the resolution, stated that: I want you to fully understand the importance of these words 'franchise in all its bearings'—for there have been one or two persons who have put forward the view-point that though the Conference can give its opinion on Franchise, as far as women are concerned, it cannot discuss the issues of either 'joint electorates' or 'the Communal Award'—for these bring us into politics. All India Women's Conference is pledged not to take part in 'party politics' and I am quite certain that we have never broken this pledge.... But if we are to eschew politics altogether we might as well as give up all our work in connection with vital questions for us— for we want our status to be fully recognized on an equal basis with men from the very beginning in the new Constitution. But the mere obtaining of the power of the vote is not enough. We must consider the basis of franchise, secondly the methods employed for the exercise of the vote and thirdly the manner in which women are to be represented, in the future councils of the country (AIWC, 1932-1933: 10).

The manner in which women are to be represented never became part of the political debate in the post-independence period. Another leader, Aruna Asaf Ali, seconded the resolution but thought reservation of seats for women to be meaningless and absurd if the demand for equality was genuine. In the pre-independence period, several women's organizations made a distinction between political participation and political a«, on or politics. Politics was a taboo word, while education and, isolative measures were considered necessary for the improvement of women's status. It is seen that the dilemma of women's organizations as to what constitutes politics and political participation continued into the post-independence period. In 1933, when the new Constitution was under consideration of the Joint Select Committee, the premier women's organizations sent three representatives to place the women's case before it.

The memorandum presented to the Committee demanded a democratic Constitution, conferring full self-governing rights on India; fundamental rights granting equal rights to women; no communal electorates; and no reservation of seats for women and no special women's constituencies or wife-hood and literacy qualification for franchise. The report of the Joint Select Committee on Indian Constitutional Reform (1933-34) made proposals for women's representation and the Government of India Act that followed in 1935 incorporated these with minor changes. Despite opposition from women's organizations, wife-hood qualifications were the main instrument for women's enfranchisement and 41 seats allocated among the minority communities were reserved for women. Under the 1935 Act, as finally adopted, 6 million women and 29 million men became eligible to vote. Seats were reserved for women on a communal basis though women could contest any of the general seats. The three major women's organizations issued a joint statement on 22 January 1935, expressing their disapproval of the wife-hood qualifications, the indirect election, the absence of a declaration of fundamental rights and communal electorates (Everett, 1981).

Furthermore, the women's movement, in the 1930s could not remain unaffected by the growing tensions between the Congress and the Muslim League in the political arena and separate all India organizations of Muslim women were formed in the late thirties. Everett also comments on the inadequate role of women's organizations in the electoral mobilization of women. The integral links between the nationalist movement and the women's movement have always been reaffirmed by political activists and analysts, but large scale mobilization of women during the freedom struggle did not resolve the question of equal representation of women in the political decision-making process. In this context she points out that AIWC leaders appeared to hold a naive view of electoral politics and the influence of their organization on mass politics before the 1937 elections.... When the parties selected their candidates, women leaders discovered that very few women were nominated from general seats and once they entered the legislatures, they considered party affiliation to be more important than sex in voting on legislation. The attitudes of politicians, policy makers and women leaders in the pre-independence period thus display an ambivalence and failure to understand the varied nature of women's constraints within the complex system of structural inequalities.

Instead, patterns of marginalization of underprivileged groups, who lack access to power, authority and decision making, were reinforced, as these did not automatically disappear with independence. The ideology of national liberation incorporated a vision of society with a liberal political agenda. Within the nationalist discourse and during the initial phase of nation-building, women received support from men for equal political rights, but the policies and programs of independent India hardly reflected the recognition of women's contribution and potentialities.

However, the ambivalence and at times contradictory approaches to the women's question has also been noted by commentators such as Joanna Liddle and Joshi who mention that: the two issues central to the women's question in Independent India were—women's suffrage and the reform of Hindu Personal Law. Votes for women united the nationalist movement with the women's movement but the nationalists were bitterly divided over personal law reform which included issues like marriage and inheritance which were of special concern to women. Male chauvinism came to the fore on the issue of family laws. Whenever patriarchal control in the family was questioned during the debate over the Hindu Code Bill, it met with opposition. While a kind of liberal ideology —of equal rights in education, the right to vote, women's welfare and so on — was promoted, it is not surprising that patriotic, cultural and nationalistic arguments were used to reject or oppose other proposals.

Demands for change in family law and property rights for women were also said to be the result of western education and influence. The perceived threat of the colonial regime to indigenous tradition and values, influenced the debate on women's roles during the pre-independence period. India's colonial experience and the manner in which men played an important role in the social reform movement, and later in the nationalist movement, in focussing on the women's question, influenced the logic and strategies of the women's movement to a considerable extent. The right to representation symbolized to many at the time an entry point into the all male-world of decision making. Omvedt accordingly suggests that Gandhi recognized the power of the women and the lower castes and used it for the cause of Independence and the freedom struggle, at the expense of caste, class and gender relations.

The Post-independence Debates

It was women's large scale participation in the civil disobedience movement, rather than any radical notion of gender equality, that tilted the balance in favor of political equality in the Constituent Assembly debates. In the first Lok Sabha (lower house of Parliament) (1952-57) of independent India, only 43 women contested and 14 were elected (of a total number of 489). Of the 216 women, who contested about 3000 assembly seats, only 82 were elected. During the fifties and sixties, several laws were passed, promising a better deal to women. Nonetheless, as an indication of how little is known about this period, some scholars have called it the "silent years" of the women's movement. The question of political reservation in favor of women died out or at least became dormant till the early seventies, when the report of the Committee on the Status of Women in India (CSWI, 1974) again debated the issue.

The All India Panchayat Parishad at its Sixth National Conference held at New Delhi in 1973 also passed a resolution recommending a fuller representation of women and a reserved percentage of not less than one-third to start with (All India Panchayat Parishad, 1995). This resolution was not followed up in any of its subsequent meetings till 1990. At the Panchayati Raj Sammelans or conferences of the Northern and Western states in January 1989, delegates expressed different views about the reservation of seats for women. The report of the CSWI pointed out that "the rights guaranteed by the Constitution have helped to build an illusion of equality and power which is frequently used as an argument to resist protective and accelerating measures to enable women to achieve their just and equal position in society" (CSWI, 1974: 354). The demand for a system of reservation came from several groups of women during the Committee's tour to different parts of the country. While the CSWI rejected, by majority voice, the proposal for statutory reservation of seats for women in legislative bodies, it recommended statutory women's *panchayats* at the village level because of the neglect hitherto of women in rural development programs. It also called upon political parties to adopt a definite policy regarding the percentage of women candidates for contesting elections. The dissenting minority of two members who advocated reservation, criticized;... the policy of 'tokenism' by having few women in the legislative and executive wings of government whose minority and dependent status offered serious obstacles to their acting as spokespersons for women's rights and opportunities. Their greater representation may also increase the women legislators' concern for problems affecting women, ensuring a body of spokespersons of the women's cause in representative bodies.

This will also help political mobilisation of women. The Committee also argued that the process of marginalization of women will result in their losing faith in the political process to change their conditions of life. They may opt out of the political system and become either passive partners or rebels. In this view, a political system cannot be based on ideology alone but must keep in touch with the actualities of the social situation.... The continuing under-representation of women prevents their proper participation in the decision making process in the country.... When one applies the principles of democracy to a society characterised by tremendous inequalities such special protections are only spear heads *to* pierce through the barriers of inequality. An unattainable goal is as meaningless as a right that cannot be exercised. In these arguments, women's representation was seen as an instrument for change and women were seen as an interest group who would take up the cause of other disadvantaged women.

It was also anticipated that once they became part of the decision-making process, they would demand participation in development decisions and a reorientation of public policies. Several of these arguments have since been thrown back and forth in the current debate on reservation for women in Parliament and in the State Assemblies. Support for reservation thus came from a group of scholars who examined women's role in the political process, as part of the CSWI exercise. Thereby, they came to the conclusion that the process of Indian women coming into their own in politics has been slow because Indian culture is apolitical and the force of tradition has been pitted against their political participation. Improving the political status of women is an integral aspect of the overall problem of socioeconomic change and of broadening the political elite structure. They noted that the failure of Indian society to "look upon women's participation with sympathy and understanding is an exceedingly retarding factor in political socialization of men and women." It was argued that 30% reservation of seats in the legislative bodies for women cannot lead to their becoming "isolated pockets in the nation" because women are not marginal to society as a minority group might be.

Such a transitional measure to break through the existing structure of inequalities will not be retrogression "from the doctrine of equality and the principle of democratic representation" (CSWI, 1974: 303). Significantly, opposition at the time came from political parties and most women legislators, the very sections who are today advocating political quotas for women. Some of these arguments were still couched in the language and discourse adopted during the nationalist struggle. Rejecting the suggestion for reservation as a retrograde step, the CSWI put forward the following views:

- the women's cause in India has always been championed by all progressive elements, men and women; separate constituencies for women will narrow their outlook; women's interests cannot be isolated from the economic, social and political interests of groups, strata and classes in society.
- it may precipitate similar demands from various other interest groups.
- the privilege once granted will be difficult to withdraw.
- women are not a community and a category and hence there is no rational basis for reservation.

The emergence of autonomous women's groups (or non-party women's organizations) in the seventies, raised radical questions about the relationship between the feminist movement, formal political institutions and power structures, and the need to organize as women. Disillusioned with party politics, many of the groups preferred to mobilize outside formal political structures. These new women's groups achieved a fair degree of success in getting amendments to laws pertaining to rape and dowry; in questioning development concepts, policies and their gender-neutrality; and pressing for a reorientation of the state. The derailment of constitutional democracy, with the declaration of the National Emergency in 1975, activated a variety of people's organizations, partly because issues such as the safeguarding of civil liberties and democratic rights and ensuring the greater participation of women and other deprived groups in the political process, took centre stage.

Several of these grassroots initiatives and people's movements, which resisted state power, are part of the dynamics of democracy in India and have their origins in unequal social and economic relationships. Their struggles started as the economic and social bases of various groups were threatened and were a direct consequence of public policies that protected the interests of the power elite. Class, caste, and gender identities provided the socio-political context for popular struggles. By partially addressing the popular demands through public policies, the state tried to co-opt dissent. For example, today, much of the terminology of the women's movement has been co-opted by the government and other agencies. Nonetheless, the experi-ences of leadership and collective action by women's groups on a variety of issues such as land, credit, literacy, and so on have made a significant contribution in enlarging the definition of 'politics,' even though a majority of women remain excluded and under-represented in formal politics. Feminists challenging the liberal models of politics argue that the present conception of politics is a male one and women's concerns cannot be accommodated within such a framework.

Thus, in 1983 a meeting of experts on the participation of women in political life, felt the need to redefine women's participation in politics and what constitutes the sphere of politics. The report pointed out that "the sphere of politics includes the social relations which create and institutionalize power relations and use them to foster, control or manipulate people's behaviour, attitudes and beliefs in order to supervise and regulate the distribution of resources" Accordingly, political participation is involvement (commitment) in respect of a deliberate and organised activity which seeks to influence (modify) the character (functioning, structure, policies, statement, behaviour) of one or more of these institutions or the mechanisms of power within one of these spheres. Attempts to overcome the obstacles and to produce new (alternative) channels of power in places where access to established channels is blocked, inadequate or ineffective should be regarded as a form of political participation. Most people's movement fall in this category. Political participation is an exercise of power.

The women's movement has to grapple with the issues of representation, governance, and the nature of politics and political institutions in a multi-party democratic system. Debates on women's representation in India are, therefore, a classic example of how politics contested around different identities can push the concern for representation on or off the political agenda. Since the 1980s, most mainstream political parties have begun viewing women as a constituency and they have introduced women's issues in their party manifestos. Political parties' heightened awareness of the importance of women's votes; the participation of women in popular movements; the pressures of the women's movement; the dynamics of grassroots organizations; judicial interventions; and executive action, all taken together, have forced varied political groups to address women's issues and revive the demand for reservation. Some policy statements on reservation for women have been made in the last two decades, for example, the draft National Perspective Plan for Women (NPP) recommended reservation of 30 percent seats at *panchayat* and *zilla* or district level and local municipal bodies through nomination and co-option (Government of India, 1988).

National women's organizations, however, rejected this as subversive of the Constitution and emphasized the need for elections at all levels to ensure the emergence of grassroots leadership (CWDS, 1989). The NPP, therefore, did not take the debate on political representation raised in the CSWI any further, though the final version did recommend 30 per cent reservation of seats at the district and lower levels, to be filled by election. But reservation in Parliament and the State Assemblies was not raised at all. It is interesting to note that the demand for reservation of seats for women in Municipalities, District and Boards was endorsed earlier as well in the pre-Independence period. In the post-CSWI period, women have definitely emerged as a distinct category in development planning, but women's experience of collective action and mobilization did not result in the greater representation of women in elected bodies. The critique of the NPP draft from the women's movement argued that the under-representation of women in elected bodies is a manifestation of their subordinate position in the family, community, and society.

As such, it undermines the democratic process. The women's groups reiterated the demand for one-third reservation for women in Panchayati Raj institutions and municipal bodies (CWDS, 1989). Subsequendy, a National Conference on Panchayati Raj and Women (1989) was addressed by the late Rajiv Gandhi who announced that 30 percent of seats in Panchayati Raj Institutions would be reserved for women. He, however, claimed that this was only the beginning and that his government would extend it to fifty per cent in two years time. It is seen that those arguing in favor of reservation for women, support it on grounds of both the historic injustice and inequalities suffered by women, as well as of women's moral superiority in providing clean politics. Echoes of these arguments have been heard at various points of time during the parliamentary debates on representation of women.

Those against the quotas called it inherendy undemocratic and against the principle of equality, while those supporting it argued that the continued under-representation of women is a failure of liberal democracy and the promise of equality of status and opportunity. During the debate on the 64th and 65th Constitution (Amendment) Bill, 1989 it was hailed as a 'historic measure,' 'a revolutionary approach' and an old dream of Mahatma Gandhi. It was opposed on the grounds that it was an attempt to usurp the powers of the state. Doubts were also raised over whether Parliament had the power to amend the Constitution, which would change the nature of the federal polity. Others said it was an election gimmick. The patronizing attitude of the male MPs during the debate on the 64th and 65th Amendments was quite obvious. A veteran MP said that they wanted to break away all these shackles and liberate their women; they should be brought to the fore in an important manner into villages, panchayats, and councils and enthroned wherever possible. In a magnanimous vein, he also said that they had done much for women earlier as well by preventing them from committing suicide and sati {*Parliamentary Debates,* 1989).

An MP, Syed Shahabuddin called the two Bills "children of political compulsion" as he saw reservation for women as nothing more than a tactical maneuver by the higher castes, the elite groups and by vested interests. The Bills could not be passed in the Rajya Sabha (the upper house of Parliament) for want of the requisite majority. Panchayati Raj thus became an election issue and when the Congress party took over the reins of government, the Constitution (72nd Amendment) Bill 1991 was again introduced in the Lok Sabha, with suggestions for insertion of new elements. The 73rd and 74th Constitutional Amendment Bills, providing for one-third reservation for women in Panchayati Raj Institutions, were finally passed in December 1992 and were ratified by all the state governments by April 1993. These two historic constitutional amendments could mark a shift from the politics of protest to proactive politics and an opportunity for women to shape the agenda at the local level.

The overwhelming response by women to these measures and the entry of nearly one million women in the Panchayati Raj Institutions encouraged the women's movement to make a similar demand for reservation of one-third seats in Parliament and the State Assemblies before the general election in 1996. The experiences and effectiveness of the first generation of elected women representatives in the panchayats have generated further debate on the issue of political quotas. However, all major political parties supported the demand and incorporated it in their election manifestos. It was also included in the Common Minimum Programme of a previous ruling coalition government at the national level. The United Front government introduced the 81st Constitution Amendment Bill that proposes reservation for women in 1996 and the debate in Parliament on it reflected stiff opposition from several quarters. The political threat to the position, power, and privileges of a male dominated Parliament brought to the fore serious divisions within political parties and various interest groups. Despite assuming a brave public posture, many party leaders conceded dissension within their ranks. The ruling party's pretence was unmasked when the champions of social justice shouted down their own Prime Minister within the Parliament. Not many were convinced that it would achieve social justice for women, as argued by the women's movement. Even the beleaguered Prime Minister relented, saying that legislation of such social importance cannot be enacted without a consensus as it requires persuasion and accommodation. The Bill was referred to the Joint Select Committee of the Parliament, composed of members from botn the Houses of Parliament. Seven national women's organizations submitted a memorandum to the Committee, expressing deep concern over the demand for a separate quota for minority and other backward classes (OBCs) within the one-third reservation for women, seen as diversionary tactics being used by certain political parties to sabotage the bill (Memorandum by Seven Women's Organizations, 1996). Under the chaipersonship of Geeta Mukherjee, a woman MP from the Communist Party (Marxist), the Committee submitted its report in December to the two Houses of Parliament and suggested several amendments (Mukherjee, 1997).

However, it did not make any recommendations as to how reserved constituencies would be determined and left it to the Government and the Election Commission. It did not accept the amendment regarding the provision of reservation for women belonging to the other backward castes and the issue of quotas for backward castes and religious minorities has dogged the Bill ever since its introduction in Parliament. The Bill for women's reservation was twice stalled in the Lok Sabha. Thus, the current political scenario, characterized by compulsions of coalition politics and the need to assuage the feelings of various interest groups within the ruling coalition, may seal the fate of the Bill. It is interesting to note that there was near unanimity on the 73rd and 74th Constitutional Amendments, which were hailed by all political parties as historic steps and as instruments for democratic decentralization. In contrast, the reactions of the intellectual elite, politicians, and the media to the 81st Constitutional Amendment are sharply divided. The women's movement has managed to keep a united front, however fragile, and despite some dissonant voices.

Is there a gender divide on the reservation issue? No, says a country-wide survey conducted by the Centre for the Study of Developing Societies. Seventy five percent men and seventy nine percent women favoured reservations in legislative bodies {*India Today,* August 31, 1996). The fate of the 81st Amendment tells a different story as the predominantly male Parliament developed cold feet and did not pass it, because opposing a move towards women's political empowerment is regarded as politically incorrect, while supporting the Bill is seen as politically suicidal. Therefore, consensus continues to elude the Bill. Behind-the-door lobbying to reduce the proposed one-third quota to a lower one, which may be more acceptable to all parties, has also not yielded any results. The women's movement, however, has taken a firm stand in that they will not accept any dilution, even if the Bill is defeated in Parliament (IAWS, 1996). Clearly, in the era of coalition politics and the continuous battle for political survival, political agendas are determined by other considerations. Paying lip service to women's causes on public platforms never gets translated into concrete strategies. The number of women parliamentarians has never exceeded more than seven percent.

The protagonists of reservation for women argue that the male dominated political system refuses to provide space for women, and reservation of seats will help in creating such political space and also lead to their social mobilization. Women are arguing for parity, not charity, and they see reservation as a vehicle for social justice. The antagonists, in contrast, are apprehensive about the whole rationale of reservation at the parliamentary and assembly levels. They not only consider it a retrograde step and a violation of the principle of equality, but are also opposed to the idea of reservation per se. As one commentator put it: "It is a horrible method of dismembering India.... The Amendment would be judged by history as one of the most important factors in destroying social cohesion in India" (*Hindustan Times,* November 30, 1994). Such a viewpoint ignores the challenges posed by other forces such as caste, ethnicity, and identity politics. Some believe that such a step promises to resurrect the Mandai ghost, although it is not perceived to be divisive enough to subvert society. Some add a note of caution that the proponents of women's reservation ought to be more concerned about the speedy acceptance and endorsement of their demand, rather than a fear of possible backlash, as it conceals the hypocrisy of neo-converts to reservation (*The Pioneer,* July 28, 1996). The realization that one-third reservation for women in Parliament and State Assemblies is going to gradually erode male power, has led to violent scenes within Parliament.

The bitter hostility to the women's quota Bill, both by casteist and fundamentalist forces, demonstrates entrenched vested interests and also warns against easy optimism. The attempt at redressing the gender balance in Parliament and the State Assemblies has evoked animated discussion on the quantity and quality of women's participation and whether or not reservation will empower women and reduce disparities. The debate has been proceeding at different levels. Some question the basic premise that a change in the gender composition will bring something distinctive to these bodies, inspire more women to enter politics, and represent and articulate women's interests better. These persons do not agree that securing greater representation is a matter of social justice. Others argue that it will introduce tensions in the social system and ask on what criteria will constituencies be designated as reserved?

In this context, a suggestion has also been made to introduce multi-member constituencies so that each constituency will have the choice to elect both men and women. The Shetkari Mahila Aghadi, the women's front of the Shetkari Sangathan (a peasant organization in Maharashtra), suggested a system of three seat constituencies combined to form a single constituency. The print media's responses were equally interesting, sometimes dramatic. The *Indian Express* called it "the mandalisation of gender, yet another manifestation of social engineering perfected to the divisive best". The same newspaper called it "wrong headed affirmative action which is ruthlessly self-aggrandizing." In this item entitled, "Hypocrisy Unlimited," *Hindustan Times* called it "competitive populism at its basest with no commitment or concern for the status and welfare of women in society" *(Hindustan Times,* 14 September 1996). Yet another newspaper said: strangely enough, on the issue of women's right to equality with men and their representation in legislature, there appears to be a close similarity of prejudice between the orthodox Hindu Pandit [Brahmin] and the anti-Hindu non-conformist. Gender justice is virtually unknown to either. It is evident here that group interests are central to the democratic process and, currently, attacks on reservation are emerging from class interests.

Similarly, in the context of the U.S., Katzenstein (1984) says that the politics of mobilization and the politics of electoral representation are not identical and that since the defeat of the Equal Rights Amendment in 1982, feminists have turned from the strategy of mobilization to the politics of representation. She describes three paradigms that seek to capture the meaning of electoral politics: elections as an instrument of social control and co-optation; elections as a means for the representation of group interests; and elections as a means of mobilization. It is significant that while elected women representatives often act collectively on controversial issues, party affiliation affects their responses. The opposition from male politicians has also been commented upon, as there is growing realization that reservations could change power equations forever.

Jayanthi Natarajan, a Rajya Sabha Member, counters the argument that the framers of the Constitution never intended reservations for women, by noting that it was women members of the Constituent Assembly who did not want a crutch of reservation, but fifty years down the road and the percentage of women members in Parliament has not even crossed the double digit. An eighty-four old ex-member of the Constituent Assembly in a recent interview admitted that her initial perception was wrong and she now believed in reservation (*Times of India,* 21 November 1996). The reactions have thus varied from excitement and high expectation, to guarded optimism and even cynicism about reservations and their impact on the formal political process, institutions, and for sharing of power and responsibilities. The biggest hurdles to transformative politics are the party system, electoral politics, and the polarization between ideological positions and the reality of women's oppression. The ardent advocates of political reservation usually downplay the nature of electoral politics and group interests and solidarities. The populist rhetoric of the political discourse on representative democracy, egalitarianism and popular participation disguises the conflict of interests. In India, the 73rd and 74th Constitutional Amendments, providing for one-third representation of women in Panchayati Raj institutions, gave impetus to the demand for similar reservation in Parliament and State Assemblies. It thus reopened the debate on the role of women in political parties, structures, and processes.

Political Representation of Women

Despite the historical ambivalence of the women's movement and the well-entrenched opposition to the reservation issue, the inequalities that characterize Indian social structure and qualify the notion of political equality are important concerns for the women's movement. The agenda of the women's movement spans issues ranging from the redistribution of resources, time and responsibilities at home, changes in electoral process, parliamentary democracy, representation, and women's political engagement with democratic institutions. Activists within the women's movement, however, believe that women's participation in the political process is crucial for women's struggle to access resources. Political parties today are more aware of women's votes, but this has not been matched numerically in their participation in decision-making or in parties nominating more women candidates in the elections.

The elections to the 13th Lok Sabha (lower house of Parliament) in 1999 clearly indicated the general apathy of most political parties in giving greater representation to women. A regional consultation on the women's movement in India noted that:... today a large number of activists see the women's movement as a political movement, however, its link with wider political processes has emerged as a major problem area. At one level, the social perception of the movement is of an apolitical struggle by various women's organizations, to improve women's status within the family. Even when sympathetic to women's resistance against familial oppression, this view questions the validity and rationale of the movement's effort to intervene in the political process. The autonomous women's groups, which had distanced themselves from political 'parties,' do not view themselves as apolitical. Many organizations and independent groups, however, see the struggle for gender equality as part of the process of wider participation of women in the political process. In the process over the years there has been an attempt to redefine popular notions of 'politics' and 'political participation from a gender perspective'. The absence of women in the internal party hierarchy and the lack of necessary means of facilitating women's participation in party activities, have led to a great deal of reluctance about accepting the idea of parity and partnership between men and women in politics.

This, in turn, is reflected in the small numbers of women in parliament and the state assemblies. Women's units within political parties, established in the seventies, are regarded as subsidiary or peripheral to the party structures and their activities are largely confined to social events, campaign work, and mobilizing women to support and defend the agenda of the party in power. But, without logistic, financial, and strategic support from the parties, women cannot succeed as candidates in the multi-party democratic system. A world-wide comparative survey conducted by the Inter-Parliamentary Union (IPU) examines three main factors in explaining the under-representation of women. These are: women in political parties, women's participation in the electoral process, and women in national parliaments. The study, based on replies from 115 countries, confirms a major discrepancy between the two sexes. With the relative exception of the Nordic countries, all countries conduct politics in a way that excludes nearly half their people. It suggests establishing of a new social contract to secure the common good. The report clearly states that "part of the answer to the limited parliamentary representation of women should be sought within political parties, especially in their hierarchy and political practices. Women are often numerous among the grassroots and are increasingly becoming aware of their electoral clout.

They are now beginning to react against the very narrow space in which they remain confined when it comes to power structures". The IPU has adopted a Plan of Action for correcting existing imbalances in the participation of men and women in political life. It is thus seen that political parties in Nordic countries introduced gender quotas for the selection of parliamentary candidates from the mid-seventies onwards. Other countries have also made some headway in this direction, for example, the African National Congress in the first election in South Africa introduced a quota system for women; the British Labour Party adopted a target of 50 percent women to be elected in the next three general elections; and the proportion of women in legislative assemblies has reached 38 per cent in Denmark, 21.3 percent in Netherlands and 15 percent in Germany. Does this perception about political parties being effective instruments for integrating women in the political process, alter their attitude towards women?

In this context, the response from Denmark in the IPU survey report, is worth quoting: The interplay between 'from above' and 'from below' is often highlighted as a fundamental characteristic of the integration of women in politics in the Nordic countries. This interplay, between the integration of women's issues in the state and the spread of women's movement activities, provides one of the explanations of the comprehensive mobilization and notable progress made in the Nordic countries. It is a combination of pressure from below, especially from the social movements and the system's comparatively high degree of responsiveness towards new groups and demands (the political opportunity structure) that are among the decisive factors with respect to the integration of women into politics. It is also important to point out an understanding of the political significance of gender focus both on changes in political culture and on changes in relation to gender. Issues of women's representation in India, as debated in the nineties, clearly demonstrate how social and economic inequalities combine with cultural values and political compulsions, making it harder for women to challenge dominant ideologies and structures.

Added to this perspective are the issues of caste, class, ethnic, and religious identity, and the tension of differing ideologies and positions. The nature of Indian party politics in a multi-party democratic system, given the kind of political institutions that consolidate vote banks along caste, religious and ethnic bases, have fostered new political divides, not always along conventional ideological grounds. Coalition politics has further demonstrated its own contradictions, as electoral arithmetic cannot always accommodate legitimate concerns in their political agenda because of their own concerns about survival. In a multi-party democracy, where the "numbers game" has significant impact on the formation of governments, the logic of selecting so-called "winning candidates" often works against women, despite lip service being paid to them in party manifestos. For example, the Congress Party President Sonia Gandhi's attempt to introduce a 33 per cent gender quota in fielding candidates for the recent parliamentary election in 1999 was scuttled, thanks to the dominant male group of the party. The final election results showed that only 48 of the 543 women were elected to the Lok Sabha (Lower House of Parliament). This is despite the agitation by women's organizations over the 84th Constitutional Amendment Bill relating to reservation of seats for women. Caste mobilization, however, cannot be ignored and needs to be understood from the women's viewpoint to expose the patriarchal overtones of casteist rhetoric.

Communal divisions and the violence stemming from identity politics pose yet another serious challenge to the women's movement, wherein gender identities are enmeshed with caste and communal identities and place women, in a peculiar position (CWDS, 1995). Violence and the criminalization of politics also tend to push women out of politics. The failure of the women's movement to forge links with mass based organizations and the initiatives taken by casteist and communal forces to mobilize women has thrown yet another challenge to the women's movement. As Agnihotri and Mazumdar point out: The wave of fundamentalist xenophobic upsurges sweeping across the world threatens the international women's movement as a whole. In India the complex social structures, economic constraints and political opportunism have provided ample breeding ground for the growth of revivalist ideologies and identity politics. It is obvious that, as a socially and economically disadvantaged section, women have begun to understand the ways in which power is shared and why greater representation is needed to influence the redistribution of power and resources.

Can policies of reservation redress the imbalance? Or is reservation an attempt to co-opt women's growing militancy? Undoubtedly, the women's movement is faced with a dilemma regarding the need to engage in politics and at the same time ask the state to intervene. Women activists believe that political representation will equip women with power to change and redefine the political agenda and articulate women's interests. The women's movement also emphasizes the need for transforming the standards of politics and governance, which remain male-dominated and can begin with the process of progressive political representation of women. Furthermore, the movement has to address issues surrounding caste, ethnicity, and religion, which, again, raise questions about politics contested around excluded identities. This is particularly important in a context where identity-based politics is a potential threat to society, wherein competing and exclusionary groups promote factionalism.

CHAPTER 6

Muslim OBCs

Introduction

The primary intent of this chapter is to look at Muslim-OBCs from the perspective of affirmative action. Therefore, the most pertinent categories are Hindu-OBCs and Muslim-OBCs. However, in order to understand the intra-community variations, it is necessary to provide comparative data regarding the rest of the Muslims. This chapter draws from a wide array of data, both secondary and primary. Sociological studies on Muslim social stratification have been drawn upon to comprehend the complexity of castes or biradaris among Muslims in India. Studies on backward class movements, analysis of Constituent Assembly Debates and the various landmark judgements of the Supreme Court and the High Courts have been of great help in understanding the historicity of the emergence of the category 'Other Backward Classes'.

Muslim OBCs: A Profile

Sociological studies on the social structure of Muslims in India have emphasized on the presence of descent based social stratification among them. Features of the Hindu caste system, such as hierarchical ordering of social groups, endogamy and hereditary occupation have been found to be amply present among the Indian Muslims as well. The Census of India, 1901 listed 133 social groups wholly or partially Muslim. The present day Muslim Society in India is divided into four major groups: (i) the *Ashrafs* who trace their origins to foreign lands such as Arabia, Persia, Turkistan or Afghanistan,

(ii) the upper caste Hindus who converted to Islam, (iii) the middle caste converts whose occupations are ritually clean, (iv) the converts from the erstwhile untouchable castes, Bhangi (scavenger), Mehtar (sweeper), Chamar (tanner), Dom and so on. These four groups are usually placed into two broad categories, namely, '*ashraf*' and '*ajlaf*'.

The former, meaning noble, includes all Muslims of foreign blood and converts from higher castes. While '*ajlaf*' meaning degraded or unholy, embraces the ritually clean occupational groups and low ranking converts. In Bihar, U.P and Bengal, Sayyads, Sheikhs, Moghuls and Pathans constitute the '*ashrafs*'. The '*ajlaf*', are carpenters, artisans, painters, graziers, tanners, milkmen etc. According to the Census of 1901, the *ajlaf* category includes 'the various classes of converts who are known as Nao Muslim in Bihar and Nasya in North Bengal. It also includes various functional groups such as that of the Jolaha or weaver, Dhunia or cotton carder, Kulu or oil presser, Kunjra or vegetable seller, Hajjam or barber, Darzi or tailor, and the like.' The 1901 Census also recorded the presence of a third category called *Arzal*: 'It consists of the very lowest castes, such as the Halalkhor, Lalbegi, Abdal, and Bediya...' A similar pattern of descent based social stratification is discernible in other regions as well.

In Kerala, the Moplahs of Malabar, are divided into five ranked sections called the Thangals, Arabis, Malbaris, Pusalars and Ossans. The Thangals trace their descent from the Prophet's daughter, Fatima, and are of the highest rank. Next in rank are the Arabis, who claim descent from the Arab men and local women and retain their Arab lineage. The Malbaris are next in rank. They have lost their Arab lineage and follow matrilineal descent. The Pusalars are the converts from Hindu fishermen called Mukkuvan, the new Muslims. They have low status. The Ossans are the barbers, and by virtue of their occupation, they rank lowest. In Andhra Pradesh, a field study conducted in 1987 found hierarchically arranged endogamous groups among Muslims. At the top of the ladder were those claiming foreign descent—Syeds, Shaikh, Pathan and Labbai (descendants of Arab traders who took native wives). At the lowest level were groups with 'unclean' occupations-Dudekula (cotton cleaners), Hazam (barbers) and Fakir-budbudki (mendicants). Muslim groups currently bracketed under the category 'OBC' come essentially from the non-ashraf section of the Muslim population.

They are the converts from the middle and lower caste Hindus and are identified with their traditional occupation. A study of a village in Uttar Pradesh could identify eighteen such groups, for example, Julahas (weavers), Mirasis (singers), Darzis (tailors), Halwais (sweetmakers), manihars (banglemakers) and so on. The 1911 Census listed some 102 caste groups among Muslims in Uttar Pradesh, at least 97 of them came from the non-ashraf category. Many such groups such as the Rajputs, Kayasthas, Koeris, Koris, Kumhars, Kurmis, Malis, Mochis, were common among both Hindus and Muslims. Since the Constitutional (Scheduled Caste) Order, 1950, popularly known as the Presidential Order (1950), restricts the SC status only to Hindu groups having 'unclean' occupations, their non-Hindu equivalents have been bracketed with the middle caste converts and declared OBC.

Thus, the OBCs among Muslims constitute two broad categories. The halalkhors, helas, lalbegis or bhangis (scavengers), dhobis (washermen), nais or hajjams (barbers), chiks (butchers), faqirs (beggars) etc belonging to the '*Arzals*' are the 'untouchable converts' to Islam that have found their way into the OBC list. The momins or julahas (weavers), darzi or idiris (tailors), rayeens or kunjaras (vegetable sellers) are *Ajlafs* or converts from 'clean' occupational castes. Thus, one can discern three groups among Muslims: (1) those without any social disabilities, the *ashrafs*; (2) those equivalent to Hindu OBCs, the *ajlafs*, and (3) those equivalent to Hindu SCs, the *arzals*. Those who are referred to as Muslim OBCs combine (2) and (3).

Kaka Kalelkar Commission (1955) and B. P. Mandal Commission (1980)

The First Backward Classes Commission submitted its report in 1955. The Report presented a list of 2,399 castes and communities considered backward, 837 of these were considered 'most backward' requiring special attention. Thus the category, backward classes, was further bifurcated into two categories-the backwards and the most backwards. The list included not only backward groups from amongst the Hindus, but also non-Hindus, including Muslims as well.

The Commission's Report was the first instance wherein the presence of 'backward communities' among Muslims (and other religious minorities) received recognition in official parlance. The caste basis did not find approval from the chairperson of the Commission and one of the reasons cited was the assumed castelessness of Muslims and Christians: "My eyes were however open to the dangers of suggesting remedies on the caste basis when I discovered that it is going to have a most unhealthy effect on the Muslim and Christian sections of the nation."

The second All India Backward Classes Commission, the Mandal Commission, submitted its report in 1980. The Commission evolved eleven indicators, a mix of caste and class features, for assessing social and educational backwardness. The Commission saw castes as the 'building bricks of Hindu social structure' that despite the Constitutional commitment to establish a casteless and egalitarian society had continued to persist. It arrived at an exhaustive list of 3,743 castes that were declared as backward. The Commission, in principle, accepted that occurrence of caste or caste-like feature was not restricted to Hindu society, its influence was also found among non-Hindu groups, Muslims, Sikhs and Christians, as well. Based on the data provided by the 1931 Census and field surveys conducted at the instance of the commission, at least 82 different social groups among Muslims were declared OBCs. The Commission however desisted from employing 'caste' as a criterion to identify non-Hindu OBCs as 'these religions are (were) totally egalitarian in their outlook'. The Commission, however, refrained from invoking 'poverty' too as the sole criterion. The 'rough and ready' criteria that the Commission evolved had two conditions:

a. All 'untouchables' converted to any non-Hindu religion. In the Muslim case, they are the *Arzals*.
b. Such occupational communities which are known by the name of their traditional hereditary occupation and whose Hindu counterparts have been included in the list of Hindu OBCs. Among Muslims, this comprises the *ajlaf* category.

By clubbing the *Arzals* and the *ajlafs* among Muslims in an all encompassing OBC category, the Mandal Commission overlooked the disparity in the nature of deprivations that they faced. Being at the bottom of the social hierarchy, the *Arzals* are the worst off and need to be handled separately. It would be most appropriate if they were absorbed in the SC list, or at least in a separate category, Most Backward Classes (MBCs), carved out of the OBCs.

Approaches to Affirmative Action for Muslim OBCs

At the all-India level, the issue of OBCs has been attempted to be addressed by instituting two backward classes commissions with the mandate to evolve the criteria of backwardness, identify social groups on that basis and suggest measures to ameliorate their condition. Of the two, the report of the first commission (Kaka Kalelkar Commission) was rejected by the Union government for having used 'caste' and not the economic criterion for identifying backward classes. The report of the second commission (Mandal Commission) was partially implemented in 1991 more than a decade after it was submitted. Besides these two attempts at the Centre, various state governments instituted their own backward classes commissions and have evolved distinct approaches to reservation of backward classes.

Muslim OBCs and Affirmative Action in the States

Tamil Nadu Model

Tamil Nadu offers a model of affirmative action for Muslims or Muslim OBCs that is slightly different from that offered by Kerala and Karnataka. Unlike Kerala and Karnataka, Muslims as a distinct category are not eligible for reservation, yet most of the Muslim biradaris are included either in the backward or in the most backward list. The state government has done away with reservation on grounds of religion, yet nearly 95% of the Muslims have been included within the fold of backward classes. To begin with, the Muslims who were educationally backward were given special treatment vide a resolution dated July 29, 1872. Later it was extended to the 'aborigines' and low caste Hindus.

As the Brahmins were grossly over-represented in high salaried jobs, a Government Order (1927) introduced compartmental reservation whereby the non-Brahmins were to have 42% of the posts available and Muslims 17%. Post-Independence, reservation was extended to only the constitutionally recognized deprived categories, such as the SCs, the STs and the Backward Classes. Separate quota for Muslims was also withdrawn; rather various communities among Muslims considered backward were included in the list of Backward Classes. The Sattanathan Commission (1970) endorsed the 1951 categorization, it identified 105 castes/ communities as backward, and recommended 31% reservation, whereas 18% was left for the SCs and STs. Tamil speaking Muslim groups, such as Labbais, Deccani Muslims and others were included in the backward list. In 1980, 31% quota for backward classes was raised to 50% taking the total to 68%. Following the recommendations of the Ambasankar Commission (1982) the backward classes were split into Backward Castes (BCs), Most Backward Classses (MBCs) and Denotified Communities. The quantum of reservation currently is 69%; far beyond the Supreme Court limit of 50%. The Tamil Nadu Backward Classes, Scheduled Castes and Scheduled Tribes (Reservation of Seats in Educational Institution and of appointments or posts in the Services under the State) Act, 1993 was included in the 9th Schedule through the 76th amendment of the Constitution.

Bihar Model

The 'Karpuri formula' as it is popularly called allows for the bifurcation of the category backward classes into its advanced section, the Other Backward Classes (OBCs) and relatively more deprived, the Most Backward Classes (MBCs). The first major effort to understand the plight of backward classes in Bihar was undertaken when the Mungeri Lal Commission was constituted in 1971. In its report submitted in 1975, the Commission recommended the bifurcation of the backward classes into Other Backward Classes (OBCs) and Most Backward Classes (MBCs). The OBC list contained 128 castes and the MBC list had 93 caste groups. The Karpoori Thakur government in 1978 accepted the classification made by the Mungeri Lal Commission. For the purposes of recruitments to jobs, 8% was set aside for the OBCs, 12% for the MBCs, 14% for the SCs, 10% for the STs, 3% for women and another 3% for the economically backward. After the carving out of Jharkhand from Bihar, the above scheme was slightly amended. The ST quota was reduced to 1%; the SC quota was now fixed at 15%, 13% for OBCs, 18% for the MBCs and 3% for backward caste women. Muslim caste groups, depending on their level of backwardness, have been included either in the OBC or in the MBC list. While 9 Muslim groups are in the state's OBC list, 27 of them form part of the MBC list.

The three different models for affirmative action for the Muslims/ Muslim backwards, as detailed above, can be summarized as:

a. Reservation of seats for the entire Muslim community (excluding the creamy layer): Kerala and Karnataka.
b. Reservation on the basis of backward caste/biradari but most of the Muslim groups included covering 95% of Muslim population: Tamil Nadu
c. Bifurcation of OBCs into backwards and most backwards (MBCs), most of the Muslim backwards in the MBC list: Bihar

Kerala and Karnataka Model

In terms of their policy of reservation for backward classes, Kerala and Karnataka stand out for having extended the benefits of reservation to their entire Muslim population. This has been achieved by including Muslims (minus the creamy layer) as a distinct group within the broad category of backward classes and then provided with exclusive quota. This distinct feature of their reservation policy dates back to the colonial period. In the erstwhile princely state of Mysore, affirmative action began as early as in 1874 when a government decision reserved 80% of the posts in the Police department for non-Brahmins, Muslims and Indian Christians. In Kerala, the demand for reservation for under-represented communities was accepted as early as 1936 in the princely states of Travancore and Cochin, and in Malabar even earlier, in 1921. Quotas were fixed not only for caste groups such as the Ezhavas, but also for religious minorities, the Muslims and sections of Christians. Post-Independence, on the reorganization of the State of Mysore as Karnataka, all non-Brahmin Hindu castes and all non-Hindu minority communities like Muslims and Christians were declared as backward classes.

In 1960, on the recommendations of the Nagan Gowda Committee, the category backward classes was bifurcated into backwards (28%) and more backwards (22%). Together with the quota for SC/ST, the magnitude of reservation rose to 68%. The

Supreme Court in a landmark judgement, however, placed 50% ceiling on the quantum of reservation. Muslims as a whole continued to be considered as among the backward communities. The Havanur Commission, 1972 recommended the creation of a distinct category of minority group with reservation not exceeding 6%. The State classified Backward Classes into three categories: (a) Most backward; (b) More backward and (c) Backward. All Muslims whose income is less than Rs. 2 lakh per annum have been declared backward and placed exclusively in one of the sub-categories of 'More Backwards' with four percent of the seats set aside for them. According to the information provided by the state government to this Committee, this measure has led to a substantive rise in Muslim share in the state government services. The number of seats Muslims get in professional courses like Medicine, Dental and Engineering has also increased to a considerable extent.

Between 1996 to 2002, 346 Muslim students were able to secure seats in Medicine, 258 in Dental and 3,486 in Engineering courses. In Kerala, the reservation scheme introduced in 1952, fixed the quantum of reservation at 45% (including 10% for SCs and STs). The beneficiaries included the Ezhavas, Kammalas, the Nadars (Hindu and Christian), other Hindu backward castes and SC and OBC converts to Christianity. On the reorganization of the State in 1956, the quota for backward classes was enhanced to 40%. Later, the scheme was modified to introduce sub-quotas for major backward groups. A separate Muslim share was fixed at 10% that later rose to 12%. At present, the reservation system in Kerala is as follows: Backward Classes 40% (Ezhavas 14%; Muslims 12%; Latin Catholics 4%; Nadars 2%; Christian converts from S.C.s 1%; Dheevaras 1%; Other Backward Classes 3%; Viswakarmas 3%) and S.C.s and S.T.s 10%.

Muslim OBCs Not Included in the State and Central Lists of OBCs

Reservations for OBCs has a longer history in the states than at the Centre. As the recommendations of the Mandal Commission came to be accepted, the Central list of OBCs, in the initial phase, was prepared by employing the principle of 'commonality'. Thus, only those castes/communities listed both in the state list and also in the list prepared by the Mandal Commission were included in the Central list. It is not surprising therefore that a number of castes/ communities that had either been listed only in the Mandal list or only in the state list were left out. This discrepancy was expected to be solved once a permanent body, namely, the National Backward Classes Commission (NCBC) was formed. The NCBC, formed in 1993, has issued a set of guidelines based on social, economic and educational indicators, for castes/communities to be included in the Central list of OBCs.

The discrepancy between the two lists, Central and State, is still evident. This is a general complaint and not confined to Muslims alone. There are many OBC groups, irrespective of their religion, that are present in the State list but missing in the Central list. Madhya Pradesh, for instance, has 91 social groups listed as OBCs in the list recommended by the State Backward Classes Commission, but only 65 such groups have found entry in the Central list. Uttar Pradesh has 79 castes in the state OBC list, but only 74 in the Central list, in Rajasthan there are 74 castes in the state list but only 65 have been accorded OBC status in the Central list. Such discrepancy also applies in the case of Muslim OBCs.

In Madhya Pradesh, for example, there are 37 communities listed in the state list as Islamic groups, however, only 27 of them are found in the Central list. In Bihar, after the recent revision of the list, there are 17 OBC groups that have not found a place in the central list. Six of them are exclusively Muslim, namely, (i) Faqir/ Diwan, (ii) Julaha/Ansari (the synonym Momin is in the Central List), (iii) Itrfarosh/Gadheri/Itpaj/Ibrahimi, (iv) Jat, (v) Gadaria and (vi) Surajpuri. In Uttar Pradesh, two Muslim groups-Mirshikar and Nanbai-have not found entry in the Central list. In Gujarat, Muslim groups such as Jilaya, Tariya-tai, Mansuri, Arab, Sumra, Tarak, Kalal and Bahvaiya are listed in the State's backward list but not in the Central list. Similarly, many Muslim groups in Maharashtra such as Mansooris, Pan Faroshs, Ataar, Sanpagarudi, Muslim Madari, Muslim Gawli, Darwesi, Hashmi, Nalband among others have not found entry in the Central list. The lists of OBCs prepared by the state governments have also missed many underprivileged castes and communities. There are a few groups among Muslims that have found place in the Central list but are yet to be included in the State lists. Kalwars in Bihar, Mansooris in Rajasthan, Atishbazs in Uttar Pradesh, Rayeens, Kalwars, Rangwas and Churihars in West Bengal are examples of such Muslim groups. There are still a number of Muslim groups that have neither been included in the State list nor in the Central list. These groups can be identified using the information collected by Anthropological Survey of India under its People of India Project. In Gujarat for instance, the Project found 85 Muslim communities, of which at least 76 are non-ashraf. In the Central list, however, only 22 of them have found entry, whereas in the State list, there are only 27 Muslim groups. In Bihar, according to the Project, there are 37 castes/communities that can be counted as non-ashraf, however, only 23 are in the Central list. In Uttar Pradesh, the Project lists 67 communities among Muslims, 61 of whom are occupational groups. Both the State and the Central lists of OBCs contain only 32 of them.

Empirical Situation

In this section, attempt has been made to quantify the relative deprivations that Muslims in general and Muslim-OBCs in particular face. Different variables have been employed, for instance, male and female work participation, representation in various levels and sectors of public employment, salaries and wages, per capita income, incidence of poverty, urban and rural land holding, relative share in education etc. to ascertain the status of Muslim OBCs vis-à-vis their Hindu counterparts and also the non-OBC Muslims or Muslim-General. Most of these variables indicate that Muslim-OBCs are significantly deprived in comparison to Hindu-OBCs.

Population Distribution of Muslim OBCs

In our analysis of population share of Muslim OBCs we will largely depend on the National Sample Survey, 61st Round.

State-wise Distribution of OBC Population

In the states of Kerala, Tamil Nadu and Haryana, Muslim OBCs constitute almost their entire Muslim population. In Kerala, this is mainly because of the fact that Mapillas, who constitute more than 90% of the Muslim population of the State, have been included in the Central list. Similarly, Meo Muslims, an OBC group, forms the bulk of the Muslim population in Haryana. The Hindi-Urdu belt comprising Bihar, Uttar Pradesh, Rajasthan, Madhya Pradesh and Jharkhand also has the majority of the Muslims listed as OBCs. On the other hand, in the two states of West Bengal and Assam, both with substantial population of Muslims, the proportion of OBCs is minuscule. Thus, the benefits attached to OBC status is denied to most Muslims residing in these states. Regional analysis reveals significant inter-state differences.

In 14 out of the 20 states for which data are presented, the share of Muslim OBCs has risen in the 61st Round as compared to the previous round of survey. The increase is the highest in Rajasthan (32 percentage points), followed by Bihar (23 percentage points) and Uttar Pradesh (18 percentage points). A fall in their share is observed in West Bengal, Assam, Jammu and Kashmir, Karnataka, Delhi and Himachal Pradesh. While the change is extremely high in Delhi (24 percentage points), it is marginal in West Bengal. The latest round of NSSO's survey (61st Round) estimates the OBC population share in the total population at 40.4%. Of these, 34% is the share of Hindu-OBCs and the remaining 6.4 of M-OBCs. In the total OBC population of the country, Muslim-OBCs have a share of 15.7%. This is not reflected in their representation either in public employment or in educational institutions.

National Sample Survey, 61st Round

The survey data on OBCs falls short of the estimate made by the Mandal Commission; also, there is considerable variation in the figures provided by the two surveys, 55th and 61st Round. Those reporting as OBCs among Muslims constitute 40.7% of the Muslim population, as per the 61st Round. Compared to the 55th Round when Muslim OBCs were reported to be only 31.7%, the growth is of 9%. The pattern remains the same in both rural and urban areas. As the NSSO provides self-reporting data, this only reflects either an enhanced awareness of their OBC status among the Muslim OBCs or substantive revision of the OBC list since the last round of survey. The growth in the population share of Hindu OBCs is also noticeable. The population share of SC/ST in the total Hindu population remains consistent in both the surveys. The category SC/ST and the benefits associated with it has a longer history, more than 50 years, and therefore the social groups included, to a large extent, are aware of their status.

The Scheduled Tribe Component among Muslims

Unlike the category Scheduled Caste, the category Scheduled Tribe, irrespective of the religious affiliation of the members of the tribe, is entitled for reservation. The criterion followed for specification of a community as scheduled tribes are indications of primitive traits, distinctive culture, geographical isolation, shyness of contact with the community at large and backwardness. The criteria is not spelt out in the Constitution but has become well established. The Muslim component of the ST population is very small.

According to the 1991 Census, it accounts for only 0.25% of the total ST population of the country. The highest proportion of Muslims declared as STs is found in Lakshadweep where Muslims constitute the entire ST population (99.74%). Muslim share in the ST population of Himachal Pradesh (7%) is also quite significant. Elsewhere, Muslim STs are minuscule in number. The Muslim ST population is only 1,70,428 whereas the total population of the STs stands at 6,77,58,285 (1991 Census). It must be noted that while STs get all entitlements irrespective of their religious backgrounds, all Muslims of tribal background do not get this benefit. There are many cases of claims of ST status by Muslim groups that have remained unattended.

Educational Conditions

Literacy Levels

Disaggregated analysis by place of residence reveal sharp differences across SRCs in urban areas; Muslims, and in particular Muslim-OBCs, are lagging behind Hindu-OBCs. The literacy levels among the Muslim-OBCs is the least in rural areas as well but the difference is not as sharp between them and other SRCs in urban areas.

Levels of Education

A comparison across SRCs suggests that the educational levels of Muslim-OBCs and Muslim-Gen are lower than those of Hindu-OBCs. In general, educational levels among Muslim-OBCs are lower than the other two SRCs; illiteracy is the highest among this group and a lower proportion of persons in this group complete school education or undertake graduate studies.

Children Not Attending Schools

Almost half of the children aged 6-12 years are not currently attending school. The proportion of Muslim OBC children not attending schools aged 12 years or less is much higher than this figure. While the difference between Muslim-OBCs and Muslim-Gen is not marked (both are about 55%), the difference in non-attendance level between Hindu-OBCs and Muslim-OBCs (49%, compared to 56%) is significant.

Achievements in Higher Education

Finally, the status of the three SRCs is examined with respect to their attainments in the field of higher education. Three levels of education have been used for this purpose-general graduates and above, technical graduates and technical diploma and certificate courses. It can be seen that all the three SRCs have a lower proportion of persons holding a technical/non-technical degree or technical diploma/certificate compared to the Hindu-OBCs. Except in the case of technical diploma/certificate courses, Muslim-OBCs have the lowest level of achievements in higher education; in general, Hindu-OBCs do better than the other two SRCs. Thus, in terms of higher education also, the Muslim-OBCs lag behind the other SRCs namely Hindu-OBCs and Muslim-Gen.

Employment Status

Work Participation and Unemployment Rates

The work participation rate (WPR, proportion of persons aged 15-64 years who are engaged in any economic activity (working), either as principal or subsidiary activity) shows the presence of a sharp difference between Hindu-OBCs (67%) and the two Muslim SRCs (about 55%), with WPR among both categories of Muslims being substantially lower at the all-India level. The difference between Muslim-Gen and Muslim-OBCs, however, is marginal (56% and 54% at the all-India level). This difference can be observed in both rural and urban areas and among females. Within the male population, however, differences in the WPR are marginal. According to the NSSO 61st Round data, while 9.2% of Muslim-OBCs of all age groups were unemployed in 2004-05, the unemployment rates were lower at 7.5 and 7.7 percent respectively for Hindu-OBCs and

Muslim-Gen. Similar differences were observed for both men and women and in rural and urban areas.

Share of Workers in the Formal Sector

The proportion of Muslim-Gen and Muslim-OBC workers engaged in the formal sector is below the corresponding proportion for.. According to the NSSO 61st Round data, within the formal sector, the share of Muslim-OBCs in government/PSU jobs was much lower than those of Hindu-OBCs and Muslim-Gen. While 7.2% of Hindu-OBC workers in rural areas were employed in such jobs, the shares of such workers among Muslim-Gen and Muslim-OBCs were 5.8 and 3.4 percent respectively. The differences in urban areas were sharper with Hindu-OBCs (11.3%) much ahead of Muslim-Gen (7%) and Muslim-OBCs (3.5%). The inferior employment situation of the Muslim-OBCs vis-à-vis the other two SRCs is also reflected in the fact that a much smaller proportion of workers among them are engaged in regular wage/salaried jobs, especially in urban areas. The proportion of workers engaged in regular employment in rural areas ranged between 6-7% for all the three SRCs. However, in urban areas, the participation of Muslim OBCs (20.4%) in regular jobs was much lower than that of Muslim-Gen (31.2%) and Hindu-OBCs (36.4%). In general, therefore, Muslim-OBCs are lagging behind Muslim-Gen and Hindu-OBC categories in terms of participation in the formal sector and jobs that provide regularity of employment (both waged and salaried).

Differentials in Earnings

Workers can be divided into two broad categories-casual and regular. Regular workers can be further subdivided into those who work in public or private sectors. There is no significant difference in wages paid to SRCs. Interestingly, wages received by Muslim-OBCs are higher than that received by Muslim-Gen and Hindu-OBCs. This can be observed for both male and female workers. Salaries paid to Hindu-OBC and Muslim employees in both the public and private sectors are lower than the average salaries. Muslim-Gen employees are marginally better off than Hindu-OBC employees. Muslim-OBC employees receive salaries that are significantly lower than the other two SRCs. This is true for both the public as well as the private sector thus indicating that more

Muslim OBCs tend to be in low salaried jobs as compared to other SRCs. Among male regular workers, Muslim-OBCs are relatively more deprived than the other two SRCs; differences between Muslim-Gen and Hindu-OBCs, however, are marginal. In the case of women workers, Muslim-OBC workers are less deprived in the public sector vis-à-vis the other two SRCs; in the private sector, on the other hand, they are deprived to a greater extent.

Muslim OBCs in Public Employment

The Committee's estimates indicate that while out of every hundred workers about eleven are Hindu-OBCs, only three are Muslim-Gen and one is a Muslim-OBC. Deprivation of Muslim-OBCs is highest in the Railways (employing more than 14 lakh workers) and in Central PSUs (for which the Committee has received data pertaining to almost 7 lakh workers). Representation is also low among candidates recommended for selection by State Public Service Commissions (SPSC). Muslim-Gen are also significantly under-represented in all sectors, and particularly in Central Security Agencies, Central PSUs, candidates recommended by SPSC and Universities (both teaching and non-teaching posts). While Hindu-OBCs are also under-represented, deprivation is less than that of Muslim-OBCs in five out of the six agencies, and less than that of Muslim-Gen in three out of the six agencies.

Distribution of Workers According to Place of Work

The distribution of male workers by place of work is not very different across SRCs. A large proportion belonging to all these SRCs either work in employer's enterprises or one's own enterprise/dwelling. A few differentials across SRCs can be noticed. For example, a relatively larger proportion of Muslim-OBC workers work in employer's enterprises while this is lower in construction sites. The bulk of women workers in all SRCs work in their own dwelling. However, the proportion of such workers among Muslims, especially Muslim OBCs, is higher.

Representation in Selected Central and State Institutions and Undertakings

All the three SRCs, Hindu-OBCs, Muslim-OBCs and Muslim-Gen, are under-represented when their share in employment is compared with that in population. Hindu OBCs constitute 34% of the population but in none of the Central Organizations is their share more than 12%. This includes even the lowest level, i.e, Group D employees. Muslim OBCs whose share in the population is 6.4%, have less than one percent presence in these organizations, with the exception of central security forces (3.6%). In the higher echelons of these services, they are nearly absent. In the central security forces (including BSF, CRPF, CISF and others), Muslim OBCs are better represented than Muslim-Gen (3.6%, compared to 1% Muslim-Gen). They however still fall short of their share in population. It is noteworthy that in the case of Muslims, even the non-OBC section of their population is significantly under-represented (varying from 3% to 4.5%).

Representation in Universities

Out of almost 1.5 lakh persons working in Universities, the representation of Hindu-OBCs among faculty members is more or less the same as their share in population. Muslims, both OBC and non-OBCs, seem to have only a token presence in the universities. This analysis indicates that while Hindu-OBCs have been able to reap the benefits of reservation of posts in universities, the representation of both Muslim-OBCs and Muslim-Gen in different sectors remains grossly inadequate.

Representation in State Services

In the states the situation is better for the Hindu OBCs. Although still short of proportionate representation, their share in the upper and middle levels is much higher than that in the central organizations. However, a large proportion of the Hindu-OBCs find employment at the Group D level. While Muslim-Gen has a comparatively better representation in Group A and D posts of state services, their representation in middle levels posts is marginal. Muslim OBCs have better share at the Group A level, but their presence is insignificant at all other levels.

Economic Status

Incidence of Poverty

The incidence of poverty is measured by the proportion of poor persons. All-India estimates show that the incidence of poverty is highest among Muslim-OBCs (38), followed by Muslim-General (35). In contrast the proportion of poor among Hindu-OBCs (27) is lower than even the national average (28). The higher incidence of poverty among Muslim-OBCs and Muslim-Gen, compared to the national average and Hindu-OBCs, can be observed in both urban and rural areas. The difference between Muslim OBCs and Hindu-OBCs is particularly striking in urban areas. The proportion of poor Muslim-Gen persons is almost 9 percentage points higher than among Hindu-OBCs. The Muslim-OBCs were even worse off with the share of poor persons being 14 percentage points higher than that of Hindu-OBCs.

Inequalities Among SRCs

At the all-India level, there are marginal differences in inequality levels between the three SRCs being analysed. Overall, the inequality levels are somewhat higher among Muslim-OBCs as compared to other SRCs. Higher levels of poverty are combined with relatively higher levels of inequality.

Monthly Per Capita Expenditure (MPCE)

The MPCE of the three SRCs is much lower than the national average. Among the three SRCs, the MPCE of Muslim-OBCs is the least. The condition of Muslim-Gen is marginally better off than the other two SRCs as reflected in their MPCE. In urban areas, also, the MPCE of the three SRCs is lower than the national average. As was the case with poverty levels, however, the difference between SRCs is striking in urban areas. The MPCE of both Muslim groups is much lower than the national average. Moreover, the MPCE of Muslim-OBCs is much lower as compared with Muslim-Gen in urban areas. In rural areas, differences between MPCE of SRCs are narrower. The MPCE of Muslim-OBCs is about the same as the national average, while MPCE of Muslim-Gen is marginally lower than that of Hindu-OBCs.

Ownership and Average Size of Land Holdings

Average land holdings of Hindu-OBCs are clearly much better (about twice) than that of Muslim-OBCs and Muslim-Gen. In fact the average land holdings of Hindu-OBCs (1.9 acres) are higher than even that of the national average (1.7 acres). The differences in average land holdings of Muslim-Gen and Muslim-OBCs are almost the same (1.0 and 0.7 acres, respectively).

Concluding Comments

As per the latest round of NSSO survey, Muslim OBCs constitute 40.7% of the total Muslim population. They are also a sizeable component (15.7%) of the total OBC population of the country. The NSSO survey however fails to provide disaggregated figures across individual castes/groups included in the OBC lists of the Centre and the various states.

As a result, intra-OBC differentials along castes/groups in terms of crucial indicators such as educational attainment and employment share cannot be estimated. The Committee therefore is of the opinion that enumeration of castes/groups as part of the decennial Census exercise is critical to assess the equitable distribution of benefits meant for groups included in the category, OBC.

It is important to underline that Muslims in India are not a monolith, and this is what our analyses across various indicators of human development also suggests. While Hindu-OBCs continue to be relatively deprived in terms of the all-India data, the Muslim community as a whole is lagging behind Hindu-OBCs. However, overall, the conditions of Muslim-OBCs are worse than those of Muslim-Gen.

The abysmally low representation of Muslim OBCs suggests that the benefits of entitlements meant for the backward classes are yet to reach them. To explore the differentials across the SRCs further, an exploratory exercise was undertaken to assess if the proportions of Muslim-OBC, Muslim-Gen and Hindu-OBC differ significantly in high and low income groups.

It is noteworthy that, as compared to other SRCs (except SC/ST), the share of Muslim-OBCs and Muslim-Gen population is significantly higher in low income groups. Within the Muslim community, a larger percentage of Muslim-OBCs fall in the low income category as compared to Muslim-Gen.

In contrast, much smaller share of Muslim persons belong to the high income category. Interestingly, a larger share of SCs/STs belong to the high income group as compared to Muslims. Within

Muslims, Muslim-OBCs are slightly lagging behind the Muslim-Gen in the high income group. Based on the arguments and data presented here, it is logical to suggest that Muslims in India, in terms of their social structure, consist of three groups-*ashrafs*, *ajlafs* and *arzals*.

The three groups require different types of affirmative action. The second group, *ajlafs*/OBCs, need additional attention which could be similar to that of Hindu-OBCs. The third group, those with similar traditional occupation as that of the SCs, may be designated as Most Backward Classes (MBCs) as they need multifarious measures, including reservation, as they are 'cumulatively oppressed'.

CHAPTER 7

Violation of Human Rights of Dalit Women

Introduction

All human beings have the right to live as human beings. Human rights are not conferred or given. They already exist in society. The concept of human rights aims at protection of rights like right to life, liberty and property. These rights are attributed to human beings irrespective of class, caste, gendeı, colour and religion. The Universal Declaration of Human Rights was unanimously adopted by the UN General Assembly on December 10th, 1948. The preamble of Indian constitution adequately empowers the central and state government to eliminate human rights violation in the country. Inspite of these international and national declarations and resolutions, human rights are violated in different countries all over the world. In Indian society, due to the social barriers such as castetism, untouchability, patriarchy, disparity, superstition, religious exploitation and class variations, specific groups are becoming weaker and marginalised.

These groups are facing the problems of identity crisis, deprivation, discrimination and atrocities. These marginalised groups are also identified and recognised as dalits, SC (scheduled castes) ST (scheduled tribes), OBC (other backward castes) NT (nomadic tribes) DT (denotified tribes) religious and linguistic minorities. Violence on human beings in any form results in violation of human rights. Human rights of dalits and women in general are normally violated by high castes and powerful communities to practice and exhibit patriarchy and castetism. But human rights of Dalit women are violated extremely and in peculiar form. Dalit women are in worst position than dalits in general, in terms of sex ratio, wages, employment, occupation, assets, education, health, social mobility and political participation. Hence, it is important to discuss the status of Dalit women and various problems they face even after 60 years of independence. This chapter makes an attempt to discuss basic facts, issues and concerns related to Dalit women to suggest some alternatives to combat violation of their rights for social justice and equality. Explanation of relevant terms such as 'Dalit', 'dalitism', and 'Dalit women', is given below to broaden understanding about the issue.

Dalit

Dalit ('oppressed' or 'broken') is not a new word. Apparently it was used in the 1930's as a Hindi and Marathi translation of 'depressed classes'. The British used this term for what are now called the scheduled caste. Dr. Ambedkar chose the term 'broken men', as English translation of 'Dalit', to refer to the original ancestors of the untouchables. Dalit Panthers, the youth activists from Dalit community revived the term and in their 1973 manifesto expanded its reference to include the scheduled tribes, neo Buddhists, the working people, the landless and poor peasants, women and also those who are being exploited politically, economically in the name of religion.

Dalitism

Dalitism essentially implies conditions of subjugation; economic, political, social and cultural. Dalitism also embodies different degrees of marginalisation. It includes not only marginalized status in the economic sphere but also in cultural, political, religious and social domains. That means Dalitism symbolizes marginalisation. It is a well known fact that marginalisation denies basic human rights and social justice.

Dalit Women

Dalit women are one of the most marginalized segments in the society. The condition of Dalit women is more vulnerable than non-Dalit women. Dalit women are suffering from multi-disadvantages:

a) of being Dalit i.e socio-economically and culturally marginalized section,

b) being women and sharing the gender based inequalities and subordination.

To explore these and other crucial issues concerning Dalit women there is need to discuss some basic facts concerning the vulnerable situation of Dalit women.

Vulnerable Status of Dalit Women

It is easy for the historically dominating caste and gender to violate human rights of Dalit women who are at the lowest rung of the hierarchical ladder. The type of violence inflicted on dalits is in the form of severest violation of human rights. Dalit and tribal women are raped as part of an effort by upper caste leaders, land lords and police to suppress movements to demand payment of minimum wages, to settle share cropping disputes or to reclaim lost lands. The recent incident of Khairlanji Massacare is not something new. A Dalit family had refused to let upper caste villagers built a road through their fields. Hence on September, 29th, 2006, Bhaiyalal Bhotmange's family, – wife Surekha, daughter Prinyanka and two sons were killed by the villagers of Khairlangi in Bhandra district of Maharashtra. They were first attacked with huge iron chains and than abused by the other caste women of the village. Surekha and Priyanka were paraded naked and raped, and later, their bodies were mutilated and thrown into a pond. This shows that Dalit women are easy targets for any perpetrator Upper caste considers them to be sexually available.

Hence they are largely unprotected by the state machinery. Further, there is prevalence of violence, making Dalit women eat human excreta, parading them naked, gang-rape, murder, dacoity, robbery and burning of their huts or communities. These are the types of crime, which violate their human rights. According to SC/ST commission report between 1981 and 1986 about 4000 Dalit women became victim of rape. In 1993 –94 this figure rose to 798 and 992 respectively. This means annually about 700 Dalit women fall prey to sexual assault by high caste people. The main complaints of the poorer Dalit women are that they have no good houses. In urban areas most of them stay in unhygienic slums and in rural areas their houses are away from main stream society. Under conditions of grinding poverty and severe exploitation at work place, Dalit women also suffer caste specific ban on water access from upper castes and may be beaten up in their own houses as well. A poem by a Dalit poetess Teressama, a teacher from Guntur puts the situation in the following words:

We go to work for we are poor
But the same silken beds mock us,
While we are ravished in broad daylight.
Ill-starred our horoscopes are
Even our tottering husbands
Lying on the cots in the corner
Hiss and shout for revenge
If we cannot stand their touch

At the outset, prevailing caste and secondary status of women in the society is largely responsible for violation of human rights of Dalit women. To understand the root cause of the situation it is essential to examine basic factors responsible for their vulnerability.

Socio-cultural and Religious Factors

First and foremost Dalit women are victims of social, religious and cultural practices like Devdasis and Jogins. In the name of these practices, village girls are married to God by their helpless parents. These girls are then sexually exploited by the upper caste landlords and rich men and directed in to trafficking and prostitution. In his autobiography, Kale (1994) has described a ritual called 'chira'. The literal meaning of the word 'chira', is to cut or break. In this ritual when a girl from the lower caste community reaches the age of puberty, an elderly prestigious man from the higher caste breaks the hymen of the girl child by sexual act. This ritual is performed in a way to make the girl accept this fact as a routine practice.

The 28th report of SC/ST commission reported that in February 1986 there were about ten thousand Jogins belonging to SC in Nizamabad district of Andhra Pradesh. The survey submitted by the district collector to Schedule Caste Finance Corporation revealed prevalence of 15,850 cases. Eighty percent of these Jogins belonged to SC. This data is just an example of one district of the country. Practices such as Chira, Jogins, Devdasi which are prevalent even today are harmful and threaten the dignity of Dalit women and violate their human rights.

Educational Status

Low level of education is a problem in itself and in turn gives rise to many other problems.. In 1991, literacy among the Dalit women was indeed quite low. In rural areas only 19.46 percentage women were literate. A report published by Ministry of Welfare, Government of India in 1998 showed that there is much difference in the literacy rate of dalits and non-dalits in general, and gender specific. Literacy rate of non-dalits is 64.13 % and literacy rate of women is 39.29 %, where as Dalit women's literacy rate is only 23.76 %. There is a large disparity in the literacy rate due to wide spread prejudice based on castetism and patriarchy against dalits and women in general and Dalit women in particular.

Economic Deprivation

A careful look at the economic situation of Dalit women reveals that their work force structure is such that they rarely own any land. A large majority of them are agricultural labourers. The rate of unemployment among them is also quite high. About 90% of women working in unorganized sector are mainly from lower castes. In 1991, about 71% of Dalit women workers in rural area were agricultural labourers.

Only 19% of them owned land. A prominent researcher and sociologist while sharing her experience from a research on gender and land issue, informed that, when she enquired with Dalit women about land owned by them in their names, they wondered about permissibility of owning land in their name. This indicates that neither do they own any land nor are they aware of their rights on land.

When enquiries were made with Stri-mukti sanghatana and Prerana, Mumbai based organizations working on the issue of rag picking and prostitution respectively, to ascertain the proportion of Dalit women in these occupations, it was learnt that NGOs usually do not keep record of caste. However, Human Rights Watch Report (1998) mentioned that a large number of Dalit women are engaged in unclean, inferior occupation such as sweeping, scavenging and working in dumping grounds, rag picking and also in prostitution. These women have to face steep discrimination in the matters of social relation and employment due to their engagement in these occupations.

Health and Nutrition Status

Dalit women's daily diet is the leftover of family meals, inadequate in quantity and quality. Health services are either not available in case of illness or unaffordable even if available. In addition to that, due to early marriage and too many pregnancies their health is always at risk. If birth control is practiced at all, 91% cases of tubetomy are performed on the women who have to carry the burden of family planning. In an overall situation where dalits are prone to ailments in general, women suffer from more serious and more varied kind of sickness. More than 80% of women in reproductive age group (15 to 45) are anemic. Poor health status of Dalit women pushes her then into more vulnerable situation.

Political Status

Women constitute half of total population, but are unable to get equal share in active politics. Their socio-economic status directly depends on their participation in politics. Political parties in India speak much about equality of women but have totally ignored the Dalit women. Traditionally, leadership in the village was confined to 'rural elites', who were aged and belonging to higher castes. In the year 1993, 73rd amendment in the constitution granted reservation to dalits, tribals and women in local government. This amendment made it compulsory that one third of the seats reserved for dalits be filled by Dalit women. In some states, there has been little or no acceptance of reservation for the lower castes and Dalit women by the upper castes. This has resulted in atrocities against panchayat members including women. Dalits who stood for election were beaten, and Dalit women were raped and ill-treated. The members of the higher castes, who are not prepared to relinquish power to the lower castes, grabbed their land. An easier method to retain power is to put-up proxy candidates but keep the control in the hands of the dominant castes, always men. The incapacity of women, particularly Dalit women, to assert their rights is at the root of the problem.

The reservation for dalits, particularly for women, is accepted in form but seldom in substance. Any change in the status quo is resisted. Dalit women's sitting on chairs is seen as threat to social hierarchy. So, the upper castes in the village vetoed chairs in the panchayat office. Dalit women also faced many problems in performing their duties due to illiteracy, lack of information and dependency on the male members of their families. An important obstacle is the no-confidence motion against Dalit women as pradhan by the dominant sections. Rural elites are unable to accept the power, which has been given into the hands of the poorer and disadvantaged women. Despite recognition and legal sanction for political rights, rigid caste system and patriarchy directly and indirectly has been suppressing Dalit women and violating their political rights. This proves that human rights of Dalit women are violated right from her family to the society at large by one and all. All these factors are largely responsible for the precarious position of Dalit women as far as their social, cultural, religious, economic, health and political status in the society is concerned. These factors force them to mutely allow violation of their civic and human rights. Thus they become victims of universal violence.

Efforts to Protect Human Rights

With the realization that violence is one of the potent threats to the peaceful existence of human beings, whole hearted and all round efforts are made at international, national and local level. The preamble to the Universal Declaration of Human Rights (UDHR) serves as a foundation and philosophy of Human rights. There are a host of international conventions including those for prevention and punishment of genocide and elimination of all forms of racial and gender based discrimination. The World Conference Against Racism (WCAR) related to racial discrimination, xenophobia and intolerance held in Durban, South Africa in 2001, brought the issue of caste and untouchability based discrimination on the agenda of UN Conference in Durban. Among the several organisations, the National Campaign on Dalit Human Rights (NCDHR) – a collective of Dalit NGOs, other NGOs, academicians', activists and large number of supporters spearheaded the national campaign in India for inclusion of the issue of caste and untouchability based discrimination in the Durban Conference. The preamble of Indian constitution adequately empowers the central and state government to eliminate human right violation in the country. Article 17 of the constitution provides for removal of untouchability. Based on this article Protection of Civil Rights Act' (PCR), was passed in 1955. However, there was no conviction/ under this Act hence, Thirty-four years after the introduction of PCR Act, the Scheduled Caste and Schedule Tribes (Prevention of Atrocities) Act 1989 was enacted to bring various forms of atrocities to an end. In this Act the complainant is given more weightage. There are stringent provisions against the police for negligence (Pandit)

Emerging Identity of Dalit Women and Formation

The focus on education of low caste women is one of the important factors responsible for the emerging identity of Dalit women. Reformist intervention by Savitribai and Mahatma Phule of opening school for untouchable girls way back in 1848 was a turning point for changing status of Dalit women. (Chakrvarti in Rao 2003). Dr. Ambedkar's thought and action made important differences in the lives of Dalit women. His movement and especially his organisations encouraged many Dalit women to become educated to be active in public life and to gain leadership, self respect in the contemporary period encouraged women to participate in organisation for Dalit women at regional, state and national level. [Zelliot in Rao 2003). After independence in 1960's and 70's, the Dalit movement and women's movement emerged to demand their rights against caste and gender respectively.

However, specific problems of Dalit women were not acknowledged by these movements. Hence in 1990's there were several special, independent and autonomous assertions of Dalit women's identity; a case in point is the formation of National Federation for Dalit Women (NFDW) and All India Dalit Women's Forum (AIDWF) at the state level. The Maharashtra Dalit Mahila Sanghatana (MDMS) was formed in 1995. A year earlier, the women's wing of Bhartiya Republican Party (BRP) and the Bahujan Mahila Sangha (BMS) was set up the Bahujan Mahila Parishad. In December 1996, at Chandrapur, a Vikas Vanchit Dalit Mahila Parishad (VVDMP) was organised and a proposal to commemorate 25th December (the day on which Ambedkar had set Manu smriti on fire) as Bhartiya Smriti Divas was advanced. The Christi Mahila Sanghatana, an organisation of Dalit Christian Women was established in 1997.

These organisations have come together on several issues such as celebration of Bhartiya Stree Mukti Divas and on the issue of reservation for OBC women in parliament bodies. Indian Association of Women Studies (IAWS) network with Dalit feminist across different regions had brought special issues on problems and identity of Dalit women. Several efforts have been made since independence to secure human rights of women in general and Dalit women in particular. Despite this, human rights of Dalit women are seen to be violated in different forms. Such infringement of human rights echoes the need of evolving suitable mechanism to empower Dalit women to assert for equal rights and justice in order to live a dignified life.

The Capacity of Dalit Women

To be human is to respond to human sufferings and pain with compassion and effective concern. It is not enough to feel with the Dalit women in their pain, There is more need for effective action, otherwise it would be just sentimentalism' says Sequeira in his article 'Human Response to Dalit Women. The needs and the problems of Dalit women differ with city, village, area and caste. It is essential to keep in mind that Dalit women are not mere individuals but belong to a sociological and dialectical system. Therefore to recognise the system and to prohibit violation, first and foremost proper perspectives about the issues has to be developed among all by considering following suggestions:

- Awareness for Assertion: Extensive reading of available literature can be done by young generation to understand the profile and problems of Dalit women. Factual incidents & success stories of Dalit women namely, 'We made History Too' by Meenakshi Moon & Urmila Pawar can be included in the educational texts.
- Access & Exposure Visits: Special exposure visits to Dalit localities can be organised for school and college students to assess basic amenities accessible to Dalit women namely, water, electricity, health and hygiene. Similarly Dalit women's

visit to urban structured colonies can be arranged to impress upon the importance of standard of living of non-dalits. Such purposeful visits will broaden their horizons resulting in improved living of marginalised section.

- Academic Activities: Academic institutions need to be encouraged to undertake studies to assess the problems of violence and atrocities against Dalit women as also the reasons therefore and to work out ways to overcome them. Thought provoking sessions on harmful social religions practices namely, Chira, Devdasi, Jogin need to be held for basic understanding and effective interventional strategies.
- Campaigns and Sessions: Campaigns for equal and rational distribution of natural resources among weaker sections can be organised to secure their rightful means of livelihood. Proper rehabilitation and shelter can be provided to those communities, which are out of the social periphery (NT/DT) to protect them from the risk of sexual abuse.
- Inclusion of Dalit Women in various system: More Dalit women in their population proportion (16.5% SC, 7.5% ST) should be given chance to enter in the system like police, judiciary, education, health and politics.

Sessions can be organised for Dalit activist and women activists to sensitize them about the magnitude of torture and oppression faced by the Dalit women. Legal education dealing with protection of human rights of dalits and Prevention of Atrocities Act (1989) can be organised to prevent the problems of castism.

Conclusion

At the threshold of 21st century it is absolutely necessary that common people need to be sensitized about the prevailing atrocities against Dalit women. There is a growing need to capture violation of human rights of Dalit women, so that talent and potential of Dalit Womens can be used for development of nation. According to Vippal (Jogdand, cited in 1995) a nation does not prosper only on fertile soil, dense forests and everflowing rivers. It is the healthy people who make a nation. A society is made up of both men and women from all states. If women from whichever state is weak and exploited, it is not a healthy society. And when a society is healthy, then the nation will march ahead. To fulfil these dreams women in general and particularly from weaker section need to be empowered for development of the nation.

Violence Against Dalit Women in Nepal

Dalit women comprise of more than half of the Dalit community in Nepal. Dalit community in general and women in particular have been treated as sub humans for ages. The women fold, as a whole became the victim of Manu order. Manubad is so deeply rooted in our society, no any sort of reference seen to bring change promptly. After the political change in 2007, the situation of women has certainly changed but not to the extent it should have been. The fact is that Dalit women also consist of one-forth of the total women population. The whole women are the victims of gender discrimination in the society. The basic difference between high caste women and Dalit women lies on the ground of caste based discrimination and untouchability, which Dalit women have to face. In comparison to other high caste women, the Dalit women have been forced to live in most vulnerable conditions. They constitute the major workforce doing hard manual labor and engage in agricultural operations. Dalit women are thrice alienated on the basis of class, caste and gender. The whole Dalit community has to struggle for survival. Thus they need helping hand from their women. Through this perspective, Dalit women deserve better position than those of higher castes. But high caste people/women perpetrates caste-based discrimination and untouchability against Dalit women. The reality of the Dalit community is that the whole family has to depend at least partly on their income. Regarding the Dalit craftsmen artists and labors, women participate in productive activities and thus become the part of economic chain. So in certain caste groups like Chamars, Badi, Pode etc. there is some respect for the women in comparison to higher caste women where they are also considered as tool of sex.

Population of Dalit Women

It is obvious that Dalit community comprises one-forth of the total population of the country. The census of the past (2001) was not based on the scientific criteria in which lot of Dalit sub-castes were included under upper caste group on the ground of similar creed (Thar) like Gautam, Ghimire, Dulal, Derlami, Khapangi, etc.

According to the census held in 2001, the total Dalit population is 2,962,591 (13.05%); of which the whole female population is 1,496,622 and the male population is 1,465,969.

Violence against Dalit Women

Dalit women have been facing lot of violence from various areas. Dalit women including male are considered untouchables by caste Hindus. They have no access to public places including drinking water sources. In some rural areas, Dalit women have to wait long in the water taps and wells until so-called high caste women are ready to serve water for her. If at all they interfere, they become the victims of violence and punishment. Dalit settlement in general is outside the village of the caste Hindus and mostly in the town areas. They face the difficulty of two basic necessities of any human being-drinking water and sanitation. It is observed that Dalits are not provided with even on tap/well for hundred of houses. Dalit women become victim of their male partners when they use alcohol.

They are also facing hardship due to the child marriage, double marriage, bride price and even dowry systems that prevail in the society. According to the research study done by S.C.F.U.S., 23% Dalits are landless whereas 48.7% have less than 5 ropanis of land. Furthermore, 15.6% Dalits have 6-10 ropanis of land, 9.6% Dalits have 11-20 ropanis of land and 3.1% have more than 21 ropanis of land. They hardly have 1% of cultivable land. 95% Madhesi Dalits are landless. Their per capita income is US.6, which is almost the lowest in the world. Higher class and caste people monopolized the national resources and all other income sources. They have enjoyed the fruit of all development. Dalits have no easy access to national resources, public services and even development projects. In such a situation, we can imagine the reality of Dalit women. They participate with their male partner's work in the agricultural field of the upper caste people. More than 90% of our Dalit women living in the village earn their livelihood by working as agricultural labors under the upper caste/class landlords. Their employers sometimes rape them. In Hindu society, some women from Badi community have become involved in prostitution in the name of religious tradition, which is alike Devdasi system in India. Their condition and enjoyment by upper caste Hindus is sanctioned by the Hindu religion. Badi women are looked down as inferior to dogs in the society. Badi

Dalit women per se are treated as untouchables in the society, however, there is no untouchability as far as sexual exploitation is concerned. Besides domestic works, Dalit women are entirely involved in agricultural work as well.

Their work is greater than the Dalit males. Every body is familiar with the sight of a sweeper woman in Kathmandu cleaning the city area carrying their small babies on their back. Similarly, we can see Dalit woman working in the paddy field leaving their small kids in the side of the field in hill and Tarai areas. In respect to Halia, Dom, Chamar women they have significant roles in terms of earning income. In terms of earning livelihood, Dalit woman can be considered as one of the wheels of the cart. We may never think the present day situation of socio-economic development in the absence of Dalit women. Dalit women get less wages in comparison to their male counterpart. Generally, Dalit women work as daily labour for transplanting seedlings, threshing paddy/wheat or even as labour in road or building construction. In the village of Tarai, Chamar women accomplish maternity job. The irony is that these women are permitted to enter the houses at the time of childbirth but as soon as the job is over they are again reverted back to the untouchables status.

Though they provide most valuable service, they get nominal fees in the form of 5-10 k.g. of food grains. Chamars and Doms are supposed to clear the village or town even by throwing away dead animals. They have to do such work free of charge but earn a little bit by selling hides and skins, bones etc. of the dead animals. Dalit women from these caste groups help their men folk in doing such works in the name of religion and tradition. Dalit women from Dom, Badi, Damai, Gaine, Hudke sub-caste groups are supposed to entertain the high caste people with various folk songs and dances. In return, they get nominal tips as the mercy from high caste people.Dom, Chamar, Mehtar, Pode/Chyame women like their men folks perform the humiliated job of clearing the houses, surroundings of the public places even to the extent of carrying the night soil. The greatest irony is that these people are considered as untouchables even by other untouchables. Patriarchal feudal system considers women folk in general as commodity, means of entertainment and second-class citizen.

That is why, even Dalit women face discrimination in justice, education, job, property rights, wages and decision-making process. Dalit women like other women get to loose their identity after marriage since their children follow their father's family name that is reflected in getting citizenship certificates. The great tragedy is that some people from Badi community face hardship in getting citizenship just because of their unknown father. Having guided by Hindu societal norms, Dalit community is also indifferent to educate girls as they think them other's property. Dalit women have to face violence in home, in public places and even at work in different occasions. However, there is no any proper legal provision as to protecting their basic human rights. The next tragedy lies in the area of women trafficking in which the high percentage of Dalit women falls. As a result of which they have to suffer a lot from dangerous diseases like AIDS. Similarly, a great number of Dalit women are being victimized in the accusation of Boxi (witchcraft). Recently, there occurred lot of such Boxi incidents in the Tarai. Dalit women have been the victims of dowry and bride price systems which are still continuing in our country.

Mostly Dalit women have been the victims of intra-caste and inter-caste marriage. So-called upper caste people engage in fake love with Dalit girls and then right after pregnancy or marriage they give up them just on the ground the caste factor. Hence, a great number of Dalit girls have been facing hardships. Any violence on the Dalit community is ultimately born by Dalit women. Specifically during the eight-year of Maoist war, many of Dalit youths have lost their lives by being the victim of both Maoists and state. It is the Dalit women who have to bear all such unbearable sufferings socially, economically, culturally and politically at great risk of her own and her children's life.

Efforts to Improving Situation of Dalit women

Despite the civil Code (1964) along with its eighth amendment and the constitution of the kingdom of Nepal (1990:11/44) ensuring equitable justice for Dalit rights, the caste-based discrimination and the practice of untouchability still continue. There are contradictory laws and by-laws which violate Dalit rights. Still there is an urgent need to formulate laws as to abolish disparity both in principles and practice. Nationa Planning Commission came out with special provisions for the whole Dalit community in Eighth Plan (1992-97), Ninth Plan (1997-2002) and the Tenth Plan (2003-007). Particularly the Ninth Five Year Plan had put some major objectives for Dalit upliftment with a view to abolishing all forms of discrimination. However, the state commitment could not be translated into reality. The Tenth Plan is focusing on Dalit empowerment and development programs. INGOs, NGOs and even government agencies have spent a big amount of money in the name of Dalit empowerment for decades. But the so-called Dalit empowerment programs seem to be mostly Kathmandu-based, activists-centred and are out of the reach of grassroots levels. Actually some forward Dalit activists including women have been benefited from several projects rather than the unaware-targeted community. It is notable that right after 1990 various Dalit organizations, along with Dalit women activists are working for the Dalit cause. The significant change so far is seen in the field of awareness raising.

The creation of Dalit Bikas Samitee in 1978 has become an asset to Dalit community, although the budget allocation to its program is nominal. In May 2002, the government constituted National Dalit Commission with a view to protecting Dalit rights. Since this Commission was created through executive decision of the government, there arises a question of its legitimacy. Thus, in reality it could not meet the minimum aspiration of Dalit community. The current government, for the first time in the history, has declared reservation policy to Dalits, indigenous and women. Definitely, from the perspective of inclusiveness this step of the government is positive one and it is hoped that it will help bring change in the life of the Dalit community. Moreover, the approach adopted by Maoists might be debatable to many but it brought certain level of awareness and practice of equity in the Nepalese society. It is praiseworthy indeed that some INGOs and NGOs have given due attention to Dalit empowerment programs in Nepal. The next important juncture was the WCAR conference where for the first time Dalit NGOs became successful in raising their voice at international level. Paper presented at a seminar organized by FES/ CETS)

CHAPTER 8

Revisiting the Women's Reservation Debate

Once again, the debate over Women's Reservation Bill has resurfaced, in the wake of the President's speech promising to enact 33% quota for women in assemblies and parliament as well as 50% quota in panchayats. After 13 years of delays and vacillations, the women's movement and progressive forces are naturally demanding that the Government and main ruling parties, who no longer have any excuse not to enact the Bill, walk their talk this time without any further delay. The cacophony of misogynistic rhetoric voiced against the Bill since 1996, and revived this time around, has rightly invited outrage. However, let us set aside the anti-women baggage for a while, and re-examine the main case against the Bill, as articulated mainly by parties and leaders claiming to represent the dalits and OBCs. The crux of the debate is: will the Women's Bill in its present form militate against OBC representation in parliament and benefit only elite, privileged women, and must it therefore include a quota within quota for OBC women, as a precondition for passing the Bill? Does the women's quota indeed represent a threat to political representation of oppressed and backward castes? In the first place, we must note that provision has already been made, in the Bill, for 33% quota for women within the existing 22% SC/ST quota. So Mulayam Singh's warning to the (Dalit woman) Speaker in his parliamentary diatribe against the Bill, that the Bill, if enacted, would prevent her own entry into Parliament, is obviously baseless.

The question of quota within quota for OBC women is more complicated – mainly because of the fact that there is no existing

OBC quota at any level in representative institutions. The question of OBC quota in assemblies and parliament is being brought up only in response to the Women's Bill. Even in Bihar, where the state government headed by the JD(U) (the party of Sharad Yadav, the most vocal opponent of the Women's Bill) has instituted 50% quota for women in panchayats, there is a quota within quota for women from SC/ST and Most Backward Castes (MBCs), not for OBCs as such. OBC representation in assemblies and parliament has, by all accounts, increased significantly since the 1980s. If 33% seats are reserved for women, will it result in a decline in OBC representation? Won't OBC women win seats which OBC men have been winning? No, say the opponents of the Bill – arguing that elite, educated, privileged, usually upper caste women will steal a march over OBC women. The lion's share of the benefits of women's quota, they say, will accrue to the more privileged upper caste women.

This argument seems to be founded on a fallacy about the nature of electoral and political mechanisms. In reservation in general, it is true, where it is individuals who compete for limited seats – in jobs or education – it is the more privileged who are likely to corner the lion's share of quotas. For instance, in the case of OBC quota, intended to correct the underrepresentation of OBCs in jobs and higher education, working class poor and women from these castes are less likely to avail benefits as compared to those from the same castes who are relatively more privileged educationally and economically.

But the question arises: while OBCs continue to be underrepresented in jobs and higher education, necessitating the OBC quota, how come they are fairly well represented in parliament and many assemblies? Why has the upper caste domination in Indian politics been decisively broken, without any quota? The reason is that OBC political forces have ridden a wave of popular social mobilization that has asserted itself since the 1980s. Politics – including electoral politics – is all about contending social mobilizations, where the caliber and privileges of individual candidates is relatively secondary. This is the reason why a Phoolan Devi (the former bandit) won electoral battles even without any OBC quota. It is one matter that parties have been reluctant to field such women candidates, thus necessitating a women's quota, but the example of Phoolan Devi suggests that when given a chance, OBC women have not fared worse than their male counterparts in electoral battles. The same social forces which benefited male OBC leaders has played in their favour too, and their lack of educational privilege has not come in the way of electoral success.

The point is that politics is not a personality contest, and there is simply no reason why OBC women should fare badly in comparison with upper caste women once the Women's Bill is brought into effect. Even the apprehension that OBC women might be denied tickets because they would be seen as less 'winnable' than more privileged women, doesn't hold water. Winnability, in our electoral process, is decided less by individual privilege alone – and more by the position of candidate and party in the social balance of forces. It is this which is the biggest factor in parties' decisions to field candidates. There is no reason why a party, in a constituency where their position in the social balance would favour an OBC candidate, would choose a non-OBC candidate in case the seat is reserved for women. Reservation for women would not alter the social balance of forces – it would only eliminate the aspect of gender discrimination from the social equation in that particular election.

Why is OBC quota proposed only in response to the Women's Bill, while it is not seen as necessary in general? Opponents of the Bill retort that it is precisely to counter the threat of growing OBC assertion in politics that the upper caste dominated parties have embraced the Women's Bill.

Again, such an argument is based on a fallacious and superficial understanding of the basis of the increased OBC representation in politics. OBC political assertion reflects the growing assertion of an emergent kulak class in agrarian India. To reduce it to the assertion of the marginalised 'backward castes' alone would be to ignore that it also reflects the assertion of a powerful emergent landed class, which represents a more privileged layer within the backward castes, while, however, positioning itself as the voice of the genuine social and political aspirations of the backward castes as a whole. The ruling class including the dominant national ruling parties have, to a large extent, accommodated this kulak class and its political representatives, which have not proved in any way a hurdle to the economic and social policy thrust of other ruling class parties. The initial expectations from some quarters, that these parties would prove a hurdle to communal politics or to neoliberal economic policy have been badly belied. Tensions might remain between powerful 'regional' players and national formations, but the latter, while they might seek to replace the regional outfits, will do so by accommodating the OBC-kulak forces rather than by jettisoning them. Moreover, the Women's Bill is highly unlikely to overturn the power of the agrarian kulak class in the balance of social forces. Rather, the same political logic and process that has benefited OBC male leaders is likely to benefit OBC women as well.

Sharad Yadav, in a recent interview in Tehelka, rephrased his 'parkati' brand of argument against educated, urbanised women leaders, in more palatable and even 'progressive' words. He said Sita-Savitri were usually seen as representative of Indian women, and he instead wanted the Draupadis – women who dared to fight Mahabharatas for justice – to find political representation. "If the weaker sections of the society are not included, only people like Sushma Swaraj and Brinda Karat will be seen in the Lok Sabha, not the true Draupadis who represent the real India," he said. Brave words. But there is a problem: Brinda Karat, a prominent leader of the left-led women's movement, cannot be called an advocate of 'Sita-Savitri' even by her worst detractors. In contrast to the considerable efforts of the women's movement and the Left-led women's groups, what has Sharad Yadav or his party ever done to mobilize the Draupadis against patriarchies? The accusation of being 'elite' and cut off from Indian culture and social reality is a favourite one to level against women's movement activists – and Sushma Swaraj would happily join Sharad Yadav in thus branding the women's movement as un-Indian! Such accusations ignore the fact that if women's movement leaders from middle class, educated backgrounds represent one kind of relative privilege in respect to their working class sisters, politicians of ruling class parties – including OBC leaders from kulak backgrounds, also represent considerable class (and gender) privilege, and are not unmediated 'natural' representatives of 'deprivation'.

The idea that educated middle class women – as leaders of the women's movement or as representatives in political institutions are somehow less authentic and less representative of the 'real Indian women' needs to be challenged very strongly, because such arguments are inevitably deployed to legitimize patriarchies in the name of 'Indian culture,' falsely suggesting that 'authentic' Indian women are those who accept and embrace such patriarchies. It is not our case that 'OBC parties' and leaders like Sharad Yadav or Mulayam are more anti-women than those from the Congress or BJP.

Rather, they are pitting the OBC agenda against women, not simply because they are anti-women or even because they feel more threat from the Women's Bill, but because they perceive a political benefit in flaunting purported concern for OBCs. Sharad Yadav, for instance, is clearly seeking to use the Women's Bill issue as a timely tool in his bid to pose as OBC messiah and step into the shoes left vacant by the decline of Laloo Yadav.

Today, in any case, there is no unity even in the camp of OBC leaders and parties, on the 'quota within quota' position. Nitish Kumar of the JD(U) has strategically chosen not to endorse his party colleague Sharad Yadav's stand on the Women's Bill. In Parliament, Mulayam Singh too said not a word about 'quota within quota' for OBC women, choosing instead to suggest the even weaker mechanism of a party-wise quota of 20% tickets to women candidates.

In his speech in Parliament, Mulayam Singh said that with 22% reserved for SC/STs, and 33% for women, there would be no space left for upper castes and backward castes. He said that leaders like Advani, Joshi, and others had reached the Lok Sabha through hard struggles, and the Women's Bill would 'destroy this leadership.'

He also employed the usual misogynistic spectre of women in parliament relegating men to domestic work, saying "those thumping tables today will tomorrow be left thumping mattresses at home," and lamented the 'state of affairs' where women like Sonia, Mamata, Jayalalitha and Mayawati were calling the shots everywhere.

Interestingly, these arguments were clearly targeted not just at OBCs but specifically at upper caste leaders (even naming them), and even more interestingly, his implication that women elected through quotas would not be the product of 'hard struggles' and would destroy able leadership, actually echoes the meritocratic arguments posed by protesters against OBC quotas. Clearly, be it Sharad Yadav or Mulayam, the arguments against the Bill are not just emanating from 'concern for OBC representation', but rather these leaders have complex and distinct motivations that have necessitated different articulations and emphases at different political junctures.

We do not oppose a 'quota within quota' on principle, nor do we reject it on the spurious argument that 'women' are an undifferentiated category uninflected by caste and class. In fact, it would be our greatest concern that women from oppressed castes and classes get their share of representation. What are objectionable are the attempts to use the OBC issue as a smokescreen to stall the Women's Bill.

To employ an analogy: would it not have been highly objectionable if the implementation of Mandal recommendations on OBC quotas in jobs and education had been stalled for years on the pretext that a quota within quota for OBC women, or for that matter economically deprived OBC students and youth, was a precondition, to accommodate the apprehension that these sections might be less able to benefit?

The need of the hour now is to pass the Women's Bill in its present form without a moment's further delay. If indeed experience reveals that women's reservation is resulting in any appreciable decline in OBC representation, OBC quota in assemblies and parliament, in general as well as within the women's quota, can be accommodated through amendment.

Reservations, OBCs, Women, and My Right

At the outset, let me state this-by birth (and to a great extent by upbringing) I am a Brahmin. I was born with the privilege of being born into a family with considerable socio-intellectual capital. So it would be easy to read anything that I write on the OBC reservations issue, as something that comes without the insight of belonging to a certain community.

However, let's say we put aside this issue of reservations for OBCs and the already existing quota for SC / STs. Suppose I pick up the issue reservations in higher education for women. As a woman and a practicing feminist-who is very passionate about getting women into the best of institutes and opening up more opportunities for them-I should support reservations for them right?

Wrong. Some reasons why.

1. The Usual Beneficiary: Higher Education in India is not the preserve of those with money. Money is usually not a barrier. Suppose I was 16 and studying for the JEE. What I really need is good quality coaching. God knows that the CBSE and State Board seem inadequate. I would really appreciate if interest groups pushed for bridge classes to overcome the entry barrier, instead of institutionalizing mechanism that help override the entry point. I would already have to some of the economic capital if I have been able to study till the 12th grade. If loans are available at extremely low interest rates, and payable over long periods of time-I have a feeling a woman would benefit far more than her being plonked into an institute where she's unable to cope with the subject matter. Moreover, it's likely that a woman like me who comes from a privileged background who will end up using this quota.
2. The Usual Suspect: Given stereotyping and traditional barriers, if I am a woman in a particular setting, it is often suspected that I got there through favours. This favour by the government is no less. Regardless of what merit I may possess, the suspect factor remains that I got there through other means. Even if it is a legitimate way to enter-it is sends signals about my merit. Whatever social capital I may appear to gain, it is overshadowed by the constant doubt over my merit. It also makes ALL women appear suspect. Irrespective of how they got there. Merit or Reservation (partial merit?).
3. Universalizing Primary Education: Education. Primary Education. The government makes feeble attempts at universalizing primary education and FAILS. It's been failing consistently since 1947. It's the worst report card a country can produce-that most of the country still can't read it. The issue with primary education is that it is so centralized, that it's difficult to hold an absentee or inefficient teacher responsible. The teacher in a school is simply not answerable to the community.
4. The Gap: If Education at the same institute is such an equalizer, why have reservations at the Under Graduate

level? If all these kids have cleared their Class 12 examinations and are at the same educational level-why the need to lower the cut-off for one section? Even more shocking-why would the women need reservations at the Post Graduate level? Wouldn't three to four years of the same education, additional bridge courses etc. have pushed the men and women to a level playing field based on merit?

Suppose a teacher discriminates against girls in a government school-the parents have no choice! Now the government either needs to clear up its act and decentralize schooling and education, or it needs to give more impetus to private schools. Every state perhaps cannot do a Himachal Pradesh, or a Kerala and maybe condemned to a cycle of inefficiency that means poor education, high drop out rates with far more heavy consequences for historically weaker sections like women. (hint!) If you tell me that private schools are expensive-think again.

The market forces are not allowed to operate. If enough parents feel that the teacher discriminates against girls in a private school-chances are that another private player will recognize the gap-and start a school that is more gender sensitive. I understand that this school, in an ideal situation need not be gender-blind. The school will need to reach out to parents to convince them to continue in the school. (Which school wouldn't want fees the next year?) The school has further reasons to push parents to send their girls to college.

Because earning women make a better case for the school to urge all parents to send their girls to school. If the fees do not appear to go down despite schools competing for children, well, in that case-let their be an open system where you apply to the government for scholarships. The government employees god-knows-how-many community workers, block resource centre workers etc in any case. Put them to some use! Either case, the government technically is supposed to monitor the progress of each child under the ICDS (Integrated Child Development Scheme)-let health workers report on a regular basis about who they can afford education. A girl will never be able to well in an IIT or in DU, unless her fundamental knowledge is clear. That knowledge is built over the many years through primary and secondary education. The government must then identify situation where market forces do not see adequate incentives and provide the incentives. The private schooling sector at the primary level can be and is regulated. The schools can still be answerable to government institutions that set standards for examination and progress-reporting.

5. Services: The government charges for a million services for women. Make sure the women actually access these services. If women charge these services (which they indirectly pay for) they resolve many of the issues that solutions like reservation attempt to address.
6. Time Bound: At what point will we establish that women and men are capable of generating similar socio-economic capital? Or that, irrespective of that capital-they will be able to leverage opportunities? When do we make the transition from "positive discrimination" to "positive action"? How do you arrive at that figure? How will you ever calculate? How will you measure when the impact of patriarchy has weakened enough for women to not need the quota?
7. Stop Gap: Working on systemic inefficiencies is far more difficult. But any other solution is a stop gap arrangement. It will never resolve the problems of the next generation. The government is distracting you from far greater issues affecting women. Property rights, political, civil, economic and rights over the person to start with. Oh, and how about opening more colleges to begin with. Why do so many people have to compete for such a small number of seats even at the undergraduate level?
8. Rights: Yes. It's against the rights of a man to be discriminated against because of the fact that he is a man. It's precisely the way women have been discriminated against always. I have no wish to perpetuate the system that is built on letting the divide be intact. A system need not be gender blind to be gender sensitive. The needs are different but need not be satisfied at the cost of the rights of the other. While patriarchy has traditionally favoured men, reservation is essentially a patriarchal solution. Oppressing is not the way out of oppression. Rights are to protect the vulnerable not to pander to them.

9. It's insulting: Don't favour me because I am a woman. Favour me because I am smarter, more intelligent and more capable. If I am as smart as the man. Treat me as an equal. Give me the same opportunity. Give me a loan to set up my business, don't bloody walk into my shop and tell me that you are going to run it for me because I can't do it for myself.

This post is essentially a spontaneous one. I wanted to write about my opposition to the notion of extending the reservation quota. But my own context would make it seem that I am doing so to protect my interest. (Yes, I am. I am always very concerned about the snatching away of my rights.) But the context of a feminist building a case against reservations for women in educational institutions helps in articulating my concerns when it comes to reservations as a whole.

CHAPTER 9 Globalization and Dalits: Changing Role and Nature of the India State

Social Compulsions

The process of India gradually getting drawn into globalization is both on account of external global pressure and internal economic or social compulsions. It was true that in early 1980s when India went for external borrowing from the World Bank, it was partly due to the failure of the Indian state to cope with the claims and counter claims of varied groups and classes on very slow moving economy. The one option open at that time was restructuring the rural economy through radical-land reforms and go for labour intensive industrialization to shift surplus agricultural labour from the rural areas. This path of development could have been something akin to the Chinese model of development.

The other option was to pump more capital from internal savings and technology through innovations to give momentum for faster economic development. The third option was to borrow from the global economic agencies and open up the market and allow free play of market forces. Indian state consciously went for third option without perhaps seriously debating the long-range implications and consequences to the people at large and more so to the marginalized sections of the society. Now with two decades of experience, it should be possible to discern the broad trends and the overall direction of development. The causes for globalization are more 'crisis' driven and not 'strategies' driven (Anand Teltumbde).

The U.S, the main actor in this whole process of globalization has been playing a diabclical role in terms of use of force during the post-second world war not only to protect capitalism but it did it for preventing rise of radical nationalism in different parts of the world. These trends were seen right in 1948 when they intervened in Italy or when they overthrew as back as 1954 first democratic government of Gautamala.

This seems to be intrinsic to the very nature of the model of development that America opted for. It is also true that from Nixon regime onwards-speculative economy had come to replace the real economy. Within two decades from 1971 to 1990 the percentage of transactions related to real economy came down from 90% to paltry 10% and further declined to 5% over next five years (Teltumbde). It is pointed out that the capitalist crisis over the last 25 years, with its shrinking profit rates, inspired the corporate elite to revive and recast economic liberalization into neo-liberalism which is operationalised through "the Washington consensus". This was worked out both by the U.S. and the international financial institutions "the de facto world government". One should realize that the principal architects of neo-liberal policy in England were the merchants and manufacturers.

The architects of neo-liberal 'Washington consensus' are the masters of private economy mainly huge corporations that control much of the international economy and have the means to dominate policy formation as well as the structuring of thought and opinion. (Teltumbde). Noam Chomsky in his work on "Political Economy of Human Rights: Washington Connection with the Third World Fascism" presents a blow by blow account of the American aggressive, undemocratic, unjust intervention in the internal matters of several of the third world societies to retain its brutal stranglehold on the world economy. One single driving force of American operations is its corporate interests.

It is tragic that a power like this should arise in the history at a time when human societies were realizing the human spirit, democratic essence, value of peace and security and dreaming for a humane and just world. That the newly emerging democracies – fruits of anti colonial struggles-were trampled upon and there was no way that they could fully blossom. Chomsky maintained as early as 1960s that the political elite of the newly emerging nations were getting denationalized. The convergence of the corporate interests and self-seeking third world political elite aided and abetted by the international financial institutions accentuated the process of neo-liberalization. The processes of globalization that started with the trade in commodities gradually got extended to services.

The incarnation of GAAT changed and its expanding role left nothing untouched. What was considered as service with all its positive essence has been turned into tradable commodity? The World Trade Organization (WTO) the key director of the global economy uses all forms and methods to convince, co-opt, and coerce the nation states to fall in line. One should see the real side of WTO as to why it insists on tuning the services into tradable commodities. D. Narasimha Reddy and others in their very lucid work on understanding WTO raised the question of why GAAT which has been functioning from 1947, suddenly brought in issues like trade in service, investment related to trade, intellectual property rights and trade in agricultural commodities into the fold of multiple trade? Analysing the process, the authors pointed out three important causes for this sudden shift: first, from the period following the second world war up to 1973, the year of first oil shock was a period of high growth and prosperity for the developed capitalist countries which received a setback and by 1980s crisis deepened, profits declined and a kind of recession set in these economies; second, there were critical changes in the structure of the economy, and by 1990s, in the highly developed G-7 capitalist countries, 70% to 80% of national income and employment were generated in non-goods producing sector, and the share of agricultural output and employment contracted to 2% to 10%, the share of manufacturing sector contracted to 15% to 20% in the national income and employment; third, a major change is found in terms of substantial increase in the share of developing countries in the global manufacturing sector and, it is estimated, by the turn of the century more than 50% of the global industrial output would come from newly industrializing countries and by 2020, it may cross 60%.

The authors conclude that if the developed capitalist countries have to maintain their global supremacy in trade, the emphasis on trade in manufacturing goods would no longer be beneficial to them. Joseph Stiglitz in his Globalization and its Discontents graphically brought out the role of the super powers particularly the international financial institutions in pushing forward the political and the so-called development agenda of the industrialized countries. Having been an economic advisor to American President and also an insider of the international financial institutions, he alerted the third world political elite not only of the manipulations in the unfair international financial dealings but the far reaching implications and the consequences to the third world societies and economies. One need not deliberate further in a short paper of this kind to point out that while there are admirers and well-paid advocates of the neo-liberal agenda, there have been equally powerful voices against the neo-liberalism. The truth lies somewhere in the unfolding experience with global development and its impact on different institutions particularly the nation state and vulnerable sections of the world. The nation state was one of the historical outcomes of liberalism. While the nation and the state are very old entities, nation-state is relatively of recent origin.

It was the eighteenth century capitalist development that threw up the nation-state as a means of protecting the local capital and mobilizes human effort to build it up. The state and the concept of sovereignty essentially, in an elementary sense, refer to the people living in a territorial boundary with common or collective memory, cultural traditions, having control over their natural resources and in shaping up their own destiny. The radical nationalism stood for the use and exploitation of the national resources for the good and only good of the nation. For nationalism cannot totally be divorced of some notion of common good. This common or collective good is supposed to be represented by the institution of the state that is precisely the reason why the contractualists in political theory brought in the whole notion of 'individual consent'. Liberalism had two streams of thinking, one privileging the individual and other the community. They had always the ambiguity of how to strike a balance between the individual liberty and collective good. As there was no way to arrive at an acceptable equilibrium, within the framework of market. The search for equilibrium brought in the state. While Marx maintained that the state represented collective corporate interest and used for providing legitimation to the ruling classes, the liberals interpret it as instrument of collective good. While market represent the unrestrained freedom of the self-seeking individual, for liberals, the state protects the collective good by guarding the territorial boundaries and provide legitimate governance to the people.

The separation of powers, rule of law, representative democracy, freedom of press more so citizenship are all a part of this legitimate governance. While the relation between the individual and the state are defined through rights, the relation between the state and market remained tense and undefined. The role of the state, therefore, has come to be largely conditioned by the balance of forces at a given point of time.

There are any numbers of versions of role of the state ranging from the corporate state of U.S. to the universal welfare state of Sweden to people centric state of Cuba. There are no dependable parameters to define and also assess nature of the state, the character of which has been constantly changing. This has been largely on account of the changing international pressures, growing conflict between the organized interests in the market place and the demands of the vulnerable sections of the society. Manoranjan Mohanty attempted to capture this complexity through his characterization of state as reactive, responsive and repressive. In the course of this persisting ambiguity came the neo-liberal agenda forcefully arguing that the state has no business to be present in the regulative and allocative domain.

This new agenda, unlike the classical liberalism, is very clear on what the state should not do. They will not have any satisfactory answer to what should be the role of the state vis-à-vis its own people. They are redefining role and intervention of the state from that of development, welfare, transformative to a mere facilitator of movement of the capital; this has hit hard the sanctity of the territorial boundaries and sources of legitimate governance. The World Development Report (1997) in its 'The State in a Changing World' points to the neo-liberal approach to the state. They argue that the state "will not be able to adapt to the demands of a globalizing world economy". They plead for an effective state and the effective state in their view is the one that "allow markets to flourish". They agree that "state is central to economic and social development not as a direct provider of growth but as a partner, catalyst and facilitator".

The report observes that in many countries "private initiative is held hostage to a legacy of antagonistic state-market relations" and add "poorly performing state enterprises are often a big drain and privatization provides an obvious solution". While developing a framework on "Rethinking the State" the report states, "A central difficulty in redefining the state's role is that the ground beneath government's feet is always changing". They add "many of the most successive examples of development, recent and historical entail states working in partnership with markets' to correct their failures, not replacing them". The rest of the framework discusses more of matching role to capability, re-innovating the state's capability, and suggest that the state evolves rules and restraints, competitive pressure, voice and partnership. This only indicates that the discussion on the state shifted from its role and purpose to that of process. The purpose defining the process is something logical, but the process becoming the purpose cannot answer any question emanating from the concerns for equity, justice, freedom and transformation. The problem with the neo-liberal approach to the state is its attack on the institution of the state.

It does maintain that its working has become obsolete, and therefore incapable of coping with the new global challenges. While it is true that the states have not done well as allocator of values, so is the case with the market. Once there is the argument for partnership, partnership for what? is the question. A profit seeking market driven by self-interest of the individual has its own laws, logic and limits. What is that the state does as partner? The more crucial question is the question of growing inequalities, inaccessibility to basic resources and non-availability of minimum provisions for the very survival. The retreating minimalist state in terms of reducing regulations on the market forces is one side of the story but the other side of the story is the shattering of the hopes of ordinary masses resulting is delegitimisation of the state. It is in this backdrop the Indian state need to be assessed. The Indian Constitution – a product of balance of social forces engendered by the freedom movement-envisages a transformative role to the state. The underlying logic and spirit of the Constitution is to bring about social, economic and cultural changes so as to move towards an egalitarian social order.

Egalitarianism as a world-view stresses on relative equality, equality of opportunities, dignity and freedom and also decent work, security – all this to ensure quality of life that makes life relatively comfortable and meaningful. As a part of this vision while part-three of Constitution guarantees fundamental freedoms, part-four promises equity and justice. This responsible and responsive role cast several responsibilities on the state. The role extends to regulatory, welfare, developmental and transformative functions. The Indian state has enjoyed considerable legitimacy in the first two decades of Independent India. Given the multi-class and multi-caste character of Indian society, the pressures and counter pressures mounted to a point that by late sixties, the state was finding it difficult to cope with the demands from different sections of the society. Indira Gandhi was a product of this crisis. Her regime responded to the crisis through rhetoric and repression. Rhetoric related to justice, repression curtailed the freedoms. The imposition of emergency was a part of this complexity. That the Indian state could turn into a totally authoritarian state is one lesson that this period taught to the Indian people.

System to the Forces of Globalization

It was in 1980s, during the second phase of Mrs. Gandhi the rhetoric for justice was gradually abandoned. This was the time that the option to borrow from the international financial agencies was exercised. This led to opening up of the system to the forces of globalization. It also produced immediate dividends in terms of rate of growth picking up. This was also a decade that witnessed relative peace on the borders, better rainfall and industrial peace. Given these favourable conditions, by the end of the eighties the nation should have been in a far better economic position to cope with the growing demands put forward by different sections of the society.

To the utter surprise of people and the nation, the economy was said to be in deep crisis and the balance of payment position became totally precarious. It was this crisis that provided justification for the Indian state to become a part of the process of not only globalisation but endorse the neo-liberal agenda with liberalization and privatization as the main driving forces. The retreat of the Indian state from its earlier role is too obvious.

This raises the question as to what happens to the egalitarian vision? What would be the new sources of legitimization? What happens to the vulnerable sections of the society? The answer of the neo liberals would be; there are costs for structural adjustment; societies have to put up with the pains of readjustment. This immediate price is worth paying as in the long run the new approach would lead to growth, prosperity and better quality of life to the people. This short term pains and long-term gains formulation seem to be a shock absorption therapy. While short term pains are evident and empirically validated long-term gains are something that the people have to wait and imagine. What does this long term constitute is also left to ones own imagination. During the last two decades there have been dramatic developments in all spheres of social life in India. The developments are so complex that the evidences in favour of the model are such that one can argue not only for proceeding with the model but widen the scope.

There are also equally, if not more, convincing evidences against the model. It is obvious that there are gainers and losers in this game. I would like to argue that the gainers are far lesser in number than the losers. However, the gainers are articulate, organized, powerful and fully supported by the media. They are so well organized that almost all the political parties including the parliamentary left with some reservations are in support of the whole process of globalisation and model of development. The other impressive evidences include the higher rate of growth, favourable balances of foreign exchange, the aggressive expansion of number of IT professionals both inside and outside India, strengthening of the urban infrastructure, widening of employment avenues in the IT sector particularly on account of outsourcing.

The incomes of the people in the overall service sector have gone up so dramatically that the living styles have drastically changed. This change is also partly due to remittances from the NRIs who are investing in housing, land and other assets. Anybody without a critical eye is straightaway impressed and carried away by the developments. A set of social scientists particularly economists are so impressed that they have come to fully back the model. A set of cautious analysts do recognize the magnitude of the problems and fallouts of the model but maintain that the whole process is a part of the larger global process and India cannot remain isolated and unaffected by it. There are others who are arguing that it is an irreversible process. One wonders as to how much of the Indian economy is integrated with the global economy and what are those parts of the economy which not only cannot be integrated but are largely hit by the process of globalization? This chapter does attempt to look at the darker side of globalisation and its implications to overall economic development at one level and the impact on the very making of the Nation-state at another level.

During the last two decades the evidences suggest that rate of decline in poverty slowed down, the landlessness particularly among the dalits has gone up, the agricultural growth fell down, the farmers suicides have gone up phenomenally on account of lack of access to the credit, poor quality seeds, pesticides, fertilizers and low market prices for agricultural commodities. While all these trends cannot directly be attributed to the model of development, one evidence is clear that most of these trends are a result of either withdrawal or indifference of the state. The retreat of the state is certainly a result of the pressure of international financial agencies, which are pushing the idea of free competition on the throat of the Indian state. This so called free competition includes economic development of any sector without governmental help particularly the subsidies. This is totally against the interests of the weak and vulnerable but the entire farming sector. Indian farmer has always been in debts for various historical and geographical reasons.

The government assistance in credit, subsidies on inputs, access to extension, support prices, investment in irrigation gave some relief and made subsistence agriculture possible. It is not that Indian agriculture reached a sustainable point nor is it in any position to compete in the international market. The export-led growth which Indian state has been compelled to encourage led to serious distortions in agricultural sector. The best example is the choice of cotton, or other commercial crops. These choices involve enormous risks and there is a need for some mechanism to absorb the uncertainties and shocks. In fact historically in several Nations transition of a traditional agrarian economy to commercial crop growing economy was fully supported and subsidized by the concerned states. Here is a situation where the global developments call for the economic transition without the state support. That is what accounts for the overall agrarian crisis and more so for the incidence of farmers suicides in different parts of India. The Indian agriculture is essentially a small peasant economy and has to support almost two thirds of the population and provide employment to the workforce. Neither the Indian state nor the global forces have any clue to this very complex question. If the economy were to be indigenous and "sovereign" then some workable solutions could be worked out.

The retreat of the state not only from the agrarian sector but also the other sectors takes away the little maneuverability in shifting the workforce from agrarian sector to either manufacturing sector or tertiary sector. This is a situation, which is bound to lead to pauperization, which in turn can give rise to endemic rural unrest challenging the state power and its legitimacy to govern. As the challenges mount the state that is left with little maneuverability depend more and more on its coercive power, a coercive power that is not legitimate. The second noticeable trend is seen in the urban sector particularly the urban poor who are mostly the rural migrants. These migrants are those who landed in the urban belt more because of the 'push' factor than the 'pull' factor. The pattern of urban economic growth is more in the service sector where the place for the unskilled, illiterate labour is zero. The growth of industry is so capital intensive that it has no place for the labour. The scope and hope for these people is either construction work or the trickle down effect in the form of domestic help or other forms of menial work. Quite a number of them end up as beggars, rag pickers, and small time criminals.

In fact, the rise in the urban crime during the last one and half decade has been very disturbing. There is yet another trend in the form of demand for urban land. The prices have unbelievably gone up giving rise to the expansion of land mafia in almost all the metropolitan cities of India. It has created its own under ground crime world. The poor caught up in slums are pushed from pillar to the post. They are facing a ruthless state which is evicting the poor from slums in the name of urban beautification, tourism, road expansion and setting up new parks and other sites of entertainment. The process is rendering not only the slum dwellers but even the lower middle and middle classes powerless and helpless. The frequent breakdown of law and order, growing tensions between the communities seem to be an inevitable fallout of this development. This is resulting in greater dependence of the state on its coercive power. This could be seen in a much more forceful form in the case of poorer sections like Dalits, who are the losers as they are on the margins of the economy.

In the losers' gainers game, some lose everything and a few gain everything. The distributions of gains are totally uneven and unjust. The dalits in general and the rural dalits in particular suffer the adverse impact in a far more severe way. Scholars working on dalits have been pointing out trends emanating from the model of development. One of the studies on "Dalits in the World of Globalisation" observed the following trends: (1) land reform measures are put on hold; (2) ceiling on land holdings have been selectively relaxed; (3) efforts are made to allow tenancies with no protection to small lessees; (4) private players have been granted entry into the field of education, particularly technical and vocational education which makes such education costly, without provisions for affirmative action for discriminated groups such as dalits; (5) entry has been promoted for private insurance companies without making them pro-poor; (6) industry, banking and insurance sectors are being privatized; (7) expenditure reduction has been introduced for many anti-poverty schemes; (8) labour reforms are being planned without taking into consideration adequate social security and other protective measures.

As a consequence to these policies the net results are: (1) landless and near landless households in 1991 accounted for around 70% of S.C. households which has increased to around 75% by 1999-2000; (2) priority lending has been reduced from 18% to 13% directly affecting the flow of funds to dalits; (3) the rate of decline of poverty has been much slower in 1990's in comparison with the earlier decades; (4) from 1990s the rural employment has come down and there was substantial reduction in regular salaried jobs in the public sector; (5)commercialization of education made education more inaccessible. These experiences suggest the direction of developments and trends of deprivation. If these trends continue, the Dalits would be one of the sections that would be hard hit in the long run. Another study points out that as a part of fiscal contraction, the capital expenditure slid from 5.10 percent of GDP in 1990-91 down to 2.74 percent in 1995-96. In percentage of total expenditure, it fell from an average of 32.8 percent during the preceding five years of reforms, to average of 22.05 percent during succeeding five years of the Reforms. In 1995-96 it was as low as 17.82 percent. Agricultural sector also bore the share of this cut.

The average annual increase in public sector outlay on agriculture and irrigation during 1985-90 fell from Rs.1.3 billion to an average of Rs.0.68 billion during 1990-92. The cut is bound to have a depressing impact on agricultural production in the coming years. It is also observed that there is increasing shift of land from agriculture production to corporate farming for export horticulture and floriculture products, which are in demand in developed countries. The reforms in banking led to severe squeeze on agricultural lending. The share of agriculture in net bank credit consistently declined and fell from 32.8 percent during the preceding five years of reforms in 1995-96, it was as low as 17.82 percent. In respect of food security, the system comprised over 4, 24, 000 fair price shops spread all over the country. The food distributed through PDS is subsidized by the government to the extent of the difference between the issue price of food grains and their economic cost to FCI, which devours significant part of the government subsidy. With the FCI costs ever increasing on transportation, storage and administration, any cut in the subsidy hit the poor directly. The problem is further aggravated by the raising of procurement price of rice and wheat by 67.56 percent and 62.8 percent respectively in 1989-90 and 1993-94. During this period the prices of these commodities were raised by 85.81 percent and 75.14 percent.

The impact of this rise was reflected in a significant fall in the off-take of food grains. The difference between the consumer-end PDS retail prices and market prices became marginal; the not-so-poor left the PDS. The resultant effect on nutrition and hunger had to be borne by the people in direct proportion to their poverty. During two years of the Reforms, there was 8.34 percent fall in per capita availability of cereals and 12.02 percent fall in that of pulses. Given the growing inequalities the vulnerable particularly dalits are affected very severely. Anand Teltumbde cites the instance of 350 mal-nutritious deaths of children in the Amaravati district of Maharastra-the most industrialized state in India. This is only one sample of the deteriorating situation. Another sad consequence of globalization is seen in the employment pattern, which is closely interrelated to the question of poverty. The rate of growth of employment in the organized sector dropped from more than 1.7 percent per annum in the late 1980s to 1.2 percent in 1991-92 and to 0.6 percent in 1992-93. Creation of jobs in the public sector fell drastically on account of free market euphoria. In the central government establishment there were 4.03 million jobs in first 1st march 1991 which went up next year to 4.14 million. But during the subsequent two years, they came down to 3.97 million and 3.84 million respectively. The National Planning Commission's Special Group on job creation estimates that the current unemployment rate is over 7% (as opposed to government 1999-2000 estimates of 2.2%), with the number of unemployed swelling to at least 45 million by 2007. Job creation in the 1990s, post-trade liberation is said to be three times less than in the 1980s refuting the claim that economic growth automatically leads to greater employment opportunities. There are statistics indicating that employment growth both in rural and urban has slowed down in the 1990s. Public sector employment has also seen sharp decline with the growth rate in 1997 set at 0.67% as compared to 12.7% in 1987. Given these trends in employment, the dalits who are mostly employed in the public sector because of protective discrimination are obviously the most affected.

The benefits of economic reforms have not trickled down, nor are there any mechanisms to facilitate the process. The protective discrimination in public employment has become increasingly ineffective because of narrowing down of the avenues and shrinkage of the work force. The National Planning Commission, in its mid-Term appraisal of the 9th five years plan has observed that changing government economic policies have affected the dalits. National Sample Survey data reveals that the unemployment rate of dalits (based on current weekly and current daily status) in 1977-78, 1983, 1993-94 and 1999-2000) is much higher as compared to non SCs / STs. Significantly, the unemployment rates had been declining between 1977-78 and 1993-94 but in the post-liberalisation period this rate has suddenly increased. These trends noticed in poverty, nutrition, unemployment could be seen in any walk of life be it health, education, drinking water, housing, communication so on. This increasing inaccessibility not only results in decline or denial of quality of life but increasing powerlessness. This, in turn, renders the dalits more vulnerable to even physical attacks. For increasing presence of the dalits and their representation particularly in the structure of state power is one safeguard. As this safeguard thins down, the dalits stand more exposed to the power of the mighty. It should also be realized that unchecked globalization widens the disparities and weakens the state power to do good.

The sate in the final analysis will remain more an instrument of coercion in the hands of the neo-rich class – the fallout of the neo-liberal forces. These new power elite lacking in vision and commitment to the people are prone to use more and more force to protect their own overnight made wealth. The implications would be-greater violence against the poor, dalits and also movements working for their emancipation. This partly manifests in the repressive laws that the state enacted during the last two decades. The post-independence laws starting with the Untouchabililty (Offences) Act 1955, to the Scheduled Castes and Scheduled Tribes (Prevention of Atrocities Act) 1989 reflect the legal progress but there has been simultaneous degeneration of social practices. It has been one of the striking characteristics of Indian governance, that when the practices degenerate the height of the human rights standards raised. However, the state has been arming itself with such arbitrary and coercive powers that are blatant negation of all the accepted civilized norms of jurisprudence. From Preventive Detention to POTA to the Unlawful Activities law is a testimony to the increasing repressive character of the Indian state. The Neo-liberal agenda which is set to marginalize the state so far as its transformative role is concerned is pushing the state into more and more repressive role. The Indian State which was historically mandated to play a positive role in terms of changing the entire gamut of social relations and more so the conditions of the dalits is turning around and play the role of a facilitator for the movement of capital and contain the people and their growing consciousness. A supposedly people centric state is fast transforming itself into their adversary. This changing context would invariably lead to withdrawal of support of the rural peasantry and urban poor to the Indian state. That they constitute the bulk of the population is a demographic reality. Legitimate governance in liberal theory, presupposes 'individual consent', providing an option for right to exit from the contract. The electoral outcomes bear a testimony to this resentment. In every election people are expressing their resentment in no vague and uncertain forms. Party after party are thrown out of power. But the forces of globalisation are so powerful that every party is ending up on the same path of development leaving no democratic options to the electorate. The Indian state is caught up in formidable pressure from the global forces at one level and that of the excluded sections at another level. The unavoidable inference is that it will lead to greater legitimacy crisis and larger suffering of the poorer sections of the society.

CHAPTER 10

Programme Undertaken for the Welfare of SCs/STs and Women

Welfare of SC/ST/OBCs

SC/ST Cell

In accordance with the policy of the Government of India, an SC/ST cell is functioning in the Department of Commerce. A Liaison Officer is nominated in the Department and in each of the organizations under the Department. So far as services and posts in the Department and organizations under its administrative control are concerned, none of the posts has been exempted from the purview of the reservation orders. The Liaison Officer examines and rectifies, wherever necessary, the roster maintained by the various organizations for ensuring representation to SC/ST/OBCs. The Liaison Officer also provides relevant guidelines to the officers in the Department of Commerce, its attached and subordinate offices and the Public Sector Undertakings, in accordance with the instructions issued by the Department of Personnel and Training (DOP&T) from time to time.

The Cell is also looking after the work regarding implementation of the Government Orders in respect of reservation for Other Backward Classes (OBCs) to the extent of 27 per cent in direct recruitment. A statement showing total number of Government employees and the number of SC/ST/OBCs as on 31.12.2006 in the Department of Commerce, its subordinate offices, Public Sector Undertakings, semi-autonomous bodies etc.. The Commodity Boards under the administrative control of the Department of Commerce have certain specific schemes under special tribal plans, which are operated with a view to supplementing the efforts of the Government in improving the socio-economic conditions of the SC/ST in the non-traditional areas.

The welfare activities undertaken by different organisations attached to this Department are given below:

Rubber Board

The various schemes operated/ activities undertaken by the Rubber Board for the welfare of SC/ST category of growers during the year 2006-07 include:

- Cash assistance of Rs. 35.75 lakh was disbursed to 1507 beneficiaries under Rubber Plantation Development Scheme. A total amount of Rs. 11.84 lakh was disbursed to 460 beneficiaries as reimbursement of cost for high yielding planting material.
- An amount of Rs. 7.35 lakh was disbursed to 94 SC/ST tappers employed in the unorganized sectors under the housing and sanitary assistance scheme.
- 466 persons were given free training in rubber cultivation, tapping, processing and manufacturing.
- Assistance of Rs 4.98 lakh was provided to 349 beneficiaries for boundary protection fencing material for rubber plantation.
- 466 persons were given free training in rubber cultivation, tapping, processing and manufacturing.

·Total area of 14.79 hectares was planted for the benefit of tribal communities in traditional area.

Projects and Equipment Corporation (PEC) Limited

- There exists a Time Scale Promotion Scheme for staff cadre. Qualifying period for promotion for employees belonging to SC & ST categories is relaxed by one year in each stage of promotion.
- There is a welfare scheme in PEC under which merit scholarship is given to the wards of the employees securing certain percentage of marks in the annual examination. In case of the wards of SC/ST employees, the merit scholarship is given with relaxed standard.

State Trading Corporation (STC) of India Limited

- A relaxation of 5 per cent in marks is allowed to the wards of SC/ST employees while considering the grant of merit scholarship.
- One-year relaxation is given to SC/ST employees in the qualifying period of service at each stage of promotion under the Time Bound Promotion Policy in the unionized cadres.
- Reservation for SC/ST employees is kept in allotment of residential apartments maintained by the Corporation at New Delhi.
- Nomination of SC/ST employees to various training programmes (including awareness programmes) held both in-house and outside.

Agricultural & Processed Food Products Export Development Authority (APEDA)

Training programmes are conducted for SC/ST personnels in India and abroad.

India Trade Promotion Organisation (ITPO)

In every Departmental Promotion/Selection Committee meeting, an officer of the appropriate level belonging to SC/ST category is being associated to look after the interest of SCs/STs.

Export Credit Guarantee Corporation (ECGC) of India Limited

Housing loan, residential accommodation and financial assistance for higher studies are provided to SC/ST/OBC employees.

Indian Institute of Foreign Trade (IIFT)

During the year 2006-07 all the three faculty members belonging to OBC category were nominated to participate in seminars/ workshops to upgrade their knowledge.

Three SC/ST employees on administrative side were also nominated to attend English/Hindi shorthand classes as also training programmes organized by DOPT.

Minerals & Metals Trading Corporation (MMTC) Limited

- Under the MMTC Employees' Welfare Scheme, a relaxation of 5 per cent in marks is allowed to the wards of SC/ST employees while considering grant of merit scholarships. There is a provision for reservation in the allotment of residential quarters to SC/ST employees.
- Training in various functional areas of work was imparted to 1226 employees out of whom 240 employees belonged to SC/ST categories. In-house training programme was organized on "Reservation for SC/ST/OBC Categories in Employment" for the benefit of Liaison Officers, SC/ST Cell members, Office Bearers of the SC/ST Associations with the help of external faculty.

Welfare of Women

Women in Public Sector (WIPS)

The Women in Public Sector (WIPS) activities within the MMTC aim at networking, experience sharing, interacting with various organisations and other PSUs and women bodies like National Commission, Women and Child Development Ministry, ILO, DPE, NGOs and other such institutes etc. seeking to enhance women's role at the workplace. Women employees from different organizations participate in the regional meet and national meet for discussons on the various developments. Committee headed by a senior female officer of the rank of CGM duly assisted by two other senior female officers of GM and DGM level is in force at Corporate Office to handle grievances and cases of sexual harassment of women at work. Similar committees are functioning at various Regional Offices also.

Women Cell

An independent 'Women Cell' has been set up in Department of Commerce with the following broad functions:

- Prevention and redressal of sexual harassment at workplace, constitution of Complaints Committee in the Department of Commerce, its attached and subordinate offices, PSUs, autonomous bodies etc., monitoring their performance and providing necessary help and guidance.

- Coordination with the Department of Women & Child Development, National Commission for Women and other concerned agencies in respect of the matters connected with welfare and economic empowerment of women and other related issues.
- Review of Plan schemes and other programmes of Department of Commerce to ensure that various aspects of women welfare, development and empowerment are promoted through the programmes and schemes of the Department.
- Preparation of Action Plan pertaining to the Department of Commerce for the overall development of women in line with the National Policy for empowerment of women.
- Other incidental matters pertaining to the subject.

The Women Cell actively participated in the various workshops / seminars on gender issues organized by National Commission for Women etc. During the year 2006, no complaint of sexual harassment at work place was received.

CHAPTER 11

Competing Claims: Quotas for Women and Minorities in India and France

Recent years have witnessed a surge of interest in patterns of political representation. At the empirical level, political transformations around the world have stimulated reflection on questions of institutional and constitutional design. At the theoretical level, scholars have challenged the dominant conventions of liberal democracy by rethinking the means and ends of the political process (Kymlicka 1995; Taylor 1994; Williams 1998). These developments, both empirical and theoretical, have led to various innovations in political participation, including the establishment of quotas for traditionally under-represented groups. Research in political science and political theory has tended to treat these groups as making similar, additive claims to representation, assuming that the recognition of one group facilitates the recognition of other groups. A closer look at quota debates reveals, however, that groups more frequently compete for representation, and often, the recognition of one group precludes the recognition of other groups.

Despite assertions that certain group identities are more important than others, the groups that compete for representation not only differ across countries, but the specific hierarchy among them varies considerably across national contexts. Seeking to compare claims for group representation, I focus on debates over quotas for women and minorities in political assemblies in India and France, two states which have historically sought to assimilate or transcend differences at the political level. In recent years, both countries have seen the emergence of claims for improved descriptive representation, yet have responded to these demands in nearly opposite ways. In India, ethnic and racial minorities quickly received guaranteed seats in all political assemblies, but women have experienced greater difficulties, primarily due to lingering questions about how to resolve caste and tribal quotas with reserved seats for women.

In France, on the other hand, women have been recognized as a group deserving greater representation in politics, to the exclusion of other groups, because advocates have framed gender as a characteristic that crosses all other groups, making it the universal difference. Through this comparison, I aim to generate insights into how some identities, and not others, are deemed relevant categories of political representation in some contexts but not in others, and how claims for the recognition of these identities are linked – either implicitly or explicitly – to the non-recognition of others. France and India are particularly crucial cases in this regard, since both states have historically been concerned with promoting national unity and the notion of university, yet have accepted justifications for the recognition of some identities in recent years. These patterns undermine broad claims about the inherent hierarchy of political identities and point instead to the discursive construction of such priorities within the already contested arena of claims to group representation.

Antecedents to the Women's Reservation Bill

Reserved seats for women have a long but disjointed history in India, appearing first in 1935 as part of the Government of India Act, disappearing in 1950 as per the provisions of the new Constitution, and resurfacing again in 1988 as part of the government's National Perspective Plan on Women. Women began to campaign for the right to vote and to stand for political office when the country was still part of the British Empire.

Although the Government of India Bill of 1919 did not enfranchise women, it empowered provincial legislatures to do so at their own discretion, which all did between 1921 and 1929, albeit with some important restrictions related to property and education (Mahan 1999). Women's groups continued to press for the right to stand for election and over the course of the 1920s raised the possibility of reserving seats for women in various political bodies.

This suggestion provoked a vivid debate between the nationalist movement and various women's groups when the British government set up the Simon Commission in November 1927 to decide whether and when self-government should be established in India. Although all major political groupings agreed with the need to extend women's right to vote and increase the number of women in elected positions, the British committee members and one section of the women's movement supported special franchise qualifications and the reservation of seats for women, while the nationalist movement and another section of the women's movement strongly opposed any mechanisms that would not provide for universal suffrage and that would recognize divisions among the population (Everett 1979). The former claimed that women would not be able to win election without the help of reserved seats, while the latter argued that women should stand for election on the same terms as men because legislators should rise above their personal identities to consider the country's best interests.

For this reason, nationalists viewed reserved seats for all groups – including Anglo-Indians, Christians, Muslims, Sikhs, and 'depressed classes' – as a strategy for creating divisions within the movement. Protesting the fact that the Simon Commission was composed entirely of British members, the Congress Party and the Muslim League rejected its activities and eventually brought about its demise. The British responded by authorizing the local parties to draft a new constitution for India on which Hindus and Muslims could both agree. Coming together in an All-Parties Conference in January 1928, however, these parties could not overcome their differences, especially with regard to the rights of minorities. After meeting several more times, the Conference eventually appointed a committee to work out the details of the constitution. The resulting Nehru Report, issued in August 1928, reserved seats for Muslims but introduced a system of joint electorates in which Hindus and Muslims would vote for the Muslim seats. The report sparked a great deal of civil disobedience, with various groups supporting reserved seats for women and minorities, supporting reserved seats for women but not for minorities, and opposing reserved seats for both women and minorities. The British sought to suppress these protests – and undermine the Congress Party – by retaining separate electorates and reserved seats for minorities and urging provincial governments to nominate women if no women were elected directly. In response, the women's group associated with the Congress Party drafted a memorandum in 1931 in which it reiterated its opposition to reserved seats for women and all other social groups.

The other faction of the women's movement, however, continued to maintain that women were unlikely to gain election without reserved seats and proposed that at least 5% of the seats in the first three legislatures be reserved for women on the basis of indirect election by the generally elected members of these legislatures (Everett 1979). To find a resolution to these debates, the British prime minister appointed the Indian Franchise Committee to tour the country and form an opinion on the questions of suffrage and political representation.

Subsequently known as the Lothian Committee, this group heard arguments for and against franchise qualifications and reserved seats for women – among other items – and recommended at the end of 1932 that women's right to vote be expanded and that 2.5% of the seats in all political bodies be set aside for women. To guarantee that these women were not drawn disproportionately from one community – i.e., the Hindus – the committee proposed electing these women on the basis of communal electorates so that, for example, Muslims would elect Muslim women and Sikhs would elect Sikh women. This overlapped with the committee's broader recommendation that all minority communities in India be assigned reserved seats on the basis of separate electorates, an idea which sparked another round of civil disobedience among all communities, including those supposedly favoured by these provisions. Wary of political instability, especially stemming from the opposition of the more conservative elements of Indian society, subsequent British government reports imposed greater restrictions on women's suffrage and right to political representation. By 1934, however, the Joint Committee on Indian Constitutional Reform had revised some of these restrictions – perhaps under the influence of British advocates for the rights of Indian women (Jenkins 1999) – to reduce suffrage requirements and reinstate reserved seats.

As a result, the Government of India Act of 1935 reserved six seats for women in the Council of State, nine seats for women in the Federal Assembly, and forty-one seats for women in the various provincial legislatures. In addition, the Act reserved seats for fourteen other groups based on profession (labor, commerce, landholders, universities), race (Europeans and Anglo-Indians), religion (Muslims, Sikhs, and Indian Christians), social backwardness (certain tribes and castes), and other minority status (Mahrattas) (Tinker and Walker 1956), such that the 145 special seats actually outnumbered the 105 open seats based on territorial representation (Clokie 1936). Although earlier Acts had set aside seats for Muslims, Sikhs, Christians, and 'depressed classes,' the dramatic increase in the number of reserved seats and recognized categories of representation led many nationalists to conclude that reservations and separate electorates were simply tactics to perpetuate British control by dividing the population into numerous special interests. For this reason, the Indian National Congress objected to special rights for any of these groups, and its women's group issued a statement denying special privileges for women for the sake of the common good.

Some minority groups, for their part, protested the requirement to include some women within their allocation of reserved seats, concerned that this effectively diluted their own quota. Congress condemned the Government of India Act on a number of grounds – most notably, because it had not been formulated by Indians and did not provide a 'national solution' to the minority problem – but eventually decided to contest the first elections to be held under the terms of the Act in 1937. The final details regarding the franchise and the shape and size of electoral constituencies were delegated by the British government to the Delimitation Committee, which recommended that special constituencies comprised of male and female voters be established for the women's seats to ensure that the women elected to these seats were more concerned with social welfare than with party politics (Everett 1979). Women's groups criticized these separate constituencies in favor of seats reserved for women in large multi-member constituencies, which they felt would enable women to learn to compete under the same conditions as men.

As parties began to prepare for the elections, however, these women turned their energies to the selection process, where they soon discovered – despite their expectations – that parties were largely unwilling to nominate women for the general seats and were disinclined to nominate any more women than necessary for the reserved seats. Concerned that women would not win any of the general seats, the non-partisan All-India Women's Conference (AIWC) met with the leaders of the various political parties to request that they nominate at least a few women to the general constituencies (Agnew 1979). As a result, fifty-six women won election across all the provincial assemblies: forty-one in the reserved seats, ten in the general seats, and five in the nominated seats. Although most of these women were affiliated with the Congress Party, the system of minority reservations ensured that both Hindu and Muslim women were elected (Agnew 1979; Everett 1979). Despite these relative successes, women's organizations came to play a reduced role in subsequent elections even as women's electoral turnout increased.

The issue of reservations remained on the agenda, however, and two years later the Women's Subcommittee within the National Planning Committee – formed to develop the future economic policy of an independent India – firmly rejected the option of quotas for women as a policy for women's empowerment (Tawa Lama-Rewal 2001). In the following years, relations between Hindus and Muslims deteriorated and both groups began to press for independence from British rule. At the end of World War II, the triumph of the Labour Party in the first post-war elections led the new prime minister to announce – among other policy innovations – that Britain would grant independence to India. As negotiations got underway, growing conflicts between the Congress Party and the Muslim League led British officials to abandon plans to transfer power to a single country and to sanction the creation of two countries, India and Pakistan, in August 1947. In the months before official independence, however, the Congress Party began organizing elections to a new Constituent Assembly that first met in December 1946. Although members of this assembly were chosen indirectly by members of the provincial legislatures, the leadership of the party – along with the AIWC – succeeded in convincing each province to send at least one female representative (Agnew 1979).

The first draft of the constitution contained provisions reserving seats for religious groups on the basis of joint electorates, as well as seats for members of various professions on the basis of appointment, but debate within the assembly following independence eventually persuaded the Muslims, Sikhs, and Indian Christians to drop their demands for special treatment (Rasul 2001; Tinker and Walker 1956). In contrast, the draft constitution enshrined equality between women and men as a fundamental right and thus did not include any special provisions for women, on the grounds that these were simply unnecessary. Despite their desire to abolish all reservations, however, delegates ultimately decided to retain those provisions in place for the Scheduled Castes (SC's) and Scheduled Tribes (ST's), the two groups that had traditionally been the most marginalized members of Indian society, distributed according to their proportion of the population in the various states and elected on the basis of joint electorates.

The resulting Constitution of 1950 also made reference to a third category – later known as the Other Backward Castes (OBC's) – who did not merit reserved seats but who had the right to other types of assistance from the state. Proposals to reserve seats for women, while not included in the constitution, resurfaced in 1957 in the context of discussions over a new system of local government, when the Mehta Committee – responsible for making recommendations for this new system – advised that all elected local councils include at least two women. Although the final version of the law passed in 1959 did not make any specific requirements regarding women's representation, it did empower local leaders to nominate women to the council if no women were elected directly. Over the next two decades, most councils adopted this practice and coopted one or two women if no women were elected, but policies varied across the states and frequently became a tool of patronage for local leaders.

This practice eventually became a crucial – and often the only– vehicle for women's participation in local government: among the 320 women in local councils in the state of Maharastra in 1978, for example, only six had been elected directly (d'Lima 1993, 22). By the 1980s, however, several states abandoned these policies in favor of seats reserved specifically for women: Karnataka introduced 25% reservation for women in local councils in 1983, Andhra Pradesh extended 9-25% reservation for women in various levels of local government in 1986, and Maharastra announced 30% reservation in local bodies in 1990.

The Origins of the Women's Reservation Bill

Despite the existence of some policies at the local level, the faith – both among women's groups and within the Congress Party– that women would be elected to national government without the need for special intervention meant that no initiatives were taken in this area in the years following independence. After the 1971 census revealed that only a small number of women had occupied positions of political power over the previous twenty years, however, the government began to view women's under-representation as a problem and – in anticipation of the United Nations Year of the Woman – set up a Committee on the Status of Women to examine the social, economic, and political standing of women in India. The Committee did not initially include a question on reserved seats in its questionnaire as it toured the country and interviewed more than 500 women in each state, but the various women's groups with whom they met repeatedly raised the issue as the only viable solution for improving women's access to political office at the local, state, and national level.

It included these arguments in its final report published in December 1974, but ultimately took the view that reserved seats were retrogressive measures that contradicted the principle of equality in the constitution. Indeed, some members went so far as to criticize the existing system of reservations for SC's and ST's as a colonial strategy that institutionalized the backwardness of these groups (Jenkins 1999). Recording two notes of dissent, the Committee more specifically rejected reservations for women on three grounds: separate constituencies for women threatened to narrow the political outlook of female voters and representatives, women's interests were not distinct from men's interests, and women were not a minority group. The Committee conceded, however, that reservations might be necessary at the local level to ensure the interests of rural and poor women (Raman 2002). For this reason, it recommended that women's councils – elected directly by local women – be formed in every village and given the responsibility of managing and administering women's and children's welfare and development programs as part of the broader system of local government.

At the same time, it encouraged political parties to increase the proportion of women among their candidates, through party-based quotas if necessary. These recommendations were passed on to the state governments, but most responded negatively and took no concrete actions to facilitate women's access to political office. Several states, however, returned to the issue of women's representation during debates over local government reform over the course of the 1980s (Sinha 2000). These initiatives were rarely preceded by a widespread mobilization of women and, interestingly, were adopted by governments across the political spectrum: the Janata Party government in Karnataka reserved 25% of seats for women in village and district councils in 1983; the Telugu Desam Party government in Andhra Pradesh reserved 9% of seats for women in the district councils in 1986; the Congress (I) Party government of Maharastra reserved 30% of seats for women in urban corporations and district, block, and village councils in 1990; and the Communist Party government in Kerala reserved 30% of seats for women in district councils in 1991 (Tawa Lama-Rewal 2001).

In the midst of these innovations, Rajiv Gandhi became the new prime minister of India, following the assassination of his mother Indira Gandhi in 1984, and identified women's status as a new priority issue. To this end, his government prepared a National Perspective Plan for Women in 1988, which drew on the positive experiences in Karnataka to propose 33% reservations for women at all levels of local government. While the report also recommended that political parties give 33% of their tickets to women, it dropped several items that had appeared in the first draft, most notably the proposal to extend 33% reservations to all levels of government, including the state legislatures and the national parliament.

According to Margaret Alva, then Minister for Women, the committee encountered a great deal of opposition to the idea of mandating reservations at all levels of government. In consultation with autonomous women's groups and the women's wings of the various political parties, therefore, the group decided to pursue reservation at the local level first and then, once women had gained experience in elected politics, to seek to extend reservation to the national level. The government introduced a package of reforms to create a more regulated structure of local government that would not only devolve decision-making power to the local level but would also provide guaranteed representation for the SC's, the ST's, and women (Manikyamba 1989).

The 64th Amendment Bill, however, was defeated in the upper house by the united opposition in 1989. Nonetheless, when new elections were organized several months later, political parties on both sides of this debate incorporated a 30% quota for women in their party manifestos, despite the lack of mass mobilization of women in favor of reserved seats (Nanivadekar 2003c). Although all parties in fact nominated less than 10% women, the new National Front government – consisting of Janata Dal and a few smaller parties – introduced a new and slightly revised version of the reservation bill in 1990.

Before this bill could be addressed, however, the governing coalition again collapsed and new elections were held that returned Congress to power in 1991. The newly elected government introduced the 73rd and 74th Amendment Bills shortly thereafter to provide for decentralization and one-third reservation in rural and urban local government, respectively. These bills passed relatively quickly without controversy through both houses of parliament, and after minor differences were reconciled by a Joint Committee of Parliament, both amendments became law in December 1992.

Many explained this rapid passage by noting that the national politicians who approved these radical amendments were unlikely to be affected personally by their implementation. More specifically, the 73rd Amendment mandated one-third reservation for women in all village, block, and district level bodies; in the posts of chairperson and vice-chairperson across all these institutions; and in the seats reserved for SC's and ST's in each body according to their proportion of the population.

The 74th Amendment extended these same provisions to municipal corporations in large urban areas, municipal councils in smaller urban settlements, and local councils in areas in transition from rural to urban. Under the terms of both amendments, the seats allocated to women were to be chosen by direct election and rotate across districts every five-year election cycle. The impact of these reforms was dramatic and immediate: after only one round of elections, more than one million women entered local government– and elected office – for the very first time.

Claims to Caste-and Gender-Based Representation

Campaigns to reserve seats for women in parliament in India cover a period of about fifteen years, with the first calls to establish quotas at the local level emerging in the late 1980s and the most recent discussions on quotas at the national level taking place in 2004. Efforts to reserve seats for women in India, however, appeared initially in the 1930s, when the country still formed part of the British Empire. Across these various periods of time, the actors involved in reservation campaigns have included civil society actors like women's movement organizations and women in the political parties; state actors like state committees, local governments, women's policy agencies, political parties, prime ministers, cabinet ministers, parliamentary representatives, parliamentary committees, and political party leaders; and international and transnational actors like the British government, the United Nations, the Inter-Parliamentary Union, and international conference delegates.

Engaged at different stages of these campaigns, these actors have supported or opposed reserved seats for various reasons, including consistency with the guaranteed representation of other groups, interest in extending colonial rule, defense of particular normative definitions of equality, attempts to make electoral gains among female voters, and empty gestures combined with interest in self-preservation. Despite relatively quick approval of a bill reserving one-third of all seats in local government for women, a bill seeking to extend similar reservations to state assemblies and the national parliament has not yet reached a vote, due outwardly to normative arguments insisting on sub-quotas for lower castes and religious minorities, but inwardly to the unstated practical concerns of male MP's, one-third of whom would lose their positions with passage of the bill.

The Debate over the Women's Reservation Bill

The relatively quick passage of the 73rd and 74th Amendments inspired women's groups in India – despite their earlier strategy – to join together to press for the immediate extension of 33% reservation to the state assemblies and the national parliament. All the major political parties – including the Congress Party, the Janata

Dal Party, the Bhartiya Janata Party (BJP), the Samata Party, and the two Communist Parties – responded, some as early as 1994, by incorporating this demand in their manifestos for the 1996 elections (Gandhi 1996; Kasturi 1998; Kishwar 1996b; Suchinmayee 2000). Although all parties presented fewer than 10% female candidates, the United Front government – another coalition led by Janata Dal – identified women's reservation as a priority issue in its Common Minimum Programme. While new Prime Minister H.D. Deve Gowda pledged to pursue legislation to this end during the first session of parliament, the government in fact delayed introducing a bill until the last days of the session, a move that many women interpreted as a lack of real commitment to the issue.

When the government finally presented the 81st Amendment Bill in September 1996, therefore, members of parliament had relatively little time to discuss or debate its provisions, which proposed to reserve one-third of the seats in the state assemblies and the national parliament for women, to rotate the reserved constituencies across districts after every election cycle, and to include the one-third requirement among the seats already reserved for the SC's and ST's. Although all the major parties had made a commitment, at least in principle, to pursuing reserved seats, a large number of MP's immediately voiced opposition to the Women's Reservation Bill. Some drew on the negative experiences of women in local government to argue that women had not proven to be effective representatives (Balasubrahmanyan 1998), but by far the most powerful objections came from Other Backward Caste (OBC) men, who argued that reservation for women would only strengthen upper caste dominance, because the women likely to benefit from reservation were likely to be those with greater social and educational opportunities. Rather than rejecting reservations altogether, however, they called for the provision to include a sub-reservation for OBC women. Muslim leaders soon echoed these arguments, claiming that the existing proposal would promote mainly Hindus if the policy did not specify sub-reservations for Muslim women.

Other minority groups followed with similar demands, including SC leaders who were apparently unaware that sub-reservation for SC women already appeared in the bill, but who perhaps sought to garner extra seats for the SC's from the women's quota, rather than yield seats to women from the existing SC quota. Women in parliament protested these attempts as disingenuous, noting that such objections had never been raised during debates over reservation at the local level and in fact had never been a focus of concern in the years since its implementation. They suggested that attention to minority women was instead simply a convenient excuse for male leaders who did not want to lose their own seats in parliament, as evidenced by the fact that none of these men had taken any steps in the past to promote women within their own parties or communities. In particular, they noted that OBC men were in an excellent position to incorporate a large number of women, given that they occupied approximately 200 of the seats in the 541-member Lok Sabha. In the days leading up to the vote, several parties issued a whip instructing its MP's to vote in favor of the bill.

Some openly declared their intentions to defy the whip (Kishwar 1996b), however, and on the day in question a number of senior male MP's stood at the main gate of parliament telling the arriving male MP's to go home unless they wanted to lose their seats. These tactics stalled the vote by ensuring the lack of a quorum and led the Minister for Parliamentary Affairs to call a meeting with the female MP's to discuss the situation. Although some women themselves opposed the bill, others felt that a meeting was unnecessary because reservations already formed part of the Common Minimum Programme (Nath 1996). When these women could not agree on the specifics of the amendment, the minister formed a Select Committee to consider whether the bill could be revised to incorporate sub-reservations for OBC's. To press their case, backward caste MP's from all the parties sent a common delegation to demand sub-quotas, but the chair of the committee pointed that no quotas currently existed for OBC's in the general category of seats. For this reason, sub-reservations for OBC women could not legally be made until a separate constitutional amendment established such a quota. In contrast, sub-reservations for SC's and ST's could be included within the bill because quotas for these groups already existed in the general category. In its final report, therefore, the committee rejected the call for OBC sub-quotas and – in addition to several small technical adjustments – recommended that the bill be passed into law as soon as possible. Female supporters pressed for an immediate vote, but the speaker of parliament allowed MP's two days to review the report. Shortly thereafter, representatives from Janata Dal – the main party within the ruling coalition – announced their opposition to the bill and threatened to defy the party whip if an OBC sub-quota was not included.

The opposition parties, in turn, alleged that the government was deliberately sabotaging the bill and the winter session ended without a vote. In February 1997, women's organizations and the National Commission for Women (NCW) launched a new campaign calling for passage of the bill in the coming session of parliament. They argued for full acceptance of the Select Committee's recommendations and accused detractors in parliament of making demands for OBC sub-quotas simply to undermine the bill. They noted that quotas were one of the few issues to bring women in parliament together from across the political spectrum, precisely because most of these women had personally witnessed discrimination in candidate selection procedures and thus had eventually come to realize that reservations were the only way to ensure women fair access to politics. Concerned that claims for other groups threatened to divide women, these women sought to expose the true motivations of male opponents by calling attention to the large gap between the official lines taken by the political parties and the actual attitudes of male party members towards reservations: while parties embraced quotas publicly in order to appear progressive to win women's votes, individual men worked secretly to subvert their adoption out of reluctance to give up their parliamentary seats.

Although reiterating many of the arguments that had already been voiced in the debates over reservation, this campaign received an unanticipated boost from a conference organized by the Inter-Parliamentary Union in New Delhi that brought together 240 delegates from 78 countries to discuss the theme "Partnership between Men and Women in Politics." The conference discussion revolved largely around the issue of quotas, and a great deal of news coverage in India carried comments from the various delegates on the positive impact of quotas in their own countries. Several weeks later, women's groups staged a rally in front of parliament to support early passage of the bill, and at an International Women's Day function later that day, Prime Minister Deve Gowda pledged to seek a 'consensus' on the Women's Reservation Bill in order to reintroduce it in parliament the following month (Balasubrahmanyan 1998). Before the bill could be introduced, however, parliament passed a motion of no-confidence against Deve Gowda and he was replaced by I.K. Gujral as the new prime minister. Shortly upon coming to power, Gujral announced that his government was committed to providing reservation for women and would also strive to reach a consensus among all the political parties to ensure smooth passage of the bill (Yadav 1997).

Despite these intentions, the all-party meeting held to discuss the bill in May 1997 only highlighted enduring differences among various groups of parliamentarians: some insisted on an OBC sub-quota within the women's quota, others suggested a reduction in the proposed reservation from 33% to 10 or 15%, and yet others remained firm on passing the bill in its current form with no sub-quotas or dilution of its proposed provisions. When Gujral nonetheless sought to introduce the bill for debate in the Lok Sabha on May 16, he was publicly heckled by two members of his own party, Janata Dal, including the party's acting president Sharad Yadav, who threatened to hold up the debate unless sub-quotas for OBC and Muslim women were incorporated into the bill. Although the votes required to pass the amendment already existed in the chamber, the prime minister responded by calling for a national debate on the bill. The left-wing parties criticized this move as unnecessary, pointing out that all major parties had committed themselves publicly to 33% reservation for women. Continuing to emphasize the need for consensus, the government announced in July that the Women's Reservation Bill would receive top priority during the monsoon session of parliament. In August, women's organizations stepped up their campaign in favor of reservation and female MP's demanded that the bill be put to a vote as soon as possible to reveal more clearly who supported reservation and who did not. Party meetings and press reports suggested that the Left and the BJP clearly endorsed quotas for women; the Shiv Sena, Rashtriya Janata Dal (RJD), Samata, and Samajwadi parties were totally opposed to quotas for women; and Janata Dal and Congress were hopelessly divided on the issue of quotas for women.

These splits led some to speculate that the Women's Reservation Bill might not be addressed in this session either, and to avoid this outcome, several parties proposed amending the People's Representation Act – instead of the constitution – to require political parties to nominate a certain proportion of women among their candidates. Six female MP's staged a walk-out to protest the Speaker's failure to take up the bill on August 14, but when the government sought to introduce the bill one week later, members of the ruling United Front again prevented the amendment from reaching the floor of parliament (Balasubrahmanyan 1998). At the end of the year, Congress withdrew its support from the governing coalition and new elections were announced for January 1998. Around this time, female opponents began to focus increasingly on the negative implications of the Women's Reservation Bill.

Although vocal during the early stages of debate, they took advantage of male opposition to the bill to call attention to its potentially negative implications for women's social and political status in India, stressing that despite media coverage that portrayed women's organizations as unequivocally supportive of gender quotas, many feminists were in fact opposed or ambivalent towards the Women's Reservation Bill. At the broadest level, they worried that setting aside seats for women would admit and reinforce the weakness of women by imposing an artificial solution to improve their access to politics that would undermine their legitimacy as political actors by implying that they were incapable of entering politics on their own. More specifically, they expressed concerns that the women who would benefit from reservation would not alter existing power structures in politics or effect policy change beneficial to women at large.

On the one hand, feminists argued, parties were likely to field the mothers, sisters, wives, and daughters of existing male politicians – the so-called *biwi-beti-bahu* brigade – to ensure that seats remained in their caste control. On the other hand, they signaled, parties of all ideologies were likely to win elections to the reserved seats and thus bring progressive as well as fundamentalist women into parliament, with positive and negative consequences for women-friendly policy change. Turning to the details of the bill itself, finally, they suggested that the rotation requirement would prevent the emergence of an enduring corps of female politicians and, even more gravely, would reduce levels of accountability among all elected officials. Drawing on evidence from the local level, they noted that men often assumed that all seats not reserved for women were reserved for men, creating a ceiling for women's representation and undermining women's opportunities to run for re-election as constituencies were de-reserved.

These problems were magnified, they pointed out, by the lottery system for allocating reservations, according to which neither men nor women would know in advance which constituencies would be open to them until just before the elections, meaning that aspirants and incumbents would have little incentive to nurse particular constituencies as they could not be held accountable for their promises or their actions. Despite their specific criticisms of the Women's Reservation Bill, however, these feminists still generally supported the goal of increasing women's representation. To this end, they offered endless suggestions for improving the bill and for devising alternative strategies to promote female candidates, focused mainly on multi-member constituencies and centrally-mandated political party quotas. These debates kept the issue of reservations on the political agenda through the January 1998 elections.

As a result, all major parties again included a commitment to women's reservation in their respective party manifestos, and following the installation of a new BJP-led governing coalition in March 1998, the new government announced that it would seek early passage of the Women's Reservation Bill (Balasubrahmanyan 1998). On the day that it introduced the 84th Amendment Bill in July 1998, however, the government was physically prevented from tabling the amendment: as Union Law Minister M. Thambi Dorai was about to present the bill, MP Surenda Prakash Yadav from the RJD ran up to the podium, snatched the bill from Dorai's hands and, passing more copies from the Speaker's table to about fifty other MP's, tore the bill to bits on the floor of the Lok Sabha. The action was applauded by RJD leader Laloo Prasad Yadav and Samajwadi (SP) leader Mulayam Singh Yadav, who press reports later revealed coordinated the action the day before in cooperation with the OBC and Muslim leaders of the other political parties (Balasubrahmanyan 1998; "Bill that reserves women's political history" 2004; "Indian parliament refuses women quotas" 1998; Rai and Sharma 2000; Sharan 2000).

Although surveys suggested that an overwhelmingly majority of male and female voters favoured reservations, the Speaker announced the following day that the bill was being deferred for the time being due to lack of consensus over the amendment. The various sides immediately blamed each other for these developments: supporters accused men of sabotaging the amendment to preserve their own seats in parliament, while opponents pointed out that no OBC or Muslim women stood up to defend the bill in solidarity with the pro-reservation women's lobby ("Indian parliament refuses women quotas" 1998; Kishwar 1998a). Leaders of several political parties criticized the BJP for abandoning the Women's Reservation Bill, while Prime Minister Atal Bihari Vajpayee faulted the Congress Party for his government's inability to pass the amendment, noting that his coalition lacked the two-thirds majority necessary for undertaking constitutional reform on its own. In the absence of any solution to these disagreements, the bill officially lapsed in April 1999 with a no-confidence vote against the government that resulted in the dissolution of parliament. New elections returned the BJP to power in October 1999, and consistent with campaign promises, the new government announced in November that it would reintroduce the Women's Reservation Bill – this time as the 85th Amendment Bill, with no changes from the 81st and 84th Amendment Bills – during the current session of parliament (Singh 1999a).

On December 20, with only four days left in the parliamentary session, Congress and left-wing MP's staged a walk-out to protest the fact that the government had not yet introduced the bill, claiming that the delay proved that the government was not serious about reserving seats for women. When Law Minister Ram Jethmalani presented the bill the following day, however, MP's from several socialist parties began to shout angrily and some ran up to the podium to snatch what they thought was the bill from the minister's hands. Demanding sub-quotas for OBC's and Muslims, they forced the Speaker to adjourn the legislature three times such that the bill could not be debated ("Hindu-Indian Regimes Introduces Women's Special Seats Bill" 1999; Singh 1999b). These disruptions forced the Minister of Parliamentary Affairs, Pramod Mahajan, to announce later that day that an all-party meeting would be convened on December 22 to work towards an agreement over introduction of the Women's Reservation Bill (Singh 1999b). This and similar meetings over the next two years, however, produced no viable compromises, despite continuing pressure from women's groups and political parties, who both frequently took to the streets to demand reservations for women (Katyal 2000). Over time, the bill's proponents grew increasingly skeptical of attempts for 'consensus,' noting that few bills ever required complete agreement among the parties and that the BJP and Congress – the two parties most visibly engaged in the campaigns for reservations – together had enough votes to pass a constitutional amendment. The government responded that it would continue to explore options that might bring all parties together on the issue, including reducing the number of seats reserved for women and abandoning a constitutional amendment in favor of a centrally-mandated party quota law (Keating 2002).

After repeated delays, the government sought to introduce the Women's Reservation Bill for the fourth time in May 2003. As with the previous two attempts, however, heated exchanges on the floor of the Lok Sabha prevented any debate on the bill, with the strongest opposition coming again from the RJD and the SP, who continued to insist that the bill be revised to include sub-quotas for OBC's and Muslims ("Bill that reserves women's political history" 2004; "Chaos over Indian women's bill" 2003). In response, the Speaker again convened a series of all-party meetings that initially failed to resolve these on-going differences but eventually achieved a breakthrough in July 2003, when representatives of four parties converged around a new proposal to create dual-member constituencies in one-third of all electoral districts – and thus increase the total number of seats in parliament by 181 – to enable the election of one man and one woman from these particular constituencies. Communicating this solution to the government, the Speaker reportedly asked the government to draft a new reservation bill, and several later, the BJP National Executive approved a resolution to pursue a constitutional amendment along these lines. The Congress and Left parties, however, soon began to express concerns that the new proposal would dilute the cause of women's reservation by reducing the proportion of reserved seats from 33% to 25%. Others acknowledged the advantages of a system that did not require sitting male MP's to surrender their seats but worried about the fate of incumbent female MP's, whose districts would now reserve additional seats for men. Yet others remarked – with great surprise – that the compromise was entirely silent on the issue of sub-reservations, the issue that had at least outwardly inspired the most powerful objections to the original bill (Nanivadekar 2003a). In his address to the nation on Independence Day on August 15, the prime minister regretted that no consensus had yet been reached on the bill and pressed again for the dual-member solution ("Vajpayee regrets women's quota bill not passed by Parliament" 2003). When the parties still could not agree by March 2004, Vajpayee blamed the main opposition Congress for stalling the Women's Reservation Bill and assured voters, as elections approached, that the BJP-led National Democratic Alliance would ensure passage of the legislation if voted into power again ("Women reservation: Long way to go" 2004; "Womens Bill differences to be sorted out: PM" 2004). Congress leader Sonia Gandhi responded by pledging that her party, if elected, would also seek to pass a women's reservation bill ("Congress will take up women's reservation bill: Gandhi" 2004; "Women reservation: Long way to go" 2004). Women's groups called both parties hypocritical, pointing out that the lists of candidates – where women formed less than 10% – told a much different story about parties' intentions regarding women's representation ("Women groups say it's not fair" 2004; "Women reservation: Long way to go" 2004). When the May 2004 elections registered a strong increase in support for the Congress Party, the party returned to power as part of the United Progressive Alliance and together with its coalition partners issued a Common Minimum Programme that included, among other demands, a promise to introduce one-third reservation for women in state assemblies and the national parliament, as well as a pledge to earmark at least one-third of all funds provided to local governments for programs related to women and children.

Quota Debates in France: Claims to Gender-and Race-Based Representation

Campaigns for the adoption and implementation of candidate gender quotas in France span a period of almost thirty years, with initial calls to adopt quotas emerging in the early 1970s and the most recent reforms on quota implementation being introduced in

2003. During this time, the actors involved in quota campaigns have included civil society actors like social movement organizations, women's movement organizations, women inside the political parties, and scholars; state actors like parliamentary representatives, government officials, women's policy agencies, and the courts; and international and transnational actors like international organizations and transnational networks. Involved in different ways at various stages of these campaigns, these actors have pursued or overturned quotas for diverse reasons, defending distinct normative definitions of equality and representation, responding to specific electoral motivations, or engaging in empty gestures of support for quota adoption and implementation. In light of a court decision in the early 1980s declaring quotas for women to be unconstitutional, both sides have focused primarily on the normative implications of reform, with opponents bolstering their position with reference to this legal precedent and advocates highlighting the need for constitutional reform. In identifying normative institutions as the main barrier to women's increased representation, however, supporters have paid much less attention to systemic and practical obstacles to change. Consequently, quota reform has proceeded in a relatively diffuse fashion, with varying combinations of rules, practices, and norms resulting in uneven implementation across parties and across levels of government.

Antecedents to the Parity Law

The parity law in France has garnered a great deal of international attention in recent years among scholars, activists, and politicians interested in gender and political representation. Their fascination with parity springs not only from the demand for equal representation of women and men, but also from the unique set of theoretical arguments developed over the course of this campaign. Importantly, these innovations did not emerge as a simple response to the question of women's under-representation in French politics, but rather as a reaction to earlier failed attempts to promote women's political presence through quotas and other types of electoral reform. As in Argentina, women's movements in France avoided electoral politics until relatively recently, focusing instead on issues related to daily life like domestic labor, reproductive choice, and sexuality. Until the 1990s, therefore, most work to increase women's representation came from women inside the various political parties, with little or no input from women's movements in civil society (Mazur 2001).

Most of these efforts were concentrated inside the Socialist Party (PS), where party feminists first began to demand gender quotas in the early 1970s. At the national party convention in 1974, two female party members proposed that the PS statutes be amended to include a 10% quota for women, both in party leadership positions and among the party's candidates for political office. They argued that the adoption of quotas was consistent with socialist ideology and would demonstrate the party's commitment to achieving equality between women and men. The proposal received unanimous support from the party committees responsible for statutory reform and was subsequently approved by a majority of the delegates to the party convention. Before voting in favor of the provision, however, delegates changed the requirement slightly so that the quota would apply only to elections governed by PR, thus excluding elections to the National Assembly which are decided by a two-round majoritarian vote. Women sought to expand these provisions at subsequent party conventions with the goal of eventually increasing the quota to reflect the proportion of women among party members.

In 1977 delegates voted to raise the quota to 15%, and in 1979 they agreed to a 30% quota for women in European Parliament (EP) elections, a 20% quota for women in the party leadership, and the nomination of as many women as possible to 'winnable' districts in two-round majoritarian elections. In 1981 Véronique Neiertz, the National Secretary for Women's Rights, proposed to increase the quota to 30% for women in the party leadership and among the party's candidates in PR elections, as well as to extend the 30% quota to elections run by majoritarian vote. Party leaders postponed discussion of this proposal until the next party convention in 1982, where it was never presented to or voted on by party delegates. At the next three national congresses in 1983, 1985, and 1987 the new National Secretary for Women's Rights, Martine Buron, repeatedly called for existing quotas to be increased to 30%, but all her proposals were rejected by party delegates. In 1990 a number of women inside the party reiterated the demand to increase existing quotas to 30%, while others proposed 40% quotas with a plan to increase to 50% by 2000, along with the creation of a commission to oversee quota implementation. Party delegates voted to raise the quota to 30%, again with no provisions to extend such measures to majoritarian elections. Despite the attention given to quotas over the 1970s and 1980s, however, the Socialist Party rarely implemented any of these policies to their fullest extent, in part because the party never established any enforcement mechanisms to ensure their application. In the few cases where the percentage of female candidates did approximate the quota – as in the 1986 regional and legislative elections – most women were placed in positions where they were unlikely to be elected, thus undermining the impact of these quotas.

At the same time that these debates got underway in the Socialist Party, several women in parliament pursued a parallel strategy to increase women's political representation through quotas at the local level. In 1975 the Secretary of State for Women's Status, Françoise Giroud, proposed limiting to 85% the percentage of candidates of the same sex who could appear on lists for municipal elections, a provision that essentially amounted to a 15% quota for women (Bird 2002; Mossuz-Lavau 1998a). In 1979 the new Minister of Women's Status and the Family, Monique Pelletier, changed this demand to 80% in an amendment to a bill on municipal election reform.

The measure was approved almost unanimously in the National Assembly, but the measure never reached the Senate before the end of the legislative term, in part because the government preferred not to pursue such a controversial reform during the 1980-1981 presidential campaign. The Socialists then came to power and, despite the party's apparent commitment to gender quotas, the new government decided not to include quotas for women in a bill that would introduce semi-proportional representation for elections at the municipal level. In 1982 an independent deputy affiliated with the PS, Gisèle Halimi, proposed that lists of candidates not include more than 70% of candidates of the same sex, applied to every three positions on the list. The Socialist group in parliament succeeded in reducing her proposal to 75% with no restrictions on the ordering of male and female candidates, but the government remained unconvinced and argued publicly that the political parties, not the

National Assembly, should decide the ratio of male and female candidates. During the parliamentary debates, Minister of the Interior Gaston Defferre, speaking on behalf of the government, requested that the measure appear as a separate article so that, if the Constitutional Council should annul it, the broader law might still be applied (Bird 2002). This suggestion fed rumors among the deputies that the court would declare the quota unconstitutional, creating an opportunity for them to appeal to female voters by supporting the quota, secure in the knowledge that it would never actually be applied. After separating the quota provision from the main legislation, they voted nearly unanimously in favor of the measure. Several months later, as expected, the court reviewed the bill on municipal electoral reform. While the review initially focused on articles other than the one providing for quotas (Gaspard 1998; Mossuz-Lavau 1998a), the Council eventually took up the quota article and declared it unconstitutional on the grounds that Article 3 of the Constitution and Article 6 of the Declaration of the Rights of Man and the Citizen together affirmed the principle of equality before the law, precluding all types of division of voters and candidates into categories for all types of political voting, including the election of municipal councilors.

While feminists paid little attention to this verdict at the time (Gaspard 1998) – partly because many women were uneasy with the idea of 25% quotas whcn women constituted more than 50% of the population (Mossuz-Lavau 1998a) – it had an enormous impact on future campaigns to increase women's political representation in France. To begin, the decision reaffirmed an interpretation of the principle of equality as equality before the law. Although the preamble of the Constitution includes the principle of equality between men and women, all subsequent Constitutional Council decisions, jurisprudence, and works of authority on the Constitution treated this principle as gender-neutral (Mazur 2001). The 1982 Council decision reinforced this view, similarly precluding attempts to institute equality of outcomes through gender-specific means.

In a related vein, the verdict cast doubt on the possibility of using legal means to compel parties to promote women's access to political office (Mossuz-Lavau 1998a), forcing advocates of quotas to develop a more fundamental critique of the existing principle of equality as a root cause of sex-based differences in political representation (Bird 2002).

The Debate over the Parity Law

The public debate on parity, combined with pressures from women inside his party, led Socialist leader Jospin to announce in May 1996 that at least 30% of the party's candidates for the 1998 legislative elections would be women, the first time that the party quota would apply to two-round majoritarian elections (Opello 2002). Although several male leaders in the party argued that they would not be able to find enough suitable women, the party approved a list of 167 female candidates in February 1997, slightly more than 30% (Gaspard 1998; Opello 2002). Despite their declarations in favor of parity, President Chirac and Prime Minister Juppé (both of Rally for the Republic, RPR) took no concrete initiatives in this direction. Indeed, Juppé became more reticent about his support following a 1997 survey showing that 75% of all deputies in the National Assembly opposed inscribing parity in the constitution, with most of this opposition coming from the conservative majority of the RPR and Union for a Democratic France (UDF) (Sineau 2001, 176). In the first parliamentary debate on parity in March 1997, consequently, Juppé stressed that he continued to support positive measures to promote women's representation, but suggested reducing the demand for parity in the constitution to some form of temporary measure to encourage female candidates. A vote never took place, however, and shortly thereafter Chirac dissolved the Assembly and called for new elections, one year ahead of schedule. Although caught off-guard by this announcement, many of the parties on the left presented relatively high proportions of female candidates, ranging between 26.8% and 32.3%. The right-wing parties, in contrast, nominated only 7.7% to 12.1% women among their parties' candidates, choosing instead to stand behind their incumbents, who were overwhelmingly male. As a result, 42 of the 63 women elected – a record 10.9% of the National Assembly – were members of the Socialist Party.

Although Chirac had anticipated that early elections would help consolidate the power of the UDF-RPR alliance, his strategy backfired when a majority of voters chose the Socialists, leading to the appointment of Jospin as the new prime minister. Within a matter of days, Jospin named more than 30% women to his new cabinet and announced that he planned to pursue an amendment to incorporate parity into the constitution. Chirac responded a month later that he too would support constitutional reform, if nothing else could be done to ensure women's access to political office (Mossuz-Lavau 1998a). Over the next two years, the issue of parity became a constant in the French media as part of a broader discussion of reforms to modernize French politics, like strengthening local democracy, bringing an end to multiple-office holding, and introducing limited electoral system reform. Although some right-wing officials claimed that the government was using parity as an excuse to change the electoral system for National Assembly elections (Ramsay 2003), public awareness of women's under-representation in politics began to grow as journalists compared the situation in France with other countries in the European Union. Many were shocked to learn that France had the lowest percentage of women in parliament, ahead of only Greece, and that the percentage of women elected to the National Assembly had barely changed since 1945, when women were first eligible to run for political office. These developments spurred both leaders to reaffirm their commitments to parity on International Women's Day in March 1998.

One month later Jospin announced that he planned to pursue a constitutional amendment for parity in positions of political, economic, and social responsibility. He argued that the best place to introduce this amendment was Article 1, which affirms the principles of the French republic and guarantees equality before the law. Because the President has the power to initiate constitutional amendments, along with individual members of parliament, Chirac considered Jospin's proposals and – despite his earlier statements – rejected the term 'parity' in favor of the term 'equal access,' and reform of Article 1 in favor of Article 34, which simply lists the policy areas in which the legislature may make law. After the two men reached a compromise to support a law guaranteeing equal access to positions of political, economic, and social responsibility, however, the Council of State argued that economic and social equality were already included in the Preamble of the Constitution. Upon further negotiation, Chirac agreed to reform Article 3, which outlines the basic rights of citizens in relation to national sovereignty, on the condition that Jospin drop his demand to introduce a new electoral system for the National Assembly, one of his long-standing political commitments. Conservatives in the Senate, further, insisted that the verb 'guarantees' be replaced with 'favours' (*favoriser*) equal access, thus reducing the claim for equal representation of women and men to the milder goal of increasing the number of female candidates.

With these changes, the amendment was submitted for its first reading in the National Assembly in December 1998. Minister of Justice Élisabeth Guigou opened the debate by reviewing the history of the parity concept. On these grounds, she argued that reform of Article 3 would not introduce a sexual cleavage into politics, but would bring an end to political exclusion, and thus finally fully realize the goals of the French Revolution.

To make her case, she criticized the 1982 Constitutional Council decision for ignoring the Preamble of the Constitution, which guarantees equal rights for men and women in all domains, and presented the current bill not as redundant but as a means for giving concrete content to this principle of equality. She pointed out that the Constitutional Council itself had cleared the way for such a measure, given its judgment in January 1997 that legislators had a duty to take the appropriate steps to prevent any departures from this principle of equality. She also noted that Article 141 of the new Treaty of Amsterdam, which has constitutional status in all EU member states and would come into force in May 1999, permits member states to adopt positive action measures to promote women's participation in professional life.

In her judgment, therefore, both national and international law supported and even obligated legislators to pass a measure to facilitate women's access to political office (Guigou 1998). Although some female politicians continued to lobby against parity, arguing that a good cause had taken the wrong path, the measure was adopted unanimously by the National Assembly in March 1999. The Senate, in contrast, rejected the measure on its first reading, but under heavy pressure from Chirac, eventually adopted it by an overwhelming majority (*The Guardian*, 6 March 1999). As per the procedure for ratifying a constitutional amendment, both houses of parliament then met in a special session at Versailles in July 1999 and approved the provision as Constitutional Law 99-569.

Passage of the constitutional amendment, in turn, set in motion a second round of debates regarding reform of the electoral law to specify and enforce equal access to electoral mandates and elective functions. In December 1999, Minister of the Interior Jean-Pierre Chevènement submitted the government's proposals for the specific types of elections to which the parity principle would be applied, the moments when compliance would be monitored, and the sanctions that would be imposed on political parties for not fully complying with these requirements.

To the disappointment of many parity advocates, the bill focused on the nomination of female candidates, rather than on the proportion of women elected, and made the weakest provisions for elections to the National Assembly, whose low percentage of women had inspired the parity campaign in the first place. More specifically, the bill mandated distinct requirements for different types of elections, according to the particular electoral system used. For elections held under proportion representation, the bill required that lists alternate between women and men in elections with only one round (European, regional, and Senate elections in departments with three or more Senate seats), and achieve parity per group of six candidates, with three men and three women in any order, in elections with two rounds (regional and municipal elections in towns with more than 3500 inhabitants).

In these elections, the penalty for non-compliance was rejection of the list, meaning that parties would not be able to participate in elections unless they complied with the law. For elections using two-round majoritarian voting, the bill mandated that parties present 50% male and 50% female candidates across all electoral districts, with no requirement as to which districts female candidates should be placed. In these elections, the penalty for non-compliance was financial, with parties losing a percentage of their state funding equal to half the difference in percentages of male and female candidates. By this arrangement, parties would still be guaranteed 50% of their financing, even if 100% of their candidates were men (Sineau 2002). This text was adopted almost unanimously, with only one vote cast against it, in January 2000 (*Le Monde*, 26 January 2000).

The Senate adopted a slightly different version in March, leading to additional votes in the Assembly in March, the Senate in April, and the Assembly again in May 2000. Upon its final approval in the Assembly, a group of sixty senators referred the bill to the Constitutional Council on the grounds that the measure instituted quotas by constraining and penalizing means, broke a constitutional tradition of not changing the electoral law less than a year before the next elections, prevented incumbents from being re-elected on their original lists, and limited the free choice of voters. Although the Council had upheld the unconstitutionality of quotas as late as January 1999 in a decision concerning provisions for regional elections, it revised this view and confirmed the constitutionality of the new parity law at the end of May 2000, leading to the promulgation of a new electoral law in June 2000.

The Origins of the Parity Law

Following the 1982 Constitutional Council decision, efforts to increase quotas inside the Socialist Party lost momentum, and for several years little progress was made at either the national-or the party-level to promote women's political representation. In 1986, however, feminists became more optimist when the electoral system for parliamentary elections was changed from two-round majoritarian to proportional representation. Many female activists anticipated that the adoption of PR would substantially increase the number of women elected, and for this reason they did not mobilize extensively within the parties to ensure that women were placed high on the candidate lists (Jenson 1996).

As a result, women comprised 24.7% of all candidates, but the percentage of women elected to the National Assembly rose only a fraction from 5.3% to 5.9%. The PS roughly approximated its 20% party quota by including 18.9% female candidates, but because party leaders had also placed most women quite far down on the candidate lists, women constituted only 9.8% of the Socialist deputies in parliament. After this disappointment, French women interested in promoting women's representation began to look for inspiration in movements outside the established parties and beyond their own national borders. Between 1986 and 1988, various women became active in the Rainbow movement, which insisted on parity, or the equal involvement of women and men, in all group decision-making.

When the group was dissolved in 1988, many adherents joined the Greens and, similar to Green parties elsewhere in Europe, inscribed the principle of parity in the party's statutes. They have subsequently applied this principle to all party lists since the 1989 EP elections (Guigou 1998).

Around the same time, the Council of Europe (COE) began a series of debates on the deepening and strengthening of democracy in Europe. In contrast to the European Union (EU), which in the late 1980s focused mainly on the rights of individuals as economic actors, the COE has long worked to promote the rights of individuals as political actors. In 1986 it organized the first European Ministerial Conference on Equality Between Women and Men, where member states identified the increased presence and participation of women in public life as a central feature of democracy and a matter of social justice. In 1988 they signed the Declaration of Equality of Women and Men calling on the COE to devise policies and strategies for integrating women into all levels of political life.

To this end, the European Committee for Equality Between Women and Men (CEEG) convened a seminar of experts in Strasbourg in 1989 to share and develop mechanisms for promoting women's access to political office. The two main contributions to these debates were papers by Marit Halvorsen, outlining Norwegian experiences in bringing more women into politics, and Élisabeth Sledziewski, elaborating new normative arguments for increasing women's political presence based on ontological differences between women and men (Steering Committee for Equality between Women and Men 1992, 17-27, 29-43).

Although the debate reflected a wider array of positions on sexual difference, as well as a more diverse set of preferences regarding party versus statutory quotas (Lovecy 2001; Steering Committee for Equality between Women and Men 1992), most subsequent accounts of this meeting equate it with the first definitive statement on 'parity democracy,' not only as a new concept in European politics but also as a set of innovative arguments for justifying positive action to promote women in politics. Many of the ideas formulated by Sledziewski – universalism as a trap for democracy, the dual nature of the human race, and the need to redefine existing notions of equality – provided inspiration for women in France, who not only perceived new ways of overcoming the 1982 Constitutional Council decision, but also recognized that COE support for parity democracy could lend important legitimacy to their efforts to increase women's political representation.

The rise of parity democracy in Europe coincided with a series of developments within France involving more critical examination of the principles and goals underlying the theory and practice of democracy in France. The bicentennial of the French Revolution in 1989, in particular, sparked a flood of books attributing women's absence from politics and other spheres of power to the Revolution itself and, especially, its core principle of the universal citizen. As scholars began to revive the history of French feminism, they focused on the exclusions inherent in French republicanism and rehabilitated work by earlier feminists calling for the equal representation of women and men in politics.

In 1990 the first parity association was formed by Régine Saint-Criq, a former regional councillor who had left the PS because of its persistent failure to implement its own party quota (Praud 2001). A number of similar organizations appeared in rapid succession several years later, following the 1992 publication of *Au pouvoir citoyennes! Liberté, égalité, parité*, a self-proclaimed manifesto for the parity movement in France. In addition to introducing the term parity to a wider public, the book addressed reasons why women were under-represented in electoral politics and, to rectify the situation, proposed that parity be inscribed in the law with the phrase "Elected assemblies, at the regional as well as the national level, are composed of as many women as men." To implement parity, the authors suggested alternating between women and men on lists for elections governed by PR, and joining current districts to create two-member slates, each with one woman and one man, for majoritarian elections.

Almost immediately, women around the country began to establish new parity associations, as well as to make parity a goal of many existing women's organizations. After the 1993 elections returned only 6.4% women to the National Assembly, activities in favor of parity multiplied with debates, roundtables, conferences, newsletters, and even demonstrations in front of the National Assembly. By the end of 1993, various women's organizations drafted the Manifesto of the 577 for Parity Democracy – a reference to the number of deputies in the National Assembly – signed by 289 women and 288 men from all points on the political spectrum to demand the incorporation of parity into the national constitution. Soon after the publication of the manifesto in *Le Monde*, one of the largest newspapers in France, a number of left-wing parties announced they would apply parity to their lists for the upcoming EP elections in 1994.

Over the course of the next year, various deputies submitted proposals in the National Assembly to institute parity or, at least, to ensure greater political representation for women. Although President François Mitterrand expressed reservations about quotas, he agreed that dramatic increases were unlikely to occur on their own (Mossuz-Lavau 1998a; Varikas 1995). To increase their influence in these debates, parity associations – including women's groups in civil society and the political parties that had adopted the goal of parity – created an umbrella organization, Tomorrow Parity, with the goal of collecting a million signatures in favor of constitutional reform. These various developments enabled parity advocates to place the issue at the forefront of political debate during the 1995 presidential elections and to gain a commitment from all the major candidates for some type of political reform.

Upon being elected, Jacques Chirac appointed Alain Juppé as prime minister and oversaw the nomination of a record number of women to the cabinet. Together they commissioned the Observatory for Parity, a state-level agency, to study and develop strategies concerning women in politics. Although the proportion of women in the cabinet soon dropped precipitously from 27.9% to 12.5%, parity advocates continued to lobby for legal reform.

In 1996 ten prominent female politicians from both the left and the right came together to outline their own proposals for attaining equal representation, which were published in *L'Express*, a major French news weekly, as the Manifesto of the Ten for Parity. Much less radical than the Manifesto of the 577, this document called for voluntary measures within the political parties rather than a parity law, an expansion in the use of PR, a drastic reduction in multiple office-holding, public financing for parties that respect parity, and a referendum on a constitutional amendment to introduce affirmative action. In the same edition, *L'Express* revealed the results of a nation-wide poll showing that 71% of the French population – with no differences between women and men – would support a law or constitutional amendment establishing equal representation. The paper also included interviews of Juppé and Lionel Jospin, the leader of the Socialist Party, both of whom endorsed a constitutional amendment and a referendum to establish measures to promote women in politics.

These public declarations in favor of parity are notable, and somewhat unusual, in that calls for parity entail a much more radical demand – equal representation for women and men – than campaigns for quotas elsewhere in the world. Nonetheless, parity gained a broad base of support, spanning women in civil society, the political parties, and the state; new and established women's groups; feminist activists and academics; politicians on the left and the right; and male and female voters. These patterns reflected the unique nature of the parity solution, which sought to redefine the principles used by the Constitutional Council to reject quotas – equality before the law and representation of the whole, rather than its parts – to devise a new normative justification for quotas consistent with the broader framework of French republicanism. To accomplish this task, advocates argued that current understandings of equality and representation – as well as their subject, the universal citizen – were originally deemed to apply only to men.

Rather than abandon these concepts entirely, they proposed reforming the constitution to provide for the equal representation of women and men in political life, on the grounds that this was the only way to recognize explicitly the two sexes of the abstract universal citizen. Instituting parity was crucial to the general welfare of society, they claimed, because 'sex' was the universal difference among human beings, a division cutting across all other groups, categories, and communities. This policy differed fundamentally from establishing quotas, because quotas implied special representation rights for minorities, while parity simply called for the equitable sharing of power between women and men, the two halves of the human race. As a consequence, the inclusion of women would provide for a more accurate reflection of the whole people and the common interest, not the representation of a distinct social category with viewpoints and interests consistently different from those of men. Inscribing parity in the constitution thus would not reverse the accomplishments of the French Revolution, but rather would finally fully realize them.

The concept of parity thus embodied a series of moves to reframe demands to promote women's political representation by establishing 'sex' as the universal division among human beings, the logic of parity as distinct from the logic of quotas, and the goal of parity as changes in patterns of participation and not in the content of public policies. These formulations, importantly, contained a number of ambiguities that not only accounted for the broad coalitions in favor of parity, but also for the particular groups opposed to including it in the constitution. The argument that 'sex' is the universal difference, for example, presented advocates with a means to justify their focus on women while also reducing the impact of criticism that recognizing parity would escalate claim-making by other under-represented groups. This solution appealed to those who sought measures to tackle gender discrimination, as well as those who feared that parity would open the way to multiculturalism and thus the erosion of cultural assimilation at the heart of French republicanism. Feminist critics of parity, however, argued that giving political value to sexual difference was invariably reactionary, not only because it reduced women to their ovaries, but also because essentializing and reifying sexual differences made it impossible to see the commonalities between women and men. Various intellectuals and politicians, for their part, refused to accept the distinction between sex and other types of political cleavage and continued to insist that a concession for women would spur 'differentialism' and 'communitarianism' among other groups, with fatal consequences for the secular and universal republic. In their view, any shortcomings in the founding principles of the French republic were a legacy of their historical implementation, a situation that would evolve naturally over time until women and men were as equal in practice as they were in theory.

In a similar vein, the claim that parity was not a quota enabled supporters to rationalize their pursuit of special measures to increase women's representation and thus overcome the negative impact of the earlier Constitutional Council decision. This argument was attractive to feminists and non-feminists who recognized the importance of taking action to promote women's access to political office, but who rejected the negative connotations of quotas or recognized the need for a semantic shift to implement a measure that – for all intents and purposes – was functionally equivalent to a quota.

Feminist opponents continually sought to demystify this distinction, asserting that parity was simply a stricter form of quota and, as such, threatened to turn women into victims who needed special help to succeed, reinforcing the same prejudices that misogynists had long used to keep women out of politics. Other critics emphasized that exclusion was not simply about numbers and ridiculed attempts to institute quotas as a misplaced desire to imitate the United States, pointing out that the countries with the highest levels of female representation had never mandated such measures by law.

The focus of parity on policy-makers, rather than on the content of public policies, finally, allowed advocates to remain agnostic as to the expected policy outcomes of the parity provision. This position appealed to male politicians concerned that parity might benefit women at the expense of men, because women in office would represent women's interests, and to feminists worried that parity falsely assumed essential differences between women and men, because not all women in office pursued women's issues.

Various feminists responded that supporting female candidates simply because they were women would draw attention away from substantive policy questions affecting women, as well as risk advancing women who were already coopted by male leaders, thus increasing the distance between elite and regular women.

Other opponents asserted that politics should revolve around ideas, not around people, and that sexual differences had nothing to do with political ideology. Despite the many efforts to reduce the appeal of parity, however, the concept remained sufficiently ambiguous to garner the support of groups who otherwise disagreed on other political issues. Indeed, one critic observed that parity was like a chameleon, able to accommodate all publics and all sensibilities (Varikas 1995). This led others to worry that not enough attention was being paid to the arguments against parity, preventing a truly democratic debate from taking place (Amar 1999).

Conclusions

A great deal of literature on group representation treats women and minority groups as making similar, additive claims to representation, and thus assumes that the recognition of one of these groups will facilitate the recognition of other groups. A closer look at quota debates in India and France, however, indicates that groups more frequently compete for representation, such that the recognition of one group often precludes the recognition of other groups. These groups not only differ across countries, but the relationship between them varies considerably across national contexts. While nation-building projects in both India and France have sought historically to assimilate or transcend differences at the political level, both countries have witnessed the emergence of claims for improved descriptive representation in recent years. Even more interestingly, these countries have responded to these demands in nearly opposite ways. In India, ethnic and racial minorities quickly received guaranteed seats in all political assemblies, but women have experienced greater difficulties, primarily due to lingering questions about how to resolve caste and tribal quotas with reserved seats for women. In France, on the other hand, women have been recognized as a group deserving greater representation in politics, to the exclusion of other groups, because advocates have framed gender as a characteristic that crosses all other groups, as the universal difference. This comparison reveals how some identities, and not others, are deemed relevant categories of political representation in some contexts but not in others, and how claims for the recognition of these identities are linked – either implicitly or explicitly – to the non-recognition of others. These patterns undermine broad claims about the inherent hierarchy of political identities and point instead to the discursive construction of such priorities within the already contested arena of claims to group representation.

CHAPTER 12

The Empirical Evidence and Dalit Exclusion

Discrimination and Caste Exclusion

In India, exclusion revolves around the societal interrelations and institutions that exclude, discriminate, isolate and deprive some groups on the basis of group identities like caste and ethnicity. It is caste-based exclusion which forms the basis for various anti-discriminatory policies. Historically, the caste system has regulated the social and economic life of the people in India. The organisational scheme of the caste system is based on the division of people into social groups (or castes) in which the civil, cultural and economic rights of each individual caste are predetermined or ascribed by birth and made hereditary.

The assignment of civil, cultural and economic rights is therefore unequal and hierarchical. The most important feature of the caste system, however, is that it provides for a regulatory mechanism to enforce social and economic organisation through the instruments of social ostracism (or social and economic penalties), and reinforces it further with justification and support from philosophical elements in the Hindu religion. The caste system's fundamental characteristics of fixed civil, cultural and economic rights for each caste, with restrictions on change, implies "forced exclusion" of one caste from the rights of the other caste, or from undertaking the occupations of other castes.

Exclusion and discrimination in civil, cultural, and particularly in economic spheres such as occupation and labour employment, are therefore internal to the system and a necessary outcome of its governing principles. In the market economy framework, occupational immobility operates through restrictions in various markets such as land, labour, credit, other inputs and services necessary for any economic activity. Labour, being an integral part of the production process of any economic activity, would obviously become part of market discrimination. This implies that the caste system involves the negation of not only equality and freedom, but also of basic human rights, particularly of low-caste untouchables, thus becoming an impediment in personal development. The principles of equality and freedom are not the governing principles of the caste system. This is because the underlying principles of the caste system assume particular notions of 'human rights'. Unlike many other human societies, the caste system does not recognise the individual and his/her distinctiveness as the centre of the social purpose. In fact, for the purpose of rights and duties, the unit of Hindu society is not an individual. Even the family is not regarded as a unit in Hindu society, except for the purposes of marriage and inheritance.

The primary unit in Hindu society is caste, and hence the rights and privileges (or lack of them) of an individual are on account of him/her being a member of a particular caste. Also, due to differential ranking and the hierarchical nature of the caste system, the entitlements to various rights become narrower and narrower as one goes down the hierarchical ladder within the caste system. Various castes get artfully interlinked and coupled with each other in a manner such that the rights and privileges of the higher castes become the causative reasons for the disadvantage and disability of the lower castes, particularly the untouchables. As Ambedkar observed, a caste does not exist in a single number, only in plural.

Castes exist as a system of endogenous groups that are interlinked with each other in an unequal measure of rights and relations in all walks of life. Castes at the top of the order enjoy more rights at the expense of those located at the bottom. Therefore, the untouchables located at the bottom of the caste hierarchy have much fewer economic and social rights. Since the civil, cultural and economic rights (particularly with respect to occupation and property rights) of each caste are ascribed, and are compulsory, the institution of caste necessarily involves forced exclusion of one caste from the rights of another. The unequal and hierarchical assignment of economic and social rights by ascription obviously restricts freedom of occupation and human development.

Social Exclusion

Social exclusion is the denial of equal opportunities imposed by certain groups of society on others, leading to the inability of an individual to participate in the basic political, economic and social functioning of society. Amartya Sen draws attention to various meanings and dimensions of the concept of social exclusion.

He draws a distinction between situations where some people are kept out (or left out), and where some people are included (forcibly) on deeply unfavourable terms. The two situations are described as "unfavourable exclusion" and "unfavourable inclusion". Sen argues that it is important to distinguish between 'active exclusion' — fostering of exclusion through deliberate policy interventions by the government or by any other wilful agents (to exclude some people from some opportunity), and 'passive exclusion', which works through the social process in which there are no deliberate attempts to exclude, but nevertheless may result in exclusion from a set of circumstances. Sen further distinguishes the "constitutive relevance" of exclusion from that of "instrumental importance". In the former, exclusion or deprivation have an intrinsic importance of their own. For instance, not bring able to relate to others and to take part in the life of the community can directly impoverish a person's life, in addition to the further deprivation it may generate. This is different from social exclusion of "instrumental importance", in which the exclusion in itself is not impoverishing but can lead to impoverishment of human life. Mainstream economists have further elaborated the concept of discrimination that operates particularly through markets.

Caste Exclusion's Forms and Discrimination

Caste/untouchability and ethnicity-based exclusion reflects in the inability of individuals and groups like former untouchables, adivasis and similar groups to interact freely and productively with others and to take part in the full economic, social and political life of a community. Incomplete citizenship or denial of civil rights (freedom of expression, rule of law, right to justice), political rights (right and means to participate in the exercise of political power), and socio-economic rights (economic security and equality of opportunities) are key dimensions of impoverished lives (Jonas Zoninsein, 2005). Caste and untouchability-based exclusion and discrimination can be categorised in the economic, civil, cultural, and political spheres as follows:

Firstly, economic exclusion can be practised in the labour market through denial of jobs; in the capital market through denial of access to capital; in the agricultural land market through denial of sale and purchase or leasing of land; in the input market through denial in sale and purchase of factor inputs; and in the consumer market through denial in the sale and purchase of commodities and consumer goods.

Secondly, discrimination can occur through what Amartya Sen describes as "unfavourable inclusion", through differential treatment in the terms and conditions of contract, one of them reflecting in discrimination in the prices charged and received by discriminated groups. Discriminated groups can get lower prices for the goods that they sell, and could pay higher prices for the goods that they buy, as compared with the market price or the price paid by other groups.

Thirdly, exclusion and discrimination can occur in access to social needs supplied by government or public institutions, or by private institutions in the fields of education, housing and health, including common property resources like waterbodies, grazing land and land for common use.

Fourthly, groups (particularly untouchables) may face exclusion and discrimination from participation in certain categories of jobs (the sweeper being excluded from household jobs) because of the notion of purity and pollution, and may be restricted to so-called "unclean" occupations.

In the civil and cultural spheres, untouchables may face discrimination and exclusion in the use of public services like roads, temples, waterbodies, and institutions delivering services like education, health and other public services. In the political sphere, untouchables could face discrimination in the use of political rights, and in participation in the decision-making process. Due to physical (or residential) segregation, and social exclusion on account of the notion of untouchability, they may suffer from a general societal exclusion. Since there is a societal mechanism to regulate and enforce the customary norms and rules of the caste system, untouchables generally face opposition in the form of social and economic boycott, violence, and such acts as a general deterrent to their right to development. Caste and untouchability-based exclusion and discrimination are essentially "structural in nature" and comprehensive and multiple in coverage, involving the denial of equal opportunities.

Empirical Evidence of Caste Exclusion and Discrimination

The question is why dalits and adivasis, categorised as scheduled castes (SCs) and scheduled tribes (STs), have poor access to resources that directly and indirectly determine the level of income. Why their ownership of agricultural land and non-land capital assets is low compared with non-SC/STs. Why unemployment rates are high compared with non-SC/STs. Why daily wage earnings of SC/STs in non-farm activities are lower compared with non-SC/STs. Why literacy rates and education levels are much lower when compared with non-SC/STs. We first need to look at the evidence on discrimination in civil, cultural and political spheres provided by official data, besides an all-India study and four regional studies. These include an all-India 2000 ActionAid study ('Untouchability in Rural India' by Ghanshyam Saha, Satish Deshpande, Sukhadeo Thorat, Harsh Mander, Amita Baviskar and research and other regional staff, Delhi), a study on Karnataka (1973-74 and 1991), Andhra Pradesh (1977), Orissa (1987-88) and Gujarat (1996). The all-India study presents evidence from 11 states. The studies based on village surveys bring out the actual magnitude of the exclusion, discrimination and atrocities against dalits.

Economic Exclusion and Discrimination

Conducted in 555 villages across 11 Indian states — found that discrimination in labour markets operates through exclusion in hiring, and unfair or low wages. In about 36% of the villages, SCs were denied casual employment in agriculture. In about 25% of villages, SCs faced discrimination in wage payments. SCs received daily wages at a rate that was less than the market wage rate, or wages paid to non-SC workers. Belief in the concept of purity and pollution also impacted hiring of SC labourers — in about one-third of villages SCs were excluded from employment in the construction of houses. In the case of other markets, the study observed discriminatory treatment of SCs in access to irrigation water and public and private services.

In a little more than one-third of the villages, SCs were denied access to water for agriculture. In case of agricultural land, selective evidence from some states brings out the restrictions placed by the high castes on SCs in the purchase of private agricultural land, and use of public land for agriculture and housing. In the case of access to common property resources like grazing land, fishing ponds, and other resources, SCs faced exclusion in about one-fifth of the sample villages. The notion of pollution and purity reflected in the exclusionary and discriminatory behaviour of higher castes in the consumer markets — in the sale and purchase of consumer goods, particularly milk, vegetables and other such goods. In 35% of the villages surveyed, SCs were not allowed to sell any kind of goods at village-level markets. In about 47% of villages, SCs were not allowed to sell milk to village cooperatives and private buyers.

The survey data also reveals some isolated evidence of exclusion and discrimination in the sale and purchase of consumer goods like bakery products and vegetables. Such restrictions compelled SCs to go to small towns and other nearby marketplaces where their caste identity was not so obvious, or was hidden. Micro-level studies such as those from Andhra Pradesh (Venketeswarlu, 1990) and Karnataka (Khan, 1995) provide some evidence on economic discrimination in occupation, employment, wages, and the credit market as well as in other economic spheres. The Andhra Pradesh study observed that SCs faced restrictions in efforts to change their occupation. Similarly, the Karnataka study revealed that nearly 85% of SC respondents continue to be engaged in their traditional occupations, with only 15% able to make a switch-over. The Orissa study (Tripathy, 1994) observed discrimination in land lease, credit and labour markets in rural areas. Nearly 96% of untouchable respondents in one village and all untouchable respondents in the second village were discriminated against in wage payment, with 28% in one village and 20% in another facing discrimination in payment of rent.

For urban areas, Banerjee and Knight (1991) observed that "there is indeed discrimination by caste, particularly job discrimination" and that "discrimination appears to operate at least in part through traditional mechanisms, with untouchables disproportionately represented in poorly-paid dead-end jobs.. Even if discrimination is no longer practised, the effects of past discrimination could carry over to the present. This may help explain why discrimination is greatest in operative jobs in which contacts are more important for recruitment, and not in white-collar jobs in which recruitment involves formal methods." Such economic discrimination had obvious impacts on the earnings of SC households, and reflected in the incidence of high poverty among them.

The Right to Food

In terms of scale, caste discrimination afflicts more than one out of three fair price shops and more than one out of three government schools serving midday meals. In terms of geographical spread, it is unquestionably a nationwide problem — from 24% in Andhra Pradesh to 52% in Rajasthan, to a vast majority in Uttar Pradesh and Bihar, respondent villages from every state reported problems of caste discrimination and exclusion in the midday meal scheme. Likewise with the FPS, no state is free of discrimination — from 17% in Andhra Pradesh to 86% in Bihar. For instance, every state reports a substantial percentage of dominant caste public distribution system (PDS) dealers practising caste-based discrimination in the distribution of PDS goods, for example preferential order of service by caste, or hierarchically segregated timings for dominant caste and Dalit customers.

While the problem is nationwide, its degree varies considerably from state to state. Where higher percentages of midday meal cooks and organisers are Dalit, and where a higher percentage of midday meals are held in Dalit colonies, a lower incidence of caste discrimination in the scheme is reported. In Andhra Pradesh, where indicators of Dalit participatory empowerment and access are relatively high (49% of respondent villages have Dalit cooks, 45% have Dalit organisers, and 46% are held in Dalit localities), reported caste discrimination in the midday meal scheme stands at 24%. In Tamil Nadu, where the same empowerment and access indicators are lower (31%, 27% and 19%, respectively), reported discrimination stands at 36%. And in Rajasthan, where the indicators are alarmingly low (8% Dalit cooks, 0% Dalit organisers, 12% held in Dalit colonies), reported discrimination was extremely high at 52%. A similar pattern emerges in access to fair price shops, where higher proportions of Dalit dealers and FPS held in Dalit colonies correspond with lower proportions of reported discrimination and 'untouchability' practices.

Civil and Political Spheres

Macro-level Evidence: During 1999-2001, an average of 28,016 cases per year were registered by untouchables in the country under the Anti-Untouchability Act of 1955 and the SC and ST Prevention of Atrocities Act. This comes to about three cases per 100,000 population and included restrictions on access to temples, wells, taps, tea stalls, restaurants, community baths, roads, and other services. The ratio of such cases was highest in Rajasthan (9.3), followed by Madhya Pradesh (7.7). The ratio was about three cases per 100,000 population in Orissa, Karnataka, Gujarat and Andhra Pradesh. The break-up of crimes against untouchables for the year 2000 include 526 cases of murder, 3,497 of grievous hurt, 290 cases of arson, 1,000 cases of sexual assault, and 11,587 cases of other offences. During a nine-year period between 1992 and 2000, a total of 252,370 cases of crime, including cases of discrimination and atrocities, were registered by untouchables.

Evidence from Primary Surveys: First, the results of the most comprehensive study based on an intensive survey of 555 villages in 11 states across India. In this section, we consider the practice of discrimination in the "secular public sphere", including access to water sources, public thoroughfares, transport, and other village-level services and amenities like tea shops, barbers' or watermen's services, and so on.

Out of all the villages surveyed, complete denial was observed in a little less than half the villages — 48.4% in terms of access to public water/drinking places, 36% in terms of access to shops, 26% in terms of the use of restaurants/hotels, 21% in terms of entry to health centres/clinics, 9.2% in terms of public transport, and 3.2% in terms of entry to cinema halls/recreation facilities, etc.

In the case of individual service-providers also, the denial was more than apparent. Out of all the villages surveyed, denial of barber services was reported in 46% of the villages, washerperson services in 46% of the villages, carpenter services in 26% of the villages, and potter services in about 20% of the villages. While complete denial of access to particular water sources (well, tank, tubewell, etc), village shops, health clinics, transport used for public purposes, services offered by washerpersons, carpenters, tailors, potters, etc, is the most evident form of social exclusion, what is more common is the imposition of differential treatment in access to these and other public services, which takes various forms. This was observed in one-third of the villages in the form of separate seating arrangements and a separate set of cups at tea stalls/restaurants for untouchables. Similar forms of discrimination were observed in purchases from shops, entry into public transport, and treatment at private health clinics, etc.

Discrimination Story of Karnataka

The Karnataka study for 1973-74 is based on a fairly large sample of 76 villages, 38 urban centres and 3,330 households. Of the total households, 73% are untouchables (Parvathamma, 1984). A little more than half the untouchable respondents were not allowed to draw water from the public well in the village. The magnitude of the problem was less severe in urban centres, but even in urban areas 15% of respondents reported restrictions on the use of public waterbodies. The practice of untouchability was more widespread in terms of access to the village temple and access to high-caste houses. More than 60% of untouchables were not allowed into the village temple. A little less than half the dalits were not allowed free access to the local village teashop. In urban areas, the discrimination was much less (only 6%). In essential services, the practice of untouchability was widespread. A little more than half of the respondents did not receive the services of a barber and washerman in the village. In urban areas, access improved considerably. In public services like postal services, health and education, the practice of untouchability was much less. Almost all had access to postal services, but half of the respondents faced some kind of discrimination insofar as postmen avoided entering Dalit residential areas. Generally, discrimination in services rendered by government doctors and nurses and the village school was less. Still, in the early-1970s, one out of 10 persons among the scheduled castes was not allowed inside the village shops. One out of 10 persons among the scheduled castes could not wear clothes or ornaments of their own choice without being harassed.

Nearly 20 years later, another study was conducted in Karnataka taking 941 respondents from 52 villages and from most of the districts (Khan, 1995). In the political sphere (that is, sitting together or drinking tea in the village panchayat office), the discrimination was much less. Otherwise, not much had happened in the two decades since the previous study was carried out. About three out of four respondents were denied entry into the village temple and also denied participation in religious processions. Social mixing or relations across caste barriers were also not allowed. Most people among the untouchables did not have free access to the water taps of the high castes, and three-fourths of them had no access to the village tank.

Discrimination Story of Orissa

The Orissa study covered 65 untouchable respondents from two villages (one small and one large) in 1987-88 (Tripathy, 1994). In both villages, the settlements of untouchables were separated from those belonging to the upper castes. An overwhelming majority — 80% — of respondents in the small village and 70% in the large village were prohibited from drinking water from the public well and public tubewell. In the large village there were separate pulleys in wells for the untouchables. At village community feasts and marriages in both the villages, the former untouchables were treated unequally. The same is true of temple worship, barber services, washerman services, priest services, etc. Sixty-four per cent in the large village and 100% in the small village were treated unequally in the village meeting. Eighty per cent of the respondents in both villages did not have access to teashops; 70% in the large village and 80% in the small village faced unequal treatment or discrimination in getting services from grocery shops. Their small number, poverty and fear (in the small village) discouraged the dalits from contesting elections. But dalits had free access to schools and hospitals in both villages.

Discrimination Story of Gujarat

The Gujarat study was conducted in 69 villages, in 1996, to observe changes in the practice of untouchability (Shah, 1998). The study examined 17 spheres of village life. The practice of untouchability in the seating arrangement of students in village schools was negligible and non-SC students mingled freely in the school. Non-SC teachers do not discriminate against SC students, but they are not easily accessible to SC students outside the school boundary. Not all schools have the facility of drinking water for students. Where it exists, all students take water from a common vessel. Nearly 10% of village schools have teachers belonging to SCs. None of them complained that their colleagues discriminated against them in school. However, except in south Gujarat, these teachers do not get accommodation in the high-caste locality of the village. They either commute from their village or the nearby town, or they rent a house in the SC locality. Almost all villages are covered by state transport. Except in 7% of the villages, untouchability is not observed whilst boarding and sitting in the bus. Open or subtle untouchability is practised at panchayat meetings in 30% of the villages.

The seating arrangement in panchayat offices is common for all members, but there is a tacit convention whereby certain seats are marked for SC members. Though tea and snacks are served to everyone, separate plates and cups are reserved for SC members, and they are stored separately. In most village temples, 75% of SCs are not allowed to enter beyond the threshold, though they may worship from a distance. Many villages with large numbers of dalits have constructed temples in their localities to avoid confrontation. In 46 villages, SCs had separate water facilities near their localities. In the remaining 23 villages in which untouchables take water from a common source, SC women take water after the upper-caste women. In seven villages (11% of the sample) SC women are not allowed to fetch water from the well. They have to wait till the upper-caste women pour water into their pots. The upper-caste women shout at them constantly and humiliate the SC women: "Keep distance, do not pollute us!" Most tailors do not practise untouchability.

However, in most cases, they do not alter the used clothes of SCs. Nearly one-third of potters observe untouchability while selling pots to SC clients. Most barbers (nearly 70%) refuse their services to SC males. The extent of untouchability has remained almost intact in the sphere of house entry. Except for a few villages, SC members of villages do not get entry beyond the outer room of the houses of high castes. Even in villages where the young folk do not believe in physical untouchability, and who serve tea to SC guests in their houses, entry into the dining room is not encouraged. The practice of untouchability has considerably reduced in some public spheres that are directly managed by state laws, such as schools, postal services and elected panchayats. The practice of untouchability on public roads, restricting free movement of SCs, has considerably declined although it is too soon to say that dalits are not discriminated against in the public sphere.

Access to Justice

A number of anti-discrimination statutes and other legal provisions exist as legal safeguards against caste and untouchability-based discrimination. As mentioned earlier, the primary piece of legislation designed to provide a measure of protection to people from scheduled castes and scheduled tribes and to enforce their rights are the Anti-Untouchability Act, 1955 (in 1979 it was re-named the Civil Rights Act) and the Scheduled Caste and Scheduled Tribes Prevention of Atrocities Act, 1989. There are limited studies that examine the effectiveness of these legislations and access to institutions of justice. However, available evidence indicates that these legislative provisions are highly underutilised. SC/STs also suffer from discriminatory access to institutions of justice such as the police and the judiciary. Studies indicate that the scheduled castes/tribes face insurmountable obstacles at various levels from village-level functionaries like sarpanchs to the police, public prosecutors and other functionaries who are extremely non-cooperative and discriminatory.

This is essentially reflected in denial of justice to SC/STs. Official data on civil rights cases shows that of the total number of cases registered in 1991, only 1.56% were convicted. The conviction rate came down to .60% in 1999 and .85% in 2000. This shows that the conviction rate in cases relating to civil rights violations and atrocities was less than 1% and close to 0%. Analysis of 100 documented cases of atrocity during 2000-2003 in Andhra Pradesh throws some light on the reasons for the low conviction rate. The case studies indicated "a disturbing trend of subversion of the rights of dalits to justice and compensation under the law once an atrocity takes place" (Agrawal and Gonsalves, Dalit Human Rights Monitor 2003). The study observed negligence and collusion at the stages of registration, chargesheeting and investigation, at seeking justice before the law in the courts and in giving compensation. About the role of the judiciary, Dalit Human Rights Monitor 2003 observed: "If the low conviction rate under the Act is any indication, the judiciary has responded poorly to the Act. Judiciary delay and dilution of the scope, applicability and meaning of the SC/ST Act has resulted in denial of justice to the dalits".

The Interface of Caste and Gender

Assessments of human development at the aggregate level hide gender differences. Women belonging to marginalised groups suffer triple deprivations arising out of lack of access to economic resources, caste and gender discrimination. SC and ST women constitute perhaps the most economically deprived section of Indian society. Most of them don't own agricultural land and work as wage labourers. In 2001, about 57% of SC and 37% of ST women respectively were agricultural wage labour in rural areas, as compared with 29% for non-SC/STs. In urban areas, 16% SC and 14% ST women were daily wage labourers as compared with only 6% from non-SC/STs. Only 21% of SC women were cultivators compared with 51% for STs and 45% for non-SC/STs. SC/ST women also faced differential treatment in wage-earning, particularly in urban areas. In 2000, SC and ST women casual labourers received daily wages of Rs 37 and Rs 34 respectively, compared with Rs 56 for non-SC/ST women; the national average was Rs 42. Besides this, a large number of SC women are engaged in so-called 'unclean' occupations, like scavenging.

Because of their association with these occupations, the women face discrimination in the social and economic spheres. Lack of educational development is another important problem. In 2000, the literacy rate among SC and ST rural females (aged 15 and above) was 24% and 23% respectively, compared with 41% for non-SC/ST women. The literacy rate among SC women in urban areas was 48%, compared with 54% and 70% for ST and non-SC/ST women respectively. The dropout rate among SC and ST women is also relatively high at every stage of education. The high dependence on casual labour, with relatively low earnings, among SC and ST women induced a high degree of deprivation and poverty among them. The gender break-up of poverty is not available.

However, the high degree of deprivation is reflected in other indicators of wellbeing — under-nutrition and health. About 65% and 56% of ST and SC women respectively suffered from anaemia compared to 47.6% of non-SC/ST women. In 1998-99, 21.2% of SC and 26% of ST children under four years of age suffered from malnutrition (based on weight-for-age). Of these underweight children, 54% of SCs and 56% of STs were severely undernourished. There is a significant difference between SC and ST children and non-SC/ST children, 13.80% and 41.1% of whom are malnourished and undernourished respectively. While the Government of India has adopted the national goal of reducing the present infant mortality rate (IMR) to 60 by 2000, the SC's IMR, child mortality and under-5 mortality is 83.00, 39.50 and 119.3, respectively. Compare this with 61.8, 22.2 and 82.6 for non-SC/STs, respectively.

Similarly, IMR, child mortality and under-5 mortality are 84, 46.3 and 126 among STs. About 72% of births to SC women and 81% of births to ST women took place at home; the corresponding figure for others is 59%. Because of their lower social status, sexual exploitation of SC/ST women is also high. There are some caste-related social customs and religious practices in Hindu society that exploit only women from Dalit communities. One of these customs is devdasi or jogini, involving religious prostitution imposed on unfortunate girls who are married to a village god and then become the subject of sexual exploitation by upper caste men in a village. A primary survey estimates the number of joginis in six districts of Andhra Pradesh at 21,421. There are similar practices in states like Tamil Nadu, Karnataka and Maharashtra where Dalit women are designated devdasis or devotees of god.

CHAPTER 13

The Oppression of Shudras/Dalits in India: A Hindu Liberationist Perspective

The caste system is as old as the Hindu religion itself, in fact, it even predates Hinduism by some centuries. One important thing to know about the caste system is that it was brought into the Indus Valley from the outside by a tribe of semi-nomadic people called the Aryans (the "Noble Ones"), who originally inhabited the steppe country of southern Russia and Central Asia and entered India, through the Indus Valley, around the year 1500 BCE.

The Aryans had a linear sense of time and had a structured caste system with three sets of castes (warrior caste on top, followed by a priestly caste, and then everyone else) and a plethora of mostly male gods, the language that the Aryans spoke was Sanskrit which latter became the basis for Hindi. When the Aryans invaded the Indus Valley the people of the Indus Valley had a religion with no caste system, a circular sense of time (hence the Hindu concept of reincarnation, etc.), and a pantheon of female goddesses.

The fact that the outsider Aryans introduced India to the caste system and was a warrior-centred culture that had a reverence for male gods is one of the reasons why scholars, such as Kalpana Kannabiran argue that "patriarchy is in fact the basis of the caste system and that the patterns of hierarchy, power and authority which characterise the caste system are derived from earlier forms of gender-based oppression."

When the Aryans first invaded the Indus Valley they called the Indus Valley people (Indians) Dasa (Sanskrit for dark-skinned) and the three-tier caste system was morphed into a four-tier caste system called the Four Varnas (which means color); Brahmins, the priestly class were now on the top, Ksatriyas, the warrior class were now below the priests, then their was the Vaishyas, skilled labor, and the Sudras, unskilled labor.

Outside of the caste system were the non-Vedic peoples and the Dalits (the untouchables). Originally the lighter one's skin color was the higher up in the caste system one was (with the Aryans obviously being at the top of the system) and the higher up in the caste system one was the more "pure" that person was (purity was of a huge concern of the Indus Valley people with many ritual and private baths having been excavated).

The majority of the people in the Indus Valley fell within the lower castes which can be seen today since 77% of Indians comprise these lower castes (as well as Dalits, scheduled castes/scheduled tribes [SC/ST], etc.). What this mini-history lesson shows us was that the concept of caste is a concept that was brought into India by outside forces (the patriarchical and warrior culture of the Aryans) which then incorporated itself into the civilization of the Indus Valley people through the Vedas (specifically the Rig Veda).

The Aryans and Brahmins needed a system to keep themselves on top and the majority of the dark-skinned Indus Valley people at the bottom, the caste system was the perfect way to do this, and in fact this had been the case until around 500 BCE when the traditions of the Vedas and the Brahmins began to be attacked by Hindu ascetics.

From around 600 BCE to 200 BCE there was an incredible Vedic development in the Hindu tradition (a philosophic development) which can be described as the "democratization of Hinduism." Out of this philosophic development came the Upanisads (upanisad implies "sitting at the feet of the teacher," Upa=down, Ni=near, and Sad=sit).

The Upanisads were focused on attaining the mystical knowledge that would free a person from "re-death" or punarmrtyu. The Brhadâranyaka Upanisad placed emphasis on the knowledge of the cosmic connection underlying ritual. "When the doctrine of the identity of atman (the Self) and brahman was established in the Upanishads, the true knowledge of the Self and the realization of this identity. substituted the ritual method." Asceticism started becoming more widespread (which was one the factors leading to the creation of the latter Upanisads) in reaction to the rigid doctrines of the Brahmin and of the Vedas.

What's important to note as that even though these ascetics were critical of the Vedas and scathing in their critiques of the Brahmins they were still very much Hindu in nature (in fact, they probably didn't consider themselves anything else, all though the term Hindu wasn't around then) and their philosophical teachings and thought derived from the Vedas.

These ascetics denied that only Brahmins could receive bliss and escape reincarnation and stated that through giving up the world and all desires anyone, whether Dalit or Vaishya, could attain psychic security, or rather, liberation through the attainment of unification with Brahman. Out of reaction to this the Brhamins devised a doctrine called the four asramas (abodes) which dived the life of the "twice born" into four stages" which would keep asceticism in check by confining it to middle-aged males. On top of these ascetics came leaders who led offshoots of Hinduism and breakaway sects such as Siddhartha Gautama (the Buddha) and Vardhamana (Mahavira, the great teacher of Jainism).

These two leaders rejected not only the pleasures of the world, but more importantly, they rejected the claims of the Brahmins and the ritualistic Brahminic schools who claimed authority and superiority over other Hindus and Indians by claiming to be pure and to have the right to perform traditional rituals and sacrifices, as well as having the rights to interpret their meanings.

While the Buddha rejected Hinduism (as well as religion) all together, Mahavira kept to the central aspects of Hinduism while abandoning the rituals that allowed the Brahmins to dominate all aspects of life. Mahavira stated that through one's own efforts one could attain liberation and freedom from rebirth, short of the Buddha, this was one of the most complete rejections of the Brahmins (and in turn their belief in ritual purity and caste) that anyone could have ever articulated.

All of this now brings us to today and to the subject of the liberation of Dalits and to the subject of my final blog in this series, a Hindu Liberationist perspective on the plight of Dalits and of their liberation from caste oppression. What disturbed me about the student protests against the further admission of lower caste and SC/ST students was that these high caste students had the wrong premise that the oppression of lower caste and SC/ST peoples was the "correct" form of Hinduism and the only form that should be practiced (all though I do recognize that some of these students could have been playing the "caste card," claiming caste privilege in order to protect their privilege in society).

Yet we have seen in the ancient history of Hinduism that caste was an outside concept placed upon the Indus Valley people by an outside tribe of semi-nomadic pastoralists, this shows us that the concept of caste didn't grow "organically" from Indian soil but was imposed from the outside, and hence, the shedding of caste ideology and caste oppression would in a sense mean the shedding of outside Aryan domination against the Indian peoples, of course many high caste Indians still adhere to their Aryan roots and view their Brahmin status as a source of pride, not something to overcome in order to help out their lower caste and Dalit sisters and brothers.

Despite the seemingly set in stone concepts of caste in the Rig Veda many Hindus over the preceding centuries fought back against the Brahminic elite and questioned the writings of the Vedas, especially the writings on ritualistic purity (a major concept in caste ideology) and on the "privileges" of the Brahmin caste. Whether it was the radical Siddhartha Gautama, who renounced Hinduism, or Vardhamana, who used acetic concepts of Hindu thought to criticize the present day establishment, thoughtful Hindus and the ever evolving Hindu religion never laid down and accepted the perverse policies of the Brahmin and their constant quest for power.

Because of this we can see that Hinduism was never a monolithic religion that accepted the Vedas sayings on caste and ritual as blindly as present day Hindu nationalist BJP (Bharatiya Janata Party) and RSS (Rashtriya Svayamsevak Sangh) supporters would like us to think. History has shown us that a thoughtful and pious Hindu can be one who rejects certain ideas of Vedic thought that are oppressive and evil and history has also shown us within the Hindu tradition there has always been an ever evolving struggle for freedom against the Brahminic caste in the realm of the physical and the realm of the spiritual, such as reclaiming concepts of freedom from rebirth and attaining liberation by being joined with Brahmin.

With this in mind I will now actually tackle (in part VI, the final part, of this series) the problems of the caste system and the oppressions Dalits have faced over the centuries (especially the 20th century and now) and how Dalits will be the ones to actually bring about change in this present day situation and how Dalits are the only ones to bring about their own salvation (not from outside help from people such as Gandhi or someone like myself) and how the Hindu religion plays a role in this, and how it can play a liberating role instead of the role of oppressor.

CHAPTER 14 Income Generating Schemes for SC, ST, OBC, Minorities and Women

Govt of India at the Centre, took up the task of the Nation as whole, with all seriousness, after Independance. Govt set up a Planning Commission at the Centre, amidst many opposition, resentments and criticisms. The Party in Power, Congress appeared to be fully committed for the Development of the Nation, Welfare of the Society as a whole, and all Sections of the Society. That appeared to be inevitable in a Democracy, and a Republic. Moreover, the Congress Party during the Freedom Movement and after, had been in all Public Statements, championing the cause of the Weaker Sections like the SCs&STs, Minorities, OBCs and Women. And Special Provisions had also been made in the Constitution, for the Development of the Poor and the Weak in the Country. Further, many specific Provisions have been incorporated in the Constitution for the Welfare, Development and Protection of different Weaker Sections of the Society, like SCs, STs, Minorities, OBCs and Women. The Constitutional Promises and Guarantees, and Legal Protections for the SCs&STs were followed by the Congress Govts, with Reservations in Services.

This has helped a good number of them in different regions to participate in different spheres of National Activities, Development, Administration and Governance, where Reservations have been allowed to operate. The Scientific Socialistic Development and Justice oriented Modern Vision of Jawaharlal Nehru, the first Prime Minister of India, and his choice to go in for Planned Development through Five-Year Plans, laid a great emphasis in Developing all the Weaker Sections. In addition, Special Programmes and Schemes were also taken for the Welfare, Growth and Development of many SCs, STs, Minorities, OBCs and Women from amongst them, as well as other Women. These helped, to improve the standards of the lives of the Weaker Sections, in a Nation where they were otherwise marginalised, neglected and oppressed, depending on the situation.

Need for Development of the Weaker Sections – the SCs STs OBCs and Minorities

The SCs STs OBCs and Minorities, have been forced to remain as the Weaker Sections of India, and the Women confined or oppressed to be the most and multiply exploited sections of the Country, for nearly four millenniums. This bad situation, can not and should not continue anymore. Definitely not in the Twenty-first Century of the third millennium, in an age of fast travel and mass communication. There is a need for the Govts to do something special and tangible, to free and liberate the Weaker Sections, from the cobwebs of oppression, marginalisation and backwardness. They have to be uplifted to the levels of normal human-beings of the World.

The Then Prime Minister Jawaharlal Nehru's Views

The need to Develop the Weaker Sections, and the sensitivity with which appropriate Policies have to be adopted, can be better appreciated by what Jawaharlal Nehru, the then Prime Minister of the Nation, wrote on 9th Oct 1958 regarding Development of the STs. We can not allow matters to drift in the Tribal Areas, or just not take interest in them. In the World of today, that is not possible or desirable. At the same time, we should avoid over-administrating these areas, and in particular, sending too many outsiders into Tribal Territory. It is between these two extreme positions that we have to function. Development in various ways there has to be, such as communications, medical facilities, education and better agriculture. These avenues of Development should, however, be pursued within the broad framework of the following five fundamental principles;

1. People should Develop along the lines of their own genius, and we should avoid imposing anything on them. We should try to Encourage in every way their own Traditional Arts and Culture.

2. Tribal Rights in Land and Forests should be respected
3. We should try to Train and Build up a team of their own people to do the work of Administration and Development. Some technical personnel from outside will, no doubt, be needed, especially in the beginning. But we should avoid introducing too many outsiders into tribal territory
4. We should not over-administer these areas, or overwhelm them with a multiplicity of Schemes. We should rather work through, and not in rivalry to, their own social and cultural institutions
5. We should judge results, not by statistics or the amount of money spent, but by the quality of human character that is evolved.

The above reflects the special sensitivity with which the then Prime Minister, approached the issue of Tribal Development. We should have by now developed adequate strategies for the Development of Scheduled Castes, OBCs, Minorities and Women. Special Strategies should have been evolved for the Women from SCs&STs, OBCs and Minority Communities, who suffer the most in the Country. Special steps should have been taken, particularly for the SC&ST Women, who were subjected to multiple exploitations as –

1. poor and helpless people
2. SCs&STs
3. at times as Minority Community SCs&STs, and
4. top of them all as easily vulnerable Women

Sadly, even today there are no special Cells in the Planning Commission even for the 260 million plus SCs&STs. How then can we really hope that, the Weaker Sections of the Country will ever be developed? The Development of the Weaker Sections have to have a bearing on their Occupation, Problems, Requirements, Needs and Aspirations.

Problems of the Weaker Sections

1. Lack of Income Generating Assets and Resources
2. Lack of Regular Income
3. Lack of Access to Finances
4. Non-availability of regular Employment

5. Low Wages
6. Indebtedness
7. Shortage of Food and Fodder
8. Difficulties in getting Water
9. Landlessness
10. Homelessness
11. Sickness, lack of timely Medical Aid and adequate Health Care
12. Illiteracy Ignorance and Superstitions
13. Cheating by middlemen and Contractors
14. Oppression of their Communities
15. Suppression of the promising and developing individuals and families
16. Discrimination
17. Non-Payment of proper Wages

General Occupations of the Weaker Sections

1. Cultivators
2. Marginal Farmers
3. Seasonal Agricultural Labourers
4. Employees in Household Industries
5. Home Services and Repairs
6. Public Services like Security and Scavenging
7. Leather Workers
8. Skilled and Unskilled Workers
9. Producers of Handicrafts
10. Process Units
11. Petty Manufacture
12. Domestic Helpers
13. Casual Workers
14. Other Workers

Strategies and Approach for Planning Development

1. Market Induced Plans
2. Trickledown Theory

3. Financial Assistance to Individuals
   a) Loans for specific Projects
   b) Bridge Loans to facilitate Financial Assistance
   c) Govt Subsidies as Incentives
   d) Govt Aid as help
   e) Grants to special Programmes
4. Promotion of Co-operatives
5. Encouraging Community Development
6. State Intervention at Community Level
7. Pro-Active Target Groups oriented Schemes

Requirements of the Weaker Sections

1. Literacy
2. General Education
3. Professional Education
4. Health Education
5. Residential and Ashram Schools
6. Book-Banks
7. Freeships for primary education
8. Scholarships for higher studies
9. Fellowships for study abroad
10. Special Hostels for SCs, STs, OBCs, Minorities for Boys
11. Special Hostels for SCs, STs, OBCs, Minorities for Girls
12. Admissions into general Students Hostels of the Colleges and Universities
13. Skills Training Centres
14. Coaching Centres for Civil Services and Banking Exams

There is a need to address these basic problems first and fully. Therefore the Programmes and Schemes being designed developed evolved and implemented, should address these problems appropriately and fully, not casually in passing or incidentally.

Weaker Sections Development Programmes

All Development Programmes can be classified as –

1. LONG-TERM PROGRAMMES

a) General Area Development Programmes
b) General Community Development Programmes
c) Special-Group Oriented Plans
   i) Tribal Sub Plans for STs
   ii) Settlement of Nomadic and de-notified Tribes
   iii) Improving the Working Conditions of Sweepers
   iv) Improving the Working Conditions of Flayers and Cobblers
   v) Special-Component Plans for SCs
   vi) Development of specific Backward Classes like Gold-Smiths, Weavers, Fishermen etc
d) Socio-Economic Programmes
e) Human-Development Programmes
   i) Upgradation of Skills
   ii) General Education and Employment
   iii) Professional Education
   iv) Management Training
   v) Entrepreneurship Training to set up Industries, set-up Business etc
   vi) Loans to start Economic activities

2. SHORT-TERM PROGRAMMES
   a) Training to impart Skills
   b) Financial Assistance to set up Rural Development Programmes
      i) Cottage Industries
      ii) Mini-Economic Activities
3. EMERGENCY PROGRAMMES
   a) To meet crisises
   b) To meet disasters and natural calamities
4. POVERTY ALLEVIATION PROGRAMMES

Development Approach

1. Individual oriented
2. Community centred
3. Cluster approach

4. Saturation approach
5. Integration approach

Need for Poverty Alieviation Programmes

The present Govt and the PM had publicly shrunk away to slip out of all Political and Community Responsibilities. They want to wriggle out of the Social Contract with the People and Society for Human Development. That includes General Education of the Children, employment, health care, environmental hygiene, housing and transportation. These and the growing Corruption in Public Services, have left the Govts short-strapped of funds. Hence, they are no more in a position to take up and find money to finance time bound tangible Developmental Programmes for Welfare Schemes. Hence, the Govts are forced to take up just a little bit of Poverty Alleviation Programmes, to keep the people satisfied a little.

Govts' Efforts to Develop Weaker Sections

General and overall Developmental Planning in the Country, was launched in 1951, in the form of Five-Year Plans. When the Five-Year Plans could not be finalised due to Political and other Considerations, Annual-plans were adopted. All these Plans, took into consideration the need to Develop the Poor and the Weaker Sections. It kept in view the concerns of the first Prime Minister of India, which was subsequently evolved as the Policy of the Govt and Planning Commission. The First Five-Year Plan, during the years of 1951-56 believed in Trickle-Down Theory.

It envisaged that Programmes under various sectors of Development would benefit all sections of Population including the Weaker Sections of Society. But sadly, this reliance failed and the expectations were belied. Benefits of Development never reached the poor and the weak, for obvious reasons. Hence, Special Programmes for the Backward Classes were formulated, especially and separately under the Backward Classes Sector, with a very Small Backward Class Division in Planning Commission, New Delhi. The Special Requirements of SCs&STs were particularly taken into account. The Second Plan over the years 1956-61, was formulated with the promise to ensure that, Economic and Social Benefits of National Development would accrue to the Backward Classes also, and to the relatively much marginalised and less privileged SCs&STs. These were expected to bridge the gaps between the dominant castes and the weaker Sections on the one hand, and lift the neglected SCs&STs at least to near the levels of the Other Backward Classes. The important component of the Second Plan, were separate Tribal Development Plans, with respect and understanding of their Culture and Traditions. This was based on the Philosophy of Panchsheel for Tribal Area Administration and Development enunciated by the first Prime Minister of the Nation.

During the Plan, 43 Special Multi-Purpose Tribal Blocks were opened, which later became Tribal development Blocks for about 25,000 Tribals as against the normal 65,000 per Block. The Third Plan of the Years 1961-66 and the three Annual Plans during 1966-69, advocated Greater Equality of Opportunities, and reduction in the Economic Disparities and differences in Income and Wealth in the Society. Its thrust was towards even distribution of wealth, reduction of inequalities in the community, and levelling up the economic power of most sections of the society. The Fourth Plan of 1969-74 envisaged, the Basic Goal of Rapid Increase in the Standard of Living of the People, through measures which also Promoted Equality and Social Justice. In 1971-71, six pilot-projects were set up in Andhra Pradesh, Bihar, Madhya Pradesh and Orissa, with a separate Tribal Development Agency for each Project. The Fifth Plan during the Years 1974-79, was a watershed for the STs.

In the Year 1975-76, Tribal Sub-Plan was launched, by keeping aside Plan Funds for the Development Scheduled Tribe Areas with exclusive allocations for specific and separate Programmes and Schemes for STs Welfare and Development. This approach, and its success was appropriately copied and adopted for the Welfare of SCs in the subsequent Plans. The Annual Plan of 1979-80, saw the launching of the Special Component Plan for SCs so that they could also receive their due share of Plan Allocations and Benefits of Development from various Developmental Sectors. This facilitated convergence and pooling of available resources and Plan Allocations from every Sector to Develop the SCs in proportion to the SC Population in the Society. The Sixth Plan 1980-85 continued with the SCP for SCs which became a significant feature of the Five-Year Plans, along with TSP for the STs.

These facilitated monitoring and evaluation of the Development of both SCs and STs. The Seventh Plan 1985-90, saw the strengthening of SCP and TSP, with the flow of funds from the State Plans, Central Plans and Special Central Assistance (SCA) and Institutional Finance, facilitating enlargement of infrastructures and expansion of their coverage to benefit more SCs&STs. In 1989, National SC&ST Finance Development Corporation (NSFDC) to provide loans to SCs&STs for taking up gainful and profitable self-employment productive activities, and business was established. The Eighth Plan 1992-97, aimed at bridging the gap between the Development of the Weaker Sections and others, by the beginning of the Twenty-first Century.

The Ninth Plan 1997-2002 was said would Empower the Socially Disadvantaged Groups to become agents of Change and Development by themselves. It was expected to create an enabling Environment Conducive for SCs&STs, Minorities and OBCs to exercise their rights freely to enjoy all privileges, and lead a life with confidence and dignity at par with the rest of the society. Disparities were to be removed, exploitation and suppression eliminated, protection provided to the disadvantaged groups of Weaker Sections, such that benefits of Development would *reach the unreached* through Equitable Distribution and Social Justice. These it was said would facilitate the weaker sections not merely as beneficiaries but also as participants in the Planning and Implementation of the Developmental Process. It was expected that funds would also flow to Women of the Weaker Sections, for their Development.

However belied till-date, were all the Promises to the People about –

1. Social Empowerment
2. Economic Empowerment, and
3. Social Justice

During the Year 1997, at the time of the 11th Lok Sabha, five Office Memorandums, affecting the Reservations in Employment of not only SCs&STs but also the OBCs were introduced.

The unkindest cut of all, came during the 12th Parliament, when this Govt brought out the sixth OM. It remains to be the most dangerous of all the Black Anti-Reservation OMs. It deprives the SCs, STs and OBCs who come up on top to be in the merit list, their position in the merit list, if they had otherwise availed of any concessions as SCs/STs/OBCs. This one, without any provocation or Court Judgement whatsoever.

Importance of Income Generating Schemes

The World is now wise to believe in the Chinese Proverb – *It is better to teach an hungry individual to fish, than give a fish to eat, least the individual may come back again for the next fish.* Therefore it is good to introduce people to Income Generating Schemes, to take up their life and future in their own hands, than help them with food or doles or any other form of financial or material assistance.

Development of Scheduled Castes and Scheduled Tribes

The basic need of the SCs&STs was to end their forced Segregation by the Caste System. The best Strategy that could be considered was Reservations for SCs & STs. Reserving the dues of SCs & STs to SCs & STs, was the only way to ensure their proportionate share in all walks of life. As a result of Baba Saheb's Struggles, and his demands in the First and Second Round Table Conferences in 1930-32, the British agreed to provide some Reservations.

Political Reservations for SCs & STs

Of these only Political Reservations, though time-bound are compulsory and inescapable, being a firm Constitutional Provision. This opened the way for the SCs & STs to participate in the Governance of the Country, directly to some extent possible, and force the Govts to take the Problems of SCs & STs seriously, and Plan for their Welfare and Development.

However, there are no Reservations for SCs in the Upper Houses in the Centre and the States. As a result, the Representation of SCs & STs in the Upper Houses are still poor. There is a need to introduce Reservations for SCs & STs in Rajya Sabha in Parliament, and Legislative Councils in the States.

RESERVATION IN EMPLOYMENT FOR SCs & STs and to OBCs at the time of making Appointments.

Reservation in Employment, though without any time-limit, is only an enabling Provision in the Constitution, that also in Public

Services. It is therefore left to the discretion of the Bureaucrats, Governments, Parliament and Legislative Assemblies. This was the Most Effective Programme for the Development of SC&ST Communities.

Reservation in Employment is a means for Community Participation in the Governance of the Country through Administration, its Executive Functions, and Decision making roles for day to day business of the Govts. It should not be-as it is often prone to – mixed with the Development of any Individual or family. It should not be seen just as a means of Employment, for getting a respectable and regular income as wages pay and allowances or salary every month. Yes, Employment of the Individuals are incidental to reservations in services. From 1990, Reservations for OBCs at the time of making Appointments had been introduced. It was challenged vehemently in all Political Fora, in every possible manner in Society, in the educational Institutions, and in the Streets. Hence the Govt of India, mad compensatory Reservations in favour of the poor amongst the dominant castes. In spite of this, the decision of the Govt in introducing Reservations for the OBCs in the matters of Appointments was challenged in the Supreme Court. The Supreme Court finally in its Judgement in 1992, upheld the Reservations for OBCs, at the time of making Appointments. But, they set aside the compensatory Reservations for the Poor amongst all other Dominant Sections of the Society.

Employment of an individual, is the best and direct method of Developing the Individual, family, the larger family associated with the person to a large extent, and the section and area of the community from where the individual hails, to a certain extent. For, it helps to provide a decent and regular income over a period of 30 to 40 years, depending upon the age of the individual at the time of recruitment and employment, and type of job employment and retirement age. And it provides encouragement, facilitates guidance and incentives for others around to study and seek better and higher employment. Therefore, it is suggested that SC & ST Institutions, should directly employ SCs & STs as much as possible, as it is in the case of other Minority Institutions.

Reservations Available

Today Reservations for the SCs & STs are available in –

1. Political Reservations in Parliament (Lower House of the People-Lok Sabha) and the State and UT Legislative Assemblies (Lower House of the People)
2. Reservations in Employment
3. Reservations in Education
4. Reservations for Economic Development
5. Some Reservations in Housing

Need for Reservations in Private Sector

It is sad that today, with Liberalisation and Privatisation of even Govt Sector, Banks, Public Sector Enterprises, the Job Opportunities where the SCs & STs can reasonably hope to get a fair-play in the selections, or get jobs at least through Reservations in Employment, have shrunk. The present Govts, are in a hurry to Privatise. It helps the Private Sector, to walk away with the Govt Enterprises at throw away prices, fixed by some private appraisers again to the advantage of the private sector. And, it has not built any Safety-Clauses to protect Reservations in Employment, in the PSUs being Disinvested or sold off, or even protect those SC & ST Employees working already in the PSUs. There is an urgent need for these.

There is a need to evolve Reservation in all establishments, that make use of the Natural Resources of the Nation, like Land, Water and Man Power, even if they bring in their own money to the extent of 100%

Sabotaging Reservations

At present, Reservations in Services are under threat. They are being directly attacked by various Unions, dominant caste Welfare Associations, private individuals and even by some individual Advocates. While some of the staff and employees manipulate the existing Reservations, particularly the Rosters meant to identify the Vacancies to be Reserved for SCs, STs and OBCs, even senior officers are not free from these prejudices. At the slightest opportunity, they change the Reservation Policy, Rules and Orders, to the disadvantage of SCs, STs and OBCs. There appears to have emerged, an unholy understanding between the dominant castes advocates, officials of the courts, judges and senior officers, to Sabotage Reservations in Services.

Reservation in Education for SCs & STs

Reservation in Education, is only part of the Directive Principles to the State in the Constitution. Therefore the same is left to the sweet will and purely for the political considerations of the Govts in Power at the centre and in the States or Union Territories. Again due to Liberalisation, and opening of Education to Private Entrepreneurs and Business People, admissions has become difficult and costly, cost of Education had gone prohibitively high, and the quality of education in most private educational institutions has become worthless turning out unemployable and unsuitable graduates. On the other-hand rich dominant castes have managed to buy their way into these private institutions to virtually purchase their professional degrees and mange even well paid jobs thereafter, leaving the SCs & STs in the lurch. Now, there is a big hostile threat to the Education of the SCs & STs, and all other Weaker Sections, including the Minorities, OBCs and Women from the SCs, STs, Minorities and OBCs. The strategies being silently adopted are –

1. Intervention through Courts and direct Administrative Orders behind the back of Parliament, without any discussions to deny Admissions in Medicine, Engineering, Science, Post-Graduate Studies, Specialities and Super-Speciality Courses
2. Prohibitive Increase of Fees including Library Hostel and Examination Fees
3. Privatisation of Education that charge very very high fees and heavy admission charges in black
4. Passing out Doctors Engineers etc, without proper teaching and training, due to lack of Teaching Faculty, Laboratories and Workshops, leaving them unsuitable for good jobs
5. Turning out Doctors Engineers etc in thousands, that there is wide-spread unemployment and under-employment even amongst them

The main aim of many dominant castes, and thrust of their thinking plans and actions is to keep the Weaker Sections, still jobless, without adequate income, helpless, hopeless, weak and dependent.

Reservation in Economic Development for SCs & STs

Reservation in Economic Development, is again only part of

the Directive Principles to the State in the Constitution. As a result the Schemes and Programmes are so lob sided, and practically serve no purpose. Fifty-five years of Independence could not develop any SC or ST really as an entrepreneur or as Industrialist or Business-Person.

The SCs & STs today lag far behind the others, though by way of Education and Employment in Public Services they might have developed much better in the past. That, thanks to the Statesmanship, Vision and Policies pursued by Baba Saheb, Babuji, Jawaharlal Nehru and Indira Gandhi. Today, with all round unrestrained liberalisation and privatisation without any human face had increased unbridled corruption in every sector. This makes all the more difficult for the SCs & STs to get any loans or plans cleared through even Govt Departments, without paying speed money and bribe. And most SCs & STs can not afford to pay any. As a result, even most educated and well-experienced SCs & STs are finding it difficult to make use of any Economic Development Programmes meant for SCs & STs.

Reservation in Housing for SCs & STs

Reservation in Housing, is also only part of the Directive Principles to the State in the Constitution. Entry of private sector in housing in a very big way because of liberalisation, is pushing the prices of houses high to the sky, leaving almost all the SCs & STs except those in good jobs, helpless. It has become impossible for many SCs & STs to think of buying any house. Not only that, the private builders are edging the SCs & STs to push them out from their small pieces of land and homes, to make way for new posh elite houses and shopping complexes. All these raise many folds the rents, forcing out the SCs & STs out of the cities or into miserable hovels in heavily congested city slums in hygienically bad and dangerous places.

Reasons for Attack on Reservations

1. Intolerance of the dominant castes
2. Jealousy about the development and progress of SCs & STs
3. Fear of the Development OBCs
4. Fear of loosing easy unlimited and cheap Labour from unemployed OBC and SC & ST Communities

5. Manipulating Staff in Administration and Establishment Sections
6. Intolerance of officials, including senior Officers
7. Interfering Judiciary
8. Collaboration between private individuals, dominant caste groups, advocates, court staff the judges and personnel officers including many senior officials, at times with the support and patronage of some political parties leaders and activists

Reservations Under Threat

Reservations to SCs & STs and OBCs have always been resisted. For, that is the one Programme, which had benefited the SCs & STs forcibly placed at the bottom of the Society in all walks of life for nearly four millennium years, to –

1. Participate in the Politics of the Country
2. Take part in the Governance of the Country in proportion to their Population in the Society
3. Force the Govt to get due Shares in at least some walks of life in proportion to their Population in the Society
4. Take some part in the Administration of the Public Services, even without political clout, or money to pay any speed money or corruption
5. Get Professional Education in proportion to their Population in the Society

General, Special, And SC & ST Financial Institutions Fail

As far as Economic Development Programmes are concerned, the Country had seen much significant progress, particularly when we take into account the infrastructure, educational, scientific, professional and managerial base of the Country, at the time of Independence in 1947. But, at the same-time, the relative development and progress of either the SC & ST Individuals, or SC & ST Community is miserably insignificant. Banks, even after Nationalisation had failed the SCs & STs. So, did the Special Financial Institutions like NABARD, SIDBI etc. The general State Financial Institutions had not bothered to look at the SCs & STs or their proposals. Some States had come up with exclusive SC & ST Financial Corporations. Apart from the initial successes and hope, these could not do much. Hence in 1989, a National SC & ST Finance and Development Corporation was established by the Govt of India, in New Delhi. Sadly, that also had let down the SCs & STs. National Safai-Karamcharis Finance and Development Corporation was established in January 1997. And in 2001, NSFDC had been split into separate SC Corporation and ST Corporation. However nothing much is being done by these Corporations. The main reasons for the failure by the SC & ST Financial Institutions are –

1. Employment of non-SCs & STs for helping develop SC & ST Dalits
2. Employment of totally unsuitable individuals, at times even anti-SCs or anti-STs or anti-SCs & STs, irrespective of the fact whether they are SCs or STs or none.
3. Corruption
4. Lack of Planning – non-existence of any Planning Department
5. Non-organisation of Entrepreneur Training Programmes
6. Absence of any Portfolio of Projects to guide and help prospective SC & ST Entrepreneurs, and
7. Unwillingness and uncooperative attitudes of many officials there in to help the SCs and STs.

In many cases, it takes anywhere four to five years, before the Loan is sanctioned. Many individuals had returned frustrated and disillusioned, without any assistance from these Corporations. On the top of these, the Financial Assistance being extended by these two National Corporations are so paltry, that they are far less than many State SC & ST Corporations. Thus, they are not in a position to Develop any SC or ST, even as a Small Scale Industry Entrepreneur.

Special Strategy for Development of SCs

During the Annual Plan of 1979-80 and subsequently from the sixth Five-Year Plan, TSP was appropriately adopted as the Special Component Plan (SCP for the Scheduled Castes Development) with SCA as additive.

Specific Strategy for Development of STs

In 1974, during the fifth Five-Year Plan, Tribal Sub-Plan (TSP for Tribal Welfare and Development) was introduced, as an important Group Oriented Part of the Plan, with Special Central Assistance (SCA) as additive.

Protection and Development of Minorities

Planning Commission has reported that non-availability of authentic data makes it difficult to assess their socio-economic status. Surveys conducted by the National council for Applied Economic Research (NCAER) New Delhi in 1994 had indicated 33,230 Rural Muslim Households in 16 States as Educationally and Economically Backward. Till date, the following Programmes and Schemes have been taken up –

1. Twenty Point Programme for Development of the Poor and Weaker Sections
2. Fifteen Point Programme for Minorities
3. Special Area Programmes
4. Area Intensive Programmes for Educationally Backward Minorities
5. Maulana Azad Education Foundation 1992-93 to run
   - i) residential schools
   - ii) construction/expansion schools
   - iii) colleges
   - iv) equipment for laboratories
   - v) polytechnics
   - vi) purchase of machinery
   - vii) vocational/technical training centres for women
   - viii) hostels mainly for girls
   - ix) remedial coaching
6. Reservations at the time of recruitments to Public Services during the Ninth Plan
7. Pre-Examination Coaching Centres
8. Pre-Metric and Post-Metric Scholarships for OBC Students
9. OBC Boys and Girls Hostels for Students
10. Modernisation of Madrasas with upgradation of syllabuses therein with science, maths, social-studies, Hindi and English, and 100% finance for appointment of qualified teachers

11. National Minorities Commission
12. National Minorities Finance and Development Corporation, established in 1994-95, for promoting self-employment and income generation activities
13. Scheme of Micro-Financing from 1998-99, through Non-Govt Organisations (NGOs) and Self Help Groups (SHGs)

Schemes and Programmes for Women and Children

Educationally Women and Girl Children from the weaker Sections of the Society lag far behind others, and their own men and boys. They still remain as the weakest link in every respect, though they are in the forefront in economic activities, both as small cultivators and landless agricultural workers. Often prejudices, biases, superstitions, ignorance, illiteracy, and the inability of their families to provide them and support them to go for education are the principal causes. This, though girls out perform boys in studies, both in the schools and colleges.

Schemes and Programmes for Development of OBCs

OBCs traditionally are part of the main workforce in agriculture and almost all other productive and service sectors. Strangely, it is for this reason of their living as workers and producers, they are treated as the Shudras and OBCs. The OBCs are generally farmers and or artisans-the small cultivators, agricultural labourers, artisans, weavers, tailors, potters, carpenters, blacksmiths, goldsmiths, mud and stone quarry workers, fishermen, construction workers etc of the Country. However, most of these occupations OBCs, often overlap in many places and parts of the Country, with that of SCs, STs and Minorities, who are the other part of the main workforce in the Country. Education of OBCs was promoted with special care by some States, particularly in the South. Specific Educational Development of OBCs started as a Central Programme, in the Ninth Plan.

The present OBC Developmental Programmes are –

1. Twenty Point Programme for Development of the Poor and Weaker Sections
2. Special Area Programmes
3. Reservations at the time of recruitments to Public Services during the Ninth Plan

4. Pre-Examination Coaching Centres
5. Pre-Metric and Post-Metric Scholarships for OBC Students
6. OBC Boys and Girls Hostels for Students
7. Commission for Backward Classes
8. National Backward Classes Finance and Development Corporation, established in 1992 for promoting self-employment and income generation activities

Schemes and Programmes for Development

Special Schemes and Programmes are required for the general and overall Welfare and Development of the Weaker Sections. Important amongst them are-

Long-Term Programmes and Schemes Required

1. Allotment of Land – Distribution of Waste and Surplus Land
2. Development and Management of Water Resources
3. Development of Fisheries and Fishing Rights for Weaker Sections
4. Watershed Development Management and Preservation
5. Soil and Moisture Conservation Measures
6. Afforestation of Waste Lands, denuded Forests and Protection of Forests, particularly from Contractors and Poachers
7. Social Forestry, Farm and Industrial Forestry
8. Livestock Development
9. Animal Husbandry-Dairy and Poultry Development
10. Development of Horticulture, Floriculture etc
11. Special Co-operatives for Development and Welfare of Weaker Sections
12. Cottage Industries, Mini-Industries and Small-Industries

Short-Term Programmes and Schemes Required

1. Rehabilitation of Displaced Persons
2. Collection and Marketing of Minor Forest Produce (MFP)
3. Traditional Rights of the Tribals, harvesting and sustainable use of Forestry
4. Development of Pasture Lands
5. Development of Subsidiary Occupations

6. Medical and Public Health Programmes in Rural and Remote Areas, including Mobile Dispensaries
7. Protected Safe Drinking Water for use by the Weaker Sections
8. Irrigation of Small and Marginal Lands of the Weaker Sections
9. All weather Approach Roads, and drainage where Weaker Sections live
10. Electrification or Solar Lighting in areas where the Weaker Sections live
11. Sanitary Facilities like at least Community Bath Rooms and Toilets for use by the Weaker Sections, particularly for Women
12. Prevention of Atrocities
13. Protection from Money Lenders
14. Grains Storage (Grain Golas) and Protection from Traders Agents and Middle-men
15. Abolition of Scavenging
16. Special Housing for and Schools for Scavengers
17. Abolition of Bonded Labour
18. Prevention of Child Labour
19. Working Women Hostels
20. Crèches for Children near work spots
21. Hostels for Children
22. Ashram and Residential Schools

Steps Taken by Govt of India

Significant steps taken by the Govt of India are –

1. Separate Ministry/ Department for Women and Child Development
2. Women's Commission
3. Integrated Child Development Services (ICDS) to provide a package of 6 basic Services –
   i) Health
   ii) Immunisation
   iii) Supplementary Feeding
   iv) Referral Services

v) Non-formal pre-School Education, and

vi) Health and Nutrition for children below 6 years and expectant and nursing mothers living in most backward and rural areas and urban slums

4. Hostels for SC Girls started in 1961-62 to improve enrolment and reduce drop-outs
5. Hostels for ST Girls to increase their enrolment and reduce drop-outs
6. Hostels for OBC Girls to encourage them to enrol and reduce drop-outs
7. Hostels for Minority Girls to help their education
8. Special-Educational Development Programmes for SC & ST Girls belonging to Low Literacy Districts introduced in 1996-97
9. Special residency Schools for SC & ST Girls to first generation learners in 48 Districts of Bihar, MP, Rajasthan and UP where literacy was less than 2% in 1981 Census
10. Central Assistance to Zilla Parishads to run schools or through NGOs
11. Pre-Examination Coaching Centres

Available Programmes and Schemes

Govt has come up, from time to time, with a number of Schemes and Programmes for the Weaker Sections. They are –

Short-term Programmes

1. Bank-Loans for Higher Education
2. Creation of Community Assets
3. Infrastructure Building

Long-term Programmes

1. Education

a) Special Schools for STs, SCs, Minorities and Girl Children

b) Residential and Ashram Schools

c) Freeships, Scholarships, Fellowships and Bank Loans at Low Interest

d) Girls' Hostels for STs, SCs, OBCs and Minorities

e) Colleges and Hostels for Women
f) Working Women's Hostels

2. Distribution of Surplus Land to SCs & STs
3. Reservation in Education
4. Reservation in Jobs for SCs & STs and OBCs
5. Reservations in Job Promotions for SCs & STs

Poverty Alleviation Programmes

1. Integrated Rural Development Programme (IRDP)
2. Drought Prone Areas Programme (DPAP)
3. Multi-Purpose Tribal Development Blocks
4. Jawahar Gram Samridhi Yojna (JGSY)
5. Pradhan Mantri Gramodaya Yojana 2000-01 (PMGY)
6. Pradhan Mantri Gramodaya Yojana – Gramin Awas (PMGY–Gramin Awas)
7. Pradhan Mantri Gramodaya Yojana – Rural Drinking Water Project (PMGY-RDWP)
8. Pradhan Mantri Gram Sadak Yojana 2000 (PMGSY)
9. Antyodaya Anna Yojana 20001 (AAY)
10. Annapurna 2000
11. Indira Awass Yojana (IAY)
12. Valmiki Ambedkar Awas Yojana 2001 (VAMBAY)

Income Generating Schemes

1. National Rural Employment Programme (NREP)
2. Rural Landless Employment Guarantee Programme (RLEGP)
3. Training of Rural Youth for Self-Employment (TRYSEM)
4. Village and Small Industries (VSL)
5. Minimum Needs Programme (MNP)
6. Employment Assurance Scheme (EAS)
7. Swarnajayanti Gram Swarozgar Yojana 1999 (SGSY)
8. Sampoorna Grameen Rozgar Yojna 2001 (SGRY with EAS and JGSY integrated)
9. Jai Prakash Rozgar Guarantee Yojana (JPRGY)
10. Swarna Jayanti Shahari Rozgar Yojana (SJSRY)

GAPS in the Implementation of PAP and IGS

Though there are multiple numbers of Poverty Alleviation Programmes, and Income Generating Programmes, in reality they are parts of the original Community Development Programmes, conceived and taken up immediately after Independence. That had been muted modified renamed or separated from the original main scheme, to make them appear new. This, just to fool the people. Sometimes, few old ones have been clubbed together, under a new name, or merged together as a new programme. All these are really confusing, to even the educated. The poor Weaker Sections are therefore totally confused, and are totally at the mercy of the Block and District Level Officials, especially those in the Rural Areas.

Implementation and effectiveness of PAP and IGS are found to be wanting in many respects, that the achievements and progress are too small and negligible. The main Reasons are –

1. Inadequacy of the Schemes
2. Absence of Appropriate Technology
3. Failure to evolve Right Strategies to implement and manage the Schemes
4. Poor Implementation
5. Absence of Guidance
6. Lack of Monitoring
7. Defects in Identification of the Target Groups
8. Faulty Selection of Beneficiaries
9. Over emphasis on Traditional Agriculture and Animal Husbandry based programmes
10. Failing to Restructure Cropping Patterns
11. Lack of Extension Work to promote and adopt profitable farm practices amongst the Weaker Sections and Small Farmers
12. Non-introduction of appropriate cash-crops
13. Not Developing Orchards and Floriculture suitable to small farmers and marginal land-holders
14. Lack of Publicity amongst the Target Groups to create Awareness about the Programmes, particularly the details of the Schemes, Subsidy, Govt Aid if any, the Loan Component, as well as the time of duration and repayment

Inadequacy of the Programmes and Schemes

Main Reasons for the failure to Develop the Weaker Sections are their inadequacies –

1. Failure to dovetail the Schemes to the Problems of the Weaker Sections and relate them to the Requirements, Needs and Aspirations of the beneficiaries
2. Leakage of Funds
3. Diversion of Funds
4. Non-Utilisation of Funds
5. Corruption

Every Programme and Scheme taken up for implementation should have a bearing, on the beneficiaries poverty levels, indebtedness and income. Only then, the benefits of development could really lift the Weaker Sections out of their poverty. That alone would make them economically independent and socially self-sufficient, to interact with others without fear and on equal terms. Otherwise, the Programmes and Schemes would not only fail, but lead to more indebtedness of the Weaker Sections.

Realities!

The Govt claims that Poverty Alleviation Programmes have been strengthened. More Funds have been provided to generate Additional Employment, create Productive Assets, impart Technical and Entrepreneurial Skills. These are expected to encourage Self-Employment, increase Jobs, reduce unemployment and raise the Income Levels of the Poor. However Govt is silent about plugging the holes in the system. There is no realistic account of the leakages and diversion of funds, mis-utilisation and non-utilisation, or surrender of funds and corruption. The money actually reaching the Weaker Sections, in spite of the Plan Outlays, Budgetary Provisions, and Funds Released is not known. But the effects of Govts' efforts are disappointing. The latest quin-quennial Survey, by National Survey Organisation on Employment and Unemployment, 55th Round 1999-2000 indicates a disappointing trend. The Rate of Growth of Employment on Current Daily Status (CDS) basis declined from 2.7% per annum in 1983-1994 to 1.07% per annum during 1994-2000. However, this decline in the Rate of Growth of Employment compares adversely to the higher growth of GDP.

The present position in the Country sadly indicate –

1. decline in labour intensity of production
2. mechanisation and automation
3. deliberate strategy by the employers to reduce employment rate per rupee invested, and every rupee of output
4. concentration of wealth in the hands of a few
5. increase in relative poverty
6. sharp decline in the rate of growth of labour force
7. increase in the number of unemployed
8. higher incidence of unemployment
9. reduced income to the poor
10. growing poverty

What we now see in the Country, should worry every sensible individuals, as these mean –

1. re-emergence of contract works as in the pre-Independent Days, or East India Company Days
2. emergence of Labour Contractors
3. growing decline of the workforce in the organised sector from the present low of only 8 to 9 percent
4. growth of un-organised labour force within the organised sector

The NSSO Survey also indicate –

1. a steady increasing trend in the number of Casual Labour
2. employment in private sector increased both in the organised and unorganised
3. negligible growth of employment in public sector which accounts for more than two-thirds of employees in the organised sector

The visible Indicators are not good, and do not bode well to the future of the Nation, Society, People and Employees. These would inevitably lead to –

1. Decline in Peace and Justice in the Society
2. Increased exploitation of the workers by the Contractors
3. Fall in the wages of the workers
4. More and more Law and Order Problems
5. Possible emergence of Police States

CHAPTER 15 The Historical Setting for Mennonite and Brethren in Christ Churhes

India is a diverse, multi-religious, multi-cultural country with a population of over one billion people. It is commonly believed that India is a Hindu country and that Hindus constitute over 80 percent of the population. But the emergence of the Dalit movement and intellectual awakening of Dalits has revealed a different reality. We now know Backward Castes, Scheduled Castes, Scheduled Tribes, and other religious minorities like Christians, Muslims, Buddhists, and Parsees constitute 85-90 percent of the total population. Only 10-15 percent are so-called Hindus. India is unique both in general history and religious history.

The ancient Indus Valley civilization dates back to 3250 B.C. Indian religions such as Hinduism, Buddhism, Jainism, and Sikhism not only influenced the philosophy and thought of Asia but also of the world. Out of 6000 spoken languages in the world, 1645 languages are spoken in India itself. The history of any church or any new movement cannot be explained or understood without studying the context or background in which the movement emerged or the event occurred. Therefore the aim of this essay is an attempt to discuss the socio-economic, political, and religious conditions in India in general and in North Bihar and Chotanagpur in particular at the advent of Christian Missions and how they paved way for the conversions to different religions and to Christianity.

Political History in Brief

The general history of India can be divided into five distinct periods. First, Ancient India (Indus valley civilization, 3250-2000);

Second, the Hindu period (2000 B.C. to 1001A.D), in which the rulers were Hindus and both Hinduism and Buddhism developed. Third, the Muslim Period (1002-1757) when Islam entered India and was firmly established. Fourth, the period of East India Company and British Colonialism (1757-1947). During this period the East India Company gained a stronghold on the country and established trade. The British were able to take supremacy in this period that lasted until 1947. The final period is independent India (1947-).

In 1947 India and Pakistan were divided as independent countries. Following independence, the 562 independent native states of India were absorbed into the central government. With the formation of three more new states (Chathishghar, Jharkhand, and Uttaranchal) in November 2000, the number of Indian states grew to twenty nine. The division of the states was made mainly along language lines. A small percent of Aryan minority (3-4 % of Brahmins) ruled this country—the largest democratic society in the world—by manipulating the rulers, parties and religions since its independence.

Advent of Christianity in India

Strong Indian tradition holds that one of our Lord's disciples, Thomas, brought Christianity to India in 52 A.D. Whether the apostle Thomas actually brought Christianity to India is still a matter of argument. Nevertheless, it seems that a church has existed in South India since the early part of the Christian era. Traditionally this is called St. Thomas Church or Syrian Church. Roman Catholicism reached India through the Portuguese explorers during the fifteen and sixteenth centuries. Their pioneering missionary was Francis Xavier and the next significant missionary was Robert De Nobili. Later several Roman Catholic missionaries stopped briefly in India on their way to China. By the end of the 18th century, the Roman Catholic Church declined in India and was not revived until about the middle of the nineteenth century. In 1793 a new era in modern mission began in India with the arrival of William Carey of the British Baptist Mission.

Other Protestant mission societies followed. The socio-cultural and religious conditions in India at the time of the arrival of modern missionaries help explain the success of their mission work. There were the centuries-old deep-rooted customs and beliefs, which were often part of the religious systems. These included child marriage, polygamy, female infanticide, suttee, the belief that education is not necessary for girls, superstitions, the caste system, and untouchability. Untouchabilty is perhaps the most important feature that needs to be understood for the conversion of Dalits who constitute approximately 70% of the Indian Christian population. About 99% of present Mennonite Brethren come from the formerly "untouchable" Dalits. The Dalits in fact were called the "untouchables."

Dalit Conversions

The Meaning of the Term Dalit and the Plight of Dalits

The term 'Dalit' has come into popular use in India in recent times. The word comes from the Sanskrit root word "dal" that means to crack, split, broken, down trodden, crushed, destroyed, oppressed, poor, and helpless. This word can be used for all three genders: masculine, feminine, and neuter. Today the term 'Dalit' is used for people who on the basis of caste distinction have been considered 'out-caste' and were not included in the Hindu four-fold caste structure. These people were called names such as *Chandalas, Panchamas, Avarnas, Dasya, Out-caste, etc,.* The British referred them as the "depressed classes." Gandhi coined the word "Harijan" and the Government named them "Scheduled Castes." But today these people preferred to use the term "Dalit" for themselves because this term became an expression of hope for them in their struggle to recover their past identity.

Through their struggle against oppression, this term Dalit gained a new connotation, which has more positive meaning. Dalit does not mean low caste or poor. It rather refers to the state of a section of people who have been reduced and now are living in that predicament. Thus the word Dalit describes a condition but not a connotation of inferiority. James Massey, a prominent Dalit theologian, explains the wide usage of the term Dalit as follows: Dalit is thus not a mere descriptive name or title, but an expression of hope for the recovery of their past identity. The struggle of these 'outcastes' has given the term Dalit a positive meaning. The very realisation of themselves as Dalit, the very acceptance of the state of 'dalitness,' is the first step on the way towards their transformation into full and liberated human beings.

Although they were the original inhabitants of the land, Dalits were oppressed, exploited, and marginalized for centuries before the beginning of modern period. Though the Dalits have interesting traditions and legendary stories to trace back their origin to high status, caste, and position in the past, they were gradually reduced to the position of "no people" in the name of the caste system and with the principal of "purity and pollution." They were considered untouchables because of the work that was assigned to them by the law of Manu and were pushed to the peripheries of the village. Dalits were subjected to do all menial work in the villages which no others were willing to do. This work included sweeping the streets of the villages, serving the caste people as bonded slaves, removing dead animals from the villages, making leather works, digging graves, etc. Because of such occupations they were considered as untouchables, unspeakables, unseeables, unapprochables, unmentionables, and even unthinkables. They were expected to maintain 66 feet distance from the Brahmins and 33 feet from the other castes.

They were denied access to public places and wells. They were not allowed to enter the colony of the caste people. When they walked in the public streets they were to tie a palm leaf around their waist so as to wipe their footprints and were to tie an earthen vessel around their neck to spit their spittle, so that they would not pollute the village. Dalit women were forbidden to wear any cloth above their waist and below knees. This however has changed over the years. Religiously Dalits were strictly barred from entry into any Hindu temples. Brahmins did not serve them as their priests. The temple entry movement was a revolt against this. The Dalits in the village have had entry into the temples only for the past thirty to forty years, and they are still not part of the temple administration, nor they are allowed to actively participate in the cults. Economically also Dalits were poor because practically they were bonded slaves attached to one master whom they served through generations.

For all their services they received their wages in kind at the time of harvest. Therefore during the droughts and famines they were the first victims. John E. Clough, Baptist missionary at Ongole of Andhra Pradesh wrote, "going hungry many a day in the year produced a willingness to eat what no one else would have touched. The consequence was that the men and women had poisoned blood in their veins. The children were full of sores." G. W. H. Brook, another Baptist missionary who worked many years among Dalits described the plight of the Dalits during the drought saying that they "compete with the dogs, jackals and foul birds of the air for the carcasses of the cattle that die in the villages." Therefore A. P. Nirmal, pioneer Dalit theologian, wrote that Dalits were not just "No people" but "No humans."

There was a series of protests and resistance movements among the Dalits from the 14th century onward. The intensity of the protests and the forms they took varied according to the social context, time, and place from which they emerged. Dalits in the past expressed their feelings of pathos and protest in various forms. The Bhakti Movement in the 14th and 16th centuries, Sanskritization, self-assertion movements, and mass movements in 19th and 20th centuries were part of such protest.

Why Dalits Converted to other Faiths

Because Dalits and other backward castes were victims of Hinduism and the caste system, they converted to other religions for self respect, human dignity, and religious identity. For Dalits, conversion appeared as the only solution. Dr. B. R. Ambedker, who was a champion of Dalit uplift, said they could not get equality by remaining as Hindu in Hinduism, so he recommended conversion to the other egalitarian religions as the only solution. He said: To reform the Hindu society is neither our aim nor our field of action. Our aim is to gain freedom. We have nothing to do with anything else. If we can gain our freedom by conversion, why should we shoulder the responsibility of reforming the Hindu religion? And why should we sacrifice our strength... the object of our movement is to achieve social freedom for the untouchables. It is equally true that freedom cannot be secured without conversion. He further said, "conversion brings happiness I tell you all very specifically, religion is for man and not Man for religion.

To get human treatment, convert yourselves. Convert for getting organized, Convert so that your domestic life may be happy." He also declared "I will not die as a Hindu." Even in death he did not want to die in the suffocating society of caste. Therefore Dalits marched towards conversion into other religious faiths. Ambedker himself choose Buddhism. Thus we have Dalits in all religions. In Punjab a substantial number of Dalits chose Sikhism. In Maharashtra they converted to Buddhism. In Kerala, Tamil Nadu, and Andhra Pradesh they turned to Christianity and Islam. Thus 70-90% of people in different faiths are from Dalit origin. The Dalit movement in the 20th century liberated and provided religious identity and individual dignity to the millions of Dalits in India who were marginalized for centuries by the caste system.

Dalits and Christian Missionaries

With the coming of the Protestant missionaries with their emphasis on the equality of all human beings and educational opportunity, a door opened for Dalits social mobility. Protestant missionaries in the modern period came with the background of the evangelical revival and industrial revolution. These events in their countries shaped their ideology and theology. These motivated the missionaries to take an active part in the struggles of the poor, exploited, and marginalized Dalits. Therefore when such missionaries came to India, they "were predisposed to interest themselves in the Dalits. Thus while all missionaries came with the zeal to convert the 'heathen,' they also involved themselves with the attempts to improve the conditions of the down-trodden and the underdogs—mainly, the Dalits." However, according to Stephen Fuchs and M. E. Prabhakar the Messianic Movements also prepared a ground for acceptance of Christianity.

Two examples were Yogi Potuluri Veerabrahmam and Yogi Nasraiah in Andhra Pradesh. Veerabrahmam belonged to a carpenter's family in the Telugu region. He lived in the first half of the nineteenth century. He was a devotee of Shiva and was said to have performed many miracles before he entered his grave alive. He preached mainly against the caste system and promoted millennial expectation of a coming time when the caste system would be destroyed and the equality of all men and women established. Thus Veerabrahmam is said to have inspired thousands of Dalits in Andhra Pradesh, somewhat in line with the millennial hope of Christianity. As a result thousands of his followers embraced the Christian faith, finding a fulfilment in Christ when missionaries arrived and preached. According to the available records Yogi Nasraiah was a Muslim. His original name was Nasar Mahommed.

He too lived in the first half of the nineteenth century in present Narasaravapeta area of Andhra Pradesh. People called him 'Guru Nasaraiah' instead of Nasar Mohammed. He preached the doctrine of one God, love, and forgiveness. He had also preached that idols were useless and advocated equality of the sexes. One of his earliest converts was a Dalit, therefore many Madigas (Dalits) became his followers. Emma Raushenbush Clough wrote that when the movement towards Christianity began among the Madigas (Dalits), the men and women who were following Nasariah sect were among the first to open their hearts to the divine life in Christ. The followers of Nasaraiah later became the Disciples of Christ.

John Everrt Clough of American Baptist Mission, when he came to Ongole of Andhra Pradesh in March 1866, was easily convinced that he should work among the Dalits (Madigas), even though he had come with a mind to concentrate on the high caste people. After seeing the misery of the Dalits (Madigas) he wrote: I saw that it had come to this: If I continued to receive the Madiga I would have to identify myself with them. Their sorrows would be laid upon me. The hardships of their position would be mine to bear. Despised on their account, rejected by the other castes, I would have to begin at the bottom round of the ladder in India, and see about climbing up, carrying the Madigas with me.

Having come to know the conviction of Clough, A. V. Thimpany, a fellow missionary at Nellore, wrote a him a letter: Go on baptizing brother those 'elect of God'. A converted Madiga is as good as, and, if more pious, better, in the eye of God and than a converted Brahman. God knows the best how to work. He is working from the bottom upward.

Eventually, the mission in Ongole became a 'Madiga Mission' and Clough became a 'Madiga Dora'. Mission work at Mahabubnagar district, which later became one of the Mennonite Brethren mission fields, was an extension station of this mission. In many ways Chute, a pioneer Baptist missionary to the district, shared the ideology and policies of Clough.

Dalits and Mennonite Brethren

The Mennonite Brethren Mission which concentrated in Mahabubnager District of Andhra Pradesh had a double reason to concentrate on Dalits. They not only had came with a modern Protestant missionary background but they also shared the Anabaptist-Mennonite tradition. The Anabaptist-Mennonite movement had been a movement of the poor, the peasants, and the exploited. Furthermore they were attracted to India by the success of Clough's mission among the Madigas (Dalits) at Ongole. Consequently Daniel Bergthold, one of the four pioneer missionaries for M. B. mission, as soon as he reached Nagarkurnool of Mahabubnagar District concentrated on Dalits: While looking for a second AMBM field, the Bergtholds were soon introduced to the Madigas, the leather worker caste.

Daniel Bergthold wrote that 'though they live in the dirt of India, we have our greatest success with them'. Observing them in their suppressed condition and comparing the caste system with an earlier civilization as he conceived of it, he became quite convinced that Darwin's theory did not apply here. His view was that the Caste system had 'reversed progress' from that earlier civilization. The American Mennonite Brethren Mission, after occupying the mission field in the district, adopted the strategies of the American Baptists. J. B. Toews commented that during the first half of the 20th century "our theology of mission, strategy, and methods and church planting were largely an adoption from the Baptists."

Factors that Led to Dalit Conversions to Christianity

As the Dalits were the poorest of the poor, some people tend to see their conversion movement as a way to get material benefits. However, historians in India today agree that the motives were deeper than the grasp for material benefits. The motives might have been social, religious, and then economic. The general consensus among historians in India is that the underlying motivation was the search for improved social status, for a greater sense of personal dignity and self-respect, or freedom from bondage from oppressive land owners. Dr. George Oommen, reflecting about the Pulayas struggle in South India, wrote of "their determination to maintain a sense of human dignity and receive better treatment from the higher castes". Thus it appears clear that along with religious identity, the main motives for conversion were human dignity, self respect, and the desire to be treated as equal human beings. When Clough hesitated to baptize the Madigas they shouted "we do not want help. By the blisters on our hands we can prove to you that we have worked and will continue to work. If the next crop fails, we shall die. We want to die as a Christians. Baptize us!"

Tribal Conversions

While Dalits of South and Central India were converting to Christianity, in Northeast India, Chotanagpur and North Bihar witnessed a substantial conversion movement of the tribal peoples of that region to Christianity.

Geographical and Political Setting

Chotanagpur and North Bihar states also were not an exception in this conversion movement. Normally the North is called "graveyard for the mission and mission movement," but the conversion movement of tribal peoples in Chotanagpur negates such argument. The people of this region positively responded to the gospel with the coming of Christian missions in the late 19th and early 20th centuries. Chotanagpur is surrounded by land on all sides—the great Himalayas in the North Madhya Pradesh and Utter Pradesh in the west, Orissa in the south and Bengal in the east. North Bihar is extremely fertile because it is constantly watered by the rivers Sarayu, Ganges, and Gandak. The large two plateaus, Ranchi and Hazaribagh, are situated almost at the centre of Chotanagpur plateau.

Bihar had a glorious ancient history. It was the home state of the Mauryan Empire. Under the great king Ashoka, Pataliputra became famous. Its fame continued under the Magada and Gupta dynasties. But under the Sultans of Delhi and later under the Mogal Emperors Bihar was reduced to the status of a province. With the decline of the Mogal empire Bihar was under the Nawabs of Bengal. In 1764 the British took the region from the Nawab of Bengal in the famous battle of Busear in Bihar. Since then Bihar was a part of Bengal Presidency. In 1911 Bihar and Orissa were separated from the Presidency of Bengal and in 1936 both became separate provinces. This is the brief history of Bihar.

According to the 1991census nearly 90% of the people of Bihar live in rural areas. This makes Bihar one of the most rural states of India. Santal, Oraon, Munda, Ho, Kharia, Bhumij, and Birhor were the tribal groups of Bihar. Most of the tribal peoples live in the Chotanagpur plateau and Santal Pargana. The tribes of Bihar ethnologically belong to a pro-Austroid group but linguistically they do not have same language affinities. Austro Asiatic is divided into two language groups, Mohn Khemer and the Munda language groups. The tribal peoples of Chotanagpur were also called Adi-Vasis. They were the original inhabitants of the region. One of the tribes—Mundas—said once they snatched the land from the fangs of the snake and from the clans of the tiger. After many centuries marauders came up from the plans to raid their positions. At the beginning, tribal peoples defended themselves with their hunting weapons, but later they could not defend themselves and lost most of their land.

Tribals and Christian Missions

At the arrival of missionaries, these tribal peoples were in an acute agrarian crisis. They were being gradually alienated from their land by moneylenders, the Zamindars, and were "thus being transformed into landless agricultural labourers." Later on burdensome taxes were imposed upon them. In their poverty they sought loans "which they often could not repay because of the high interest charged." Thus the lands were taken over and they were forced to become bonded laborers in some cases. "There was no limit to their exploitation. There was also no social intercourse between these adivasis and the Hindu or Muslim inhabitants of Chotanagpur," wrote Sivaji Koyl. It was in this context and among these economically exploited and socially oppressed tribal peoples that the missionaries arrived and preached the gospel of liberation. Christian missionaries started to arrive in Chotanagpur from the middle of the 19th century.

The first who arrived were the missionaries of the Gossner Evangelical Lutheran Mission. Four Lutheran missionaries arrived in Chotanagpur in November 1845. They were the first Protestant Christian missionaries in that part of India. These four young missionaries were E. Schutz, F. Batsch, A. Brandt and H. Jamke. They came and settled down at Ranchi. For a few years there was not a single convert. Then a strange incident occurred. One day four men of the Oran tribe came to the mission house asking to see Jesus, of whom the missionaries had been preaching. They were asked to attend the church service. Having done so, they were deeply impressed but still unsatisfied. "They wished and said to see Jesus with their own eyes." One of the missionaries took them into an inner room and prayed fervently that they might be guided to the light. They went away quietly. Some time later the same men reappeared and asked again to be allowed to participate in worship service. At its close they came forward with great joy in their faces saying now they had found Jesus.

Now they were satisfied and they desired to become Christians. After further instruction and teaching they were baptized on June 9,1850. From then on the number of converts rapidly increased and by 1857 there were 700 baptized Christians. A church had been established in 1855. In the next ten years people movements among the Oraons and Mundas brought many converts and within ten years the baptized Christians numbered about 10,000. Thus the mission work continued, spread, and flourished. Apparently the tribal people came with their desire to become Christians. Sometimes a whole village came to missionaries asking for baptism. An Anglican mission (The Society for the Propagation of the Gospel) arrived in this region in 1869. By 1872, the Anglican Church had consolidated their position and reported that they had 5,000 converts. The Roman Catholic Church entered the region only in 1887 and established the mission work.

Factors that Led to the Conversion of Tribal Peoples

C. F. Andrews, analyzing the factors for conversions in this region, wrote that one of the main factors leading to conversion was religious. Citing the incident of four men who came to find Jesus and returned saying "Now we have found Jesus, now we are satisfied and now we desire to become Christians," Andrews wrote that spiritual satisfaction was the primary motive for the conversion of tribal peoples in the Chotanagpur region. Further, however, he says that they might have come with the desire for the material help from the missionaries. But this was not without spiritual value: However unworthy may have been the early motives of many in embracing Christianity, in embracing it they have found life: moral, intellectual and spiritual even now some of the Kol converts are being used for work as Catechists among the Gonds of the central provinces as well as in Calcutta and Assam. Andrews seems to be generalizing one isolated incident. It may not be true with all. Shivaji Koyal wrote that when the missionaries did not offer the people expected solutions to their problems, they broke away from the church. Hence for him the factors would be more than spiritual. At the arrival of missionaries in Chotanagpur the tribal peoples in that region were passing through an acute agrarian crisis.

These missionaries who came from the background of the evangelical awakening began to give serious attention to economic and social problems. Therefore they sided with the peasants in those struggles against exploitation. Missionaries provided them with lawyers to plead their cases, gave advice, and helped them financially to fight for their cases. Missionaries for this purpose founded a mutual help society and co-operative credit societies for the mutual uplift of the converts. Establishment of schools, educational institutions, and the churches played a positive impact with regard to the intellectual awakening of the converts. Their primitive tribal superstitions with regard to spirits disappeared. According to C. F. Andrews the work of the mission not only raised the social and intellectual status of the converts but their whole life. Body, soul, and Spirit were raised after their conversion to Christianity. As the missionaries supported the cause of the oppressed tribal peoples in this area and helped them in their struggles against their economic exploitation, it was natural for the tribal peoples to convert to Christianity in large numbers. Substantial adherents of six Mennonite Brethren and Brethren in Christ groups in India come from either Dalit or Tribal background. The history and witness of these six groups need to be studied in their broader social context.

Bibliography

Ahir, D.C.: *Dr B.R. Ambedkar: Buddhist Revolution and Counter-Revolution in Ancient India*, B.R. Publishing, Delhi, 1996.

Ainapur, L. S.: *Dynamics of Caste Relations in Rural India*, Rawat Publications, Jaipur, 1986.

Aiyappan, A.: : *Social Revolution in a Kerala Village: a Study in Culture Change*, Asia Press, Bombay, 1965.

Ambedkar, B. R.: *Annihilation of Caste: An Undelivered Speech,* Arnold Publishers, New Delhi, 1990.

Anand, J. H.: *Dalit Literature is the Literature of Protest*, Dalit Solidarity, Delhi, 1995.

Anandhi, S. *Contending Identities: Dalits and Secular Politics in Madras Slums*, Indian Social Institute, New Delhi, 1995.

Atal, Yogesh: *The Changing Frontiers of Caste*, National Publishing House, Delhi, 1968.

Bailey, F. G.: *Caste and the Economic Frontier: A Village in Highland Orissa*, University of Manchester, Manchester, 1957.

Bari, S.A.: *Gandhi's Doctrine of Civil Resistance*, Kalamkar Prakashan, New Delhi, 1971.

Benjamin, Joseph: *Scheduled Castes in Indian Politics and Society,* Ess Ess Publications, New Delhi, 1989.

Beteille, Andre.: *Caste: Old and New*, Asia Publishing House, Bombay, 1969.

Bhatt, Anil: *Caste and Political Mobilisation in Gujarat District,* Orient Longman, Delhi, 1970.

Bhatt, V.: *The Harijans of Maharashtra*, All India Harijan Sevak Sangh, Delhi, 1941.

Blunt, E. A. H.: *Caste System of Northern India*, Oxford University Press, London, 1931.

Brown, Judith M.: *Gandhi and Civil Disobedience*, Cambridge University Press, London, 1977.

Fiske, A.: *The Untouchables in Contemporary India*, University of Arizona Press, Tucson, 1972.

Gandhi, M. K.: *The Removal of Untouchability*, Navjivan Publishing House, Ahmedabad, 1954.

Ganesan, L.: *Relevance of Reservation*, Valentina Publications, Madras, 1991.

Gawali, P.A.: *Society and Social Disabilities under the Peshwas*, National, New Delhi, 1988.

Ghurye, G. S.: *Caste and Class in India*, Popular Books, Bombay, 1950.

Gorhe, Neelam: *Social Development and Dalit Women*, Gyan Pub. House, New Delhi, 1995.

Gurukal, Rajan: *The Formation of Caste Society in Kerala*, Rawat Publications, New Delhi, 1994.

Hutton, J. H.: *Caste in India: Its Nature, Function and Origins*, Cambridge University Press, London, 1946.

Jogdan, Prahlad G.: *Dalit Movement in Maharashtra*, Kanak Publications, New Delhi, 1991.

Jogdand, P.G.: *Dalit Women in India: Issues and Perspectives*, Gyan Pub., New Delhi, 1995.

Kamble, J.R.: *Rise and Awakening of the Depressed Classes in India*, National, New Delhi, 1979.

Karve, Irawati: *Hindu Society: An Interpretation*, Sangam Press, Poona, 1961.

Kshirsagar, R. K.: *Dalit Movement in India and Its Leaders (1857-1956)*, MD Pub. Pvt. Ltd., New Delhi, 1994.

Lal, Shyam: *Caste and Political Mobilisation: The Bhangis*, Panchsheel Prakashan, Jaipur, 1981.

Lokhande, G.S.: *Bhimrao Ramji Ambedkar: a Study in Social Democracy*, Intellectual Publishing House, New Delhi, 1977.

Mann, K.: *Tribal Women in a Changing Society*, Mittal Publications, Delhi, 1987.

Moffatt, Michael: *An Untouchable Community in South India: Structure and Consensus*, Princeton University Press, NJ, 1979.

Mohan, P.E.: *Scheduled Castes: History of Elevation, Tamil Nadu, 1900-1955*. New Era Pub., Madras, 1993.

Murugkar, Lata. *Dalit Panther Movement in Maharashtra: A Sociological Appraisal*, Popular Prakashan, Bombay, 1991.

Nagaraj, D. R.: *The Flaming Feet: A Study of the Dalit Movement*, South Forum Press, Bangalore, 1993.

Naidu, A. Nagaraja: *Caste and Land in Colonial South India*, Rawat Publications, New Delhi, 1994.

Omprakash, S.: *Development of the Weaker Section: Problems, Policies and Issues*, Uppal Publishing House, New Delhi, 1989.

Paranjpe, A. C.: *Caste, Prejudice and the Individual*, Lalvani Publishing House, New Delhi, 1970.

Punalekar, S. P.: *Dalit Women in India: Issues and Perspectives*, Gyan Publishing House, New Delhi, 1995.

R. Barbara: *Untouchable! Voices of the Dalit Liberation Movement*, Zed Books, London, 1986.

Robb, Peter: *Dalit Movements and the Meanings of Labour in India*, Oxford University Press, New Delhi, 1993.

Shah, Ghanshyam: *Politics of Scheduled Castes and Scheduled Tribes*, Vora and Co. Pvt. Ltd., Bombay, 1975.

Sharma, K. L.: *Caste, Class and Social Movements*, Rawat Publications, Jaipur, 1986.

Shetty, V. T. Rajshekar: *Dalit Movement in Karnataka*, Christian Literature Society, Madras, 1978.

Silverberg, James: *Social Mobility in the Caste System in India*, Mouton Publishers, The Hague, 1968.

Srinivas, M. N.: *Caste in Modern India and Other Essays*, Asia Publishing House, Bombay, 1962.

Tripathi, R. S. and Tiwari, P. O.: *Dimensions of Scheduled Caste Development in India*, Uppal Publishing House, New Delhi, 1991.

Tripathy, R. B.: *Dalits: A Sub-Human Society*, Ashish Publishing House, New Delhi, 1994.

Venkateshwarlu, D.: *Harijan-Upper Class Conflicts*, Discovery, New Delhi, 1990.

Webster, John: *The Christian Dalits: A History*, Indian Society for Promoting Christian Knowledge (ISPCK), Delhi, 1994.

Index

♦♦♦